WINNING IDE

Professional Approach in Housing, Support and Care Management

Interview Questions and Answers
Housing, Supported Housing, and Care

This volume of Winning Ideas contains questions used in previous interviews
Scenarios used in this book reflect real situations

Winning Ideas is a complete guide for today's staff

Winning Ideas
A resource book for use as:
**A source for co-corporate policy and procedure
Self development and educational tool
Staff development and training tool
Staff induction and instruction source
Staff recruitment and staff care guide
A reference material for operational staff
A tool for promoting good practice and a customer focused service**

By
Kenneth Agyekum-Kwatiah
*MCCR, Msc.OM, PGD.MS, PGD. Arch, Bsc.Design, Cert.PL CHWM
CUK, RIBA*
Director of Shelter Two Associate Services

WINNING IDEAS

Published in the UK by
Shelter Two Associate Services
4 Suffolk Road London E13 0HE
Tel. 0207 474 5411

ISBN: 0-9543659-0-9 Volume three of
Winning Ideas: Professional Approach in Housing, Support and Care Management

Obtaining copies of Winning Ideas
To order a copy of Winning Ideas or any publication authored by
Kenneth Agyekum-Kwatiah, or published by Shelter Two Associate Services, call S2S on

0207 474 5411.

Alternatively, write to S2S at 4 Suffolk Road London E13 0HE
Housing training and publications by S2S are also available on
0208 519 0089 (HEARTS, Stratford E15)
0208 980 2299 (Transatlantic College, Bethnal Green E2)

Designed and typeset by
Shelter Two Associate Services. 4 Suffolk Road London E13 0HE

Printed and bound by
Caric Press Ltd. Rickits
Green. Lionheart Close. Bearwood. Bournemouth. Dorset. BH11 9UB
Tel. 01202 574577 Fax 01202 574578 Web Site WWW. Caricpress.co.UK

Cover design and artwork by
Kenneth Agyekum-Kwatiah

Proof reading and editing
Stephen Dawuda and Shelter Two Associate Services

DEDICATION

This marvellous piece of work is dedicated to my lovely wife and best friend

Comfort

who made us all proud with a landmark success in her recent professional exams. With your support and unfailing love you have been an anchor behind Winning Ideas.
God bless you richly.

ABOUT KENNETH AGYEKUM-KWATIAH

Kenneth Agyekum-Kwatiah is the author of Winning Ideas, which has won the admiration of many senior managers of leading housing and care organisations in the UK. His strategic and conceptual approach to research and publications stands for genuine emphasis on practical issues in preference to theories. Ken has tremendous experience working in various capacities in housing and housing-related positions which puts him in a very commanding position on numerous topics of which the UK Welfare Benefits is one. Ken is known to many people as a Housing management consultant, an architect, business management consultant and a lecturer.

Despite all his achievements and successes Ken preserves his beliefs in practicalities by working in a front line role as a member of Look Ahead Housing and Care Ltd. team. This provides him with the necessary avenues for testing ideas as well as generating fresh ones. Hundreds of people have already benefited from Ken's skills and knowledge especially as students, mentees, colleagues, business partners and clients through his educational books, lecturing and training sessions.

Ken has spent quality time campaigning for sponsorship for organisations providing for the vulnerable socially excluded like the homeless, mental health and HIV victims. His activities have earned him compelling admiration from organisations like Crisis UK, Plan International UK, and the World Development Movement. In the coming years Ken plans to take Shelter Two Associate services into a new arena where it will operate as the Institute of Supported Housing. With this status he will be more able to make directly available to front line staff those practical winning service ideas that have already won the admiration of many.

Emma Rogers
Trustee. Shelter Two Associate Services (S2S)

THANK YOU

A big *thank you* to my staff, students, and colleagues who one way or the other contributed to the production of *Winning Ideas volume three*. Special *thank you* to Prince and Janet of TransAtlantic College, as well as all the staff working there. I also remember Bola and Ade of HEARTS whose selfless support was immensely important. The business of S2S has received unfailing support from Linda Pole and Trevor Humphrey (both of the Charted Institute of Housing).

I feel indebted to the many managers and leaders whose encouraging comments about Winning Ideas continue to give me the energy to put in more. I remember Richard Brook (Chief executive of Christian Alliance), Helen Buckley (Housing 21) and Liz William (Plan International UK).

I also wish to thank Ronnie Adrien, Courage Oye, and Ike Ezerioha of Look Ahead Housing and Care for making my connection with Warton House very special. I cannot forget my own team members at the Areas East office. Every member of the team showed relentless devotion towards creating a healthy working atmosphere, which made me feel very special. I cannot forget Nurun Nehar, Lena Hatch, and Sharon Odumosu,. Also, June Crawford, Dawn Clark, Kemi Gorge-Simpson, Ronie and Winston Jackman. They provided me with much needed friendship which greatly resourced this publication. *Thank you* to Princess Asare-Buafo for your friendship and love throughout these moments. *Thank you* also to Mr. Richard Batchelor (Managing Director of Garic Press) for his efforts in getting this print work out on schedule.

QUOTES AND COMMENTS ABOUT WINNING IDEAS

'Winning Ideas – Issues in the management of Housing and Care has been widely accepted for its simplicity and realistic application to issues of the industry. They are not textbooks. They avoid academics in favour of day-to-day practical professional matters, whilst placing firm emphasis on how to maximise quality service delivery. With every employer looking for staff with genuine understanding and practical awareness, and working knowledge of how to achieve success in a highly competitive market, it is just what you need'.

'Excellent – Very useful reference books'
Richard Brook (Chief Executive)
Christian Alliance Housing Association Ltd.

'This book covers a very practical approach to addressing many operational issues both at the front line and managerial level. It guides the reader through use of questions and scenarios which could be used both to help staff in post as well as providing very useful and relevant material around which interviews can be structured to address competency...... Its application covers all aspects of our work both in housing and Care'
Source: Helen Buckley (Training Assessor)
Housing 21

'I would like to take this opportunity to thank you and all those who work at S2S, and we wish you well in your valuable work'
Liz Williams.
Plan International UK.

'We are very grateful to you and all the staff at S2S'
Julie Roberts. **World Development Movement**

'Thank you for sharing our vision'
Maggie Stevenson.
Crisis (Working for Homeless People)

'I could never find a book on Housing and Supported Housing. I searched the libraries, spoke to my friends, and my mentor.......... There seemed to be nothing out there that brings all the facts into one simple book, and one simple language like Winning Ideas does'.

'Winning Ideas brings together all you needs onto one simple platform....... Quality, Good practice, Customer care, and Best value .... and it is easy to use'

'Winning Ideas contains everything practical that anyone who wishes to take up a career in housing and care will need. It provides solutions to everyday problems that staff may encounter whilst on duty, prepare people for interviews and be a reference guide for trainers, consultants and manager'
Property people magazine, The Human Voice of Housing, October 1999

Winning Ideas is now used in over 200 leading UK housing and care organisations, including St Mungo's, River Point, and Centre Point. See our publication *Evidence of Performance* for an extensive list.

Questions featured in Winning Ideas are sent to the publishers by interviewers and interviewees. Topics covered are based on current issues and concerns of employers and operational staff of the industry.

If you like to see a new topic or a question answered in
Winning Ideas please write to us.

WINNING IDEAS VOLUME 3
Content

INTRODUCTION

Part 1

TENANT AND RESIDENTS WELFARE ISSUES

Part 2

TEAM MANAGEMENT & STAFF MANAGEMENT ISSUES

Part 3

PROJECT MANAGEMENT ISSUES

Part 4

SCENARIOS QUESTIONS

Part 5

PRACTICE QUESTIONS

INTRODUCTION

This volume of Winning Ideas contains more scenario questions and answers. Today's employers seek staff with experience and genuine professional skills. This is why Winning Ideas emphasise on three main areas which are extremely important to the industry:

- Customer care and customer involvement

- Professional practice and procedures

- Quality in service design and service delivery

The use of scenarios enables employers to assess applicants ability to use initiative, work independently and reliably, and above all the level of confidence and motivation with which applicants are able to carryout their work. Therefore one cannot emphasise enough the need for all job hunters to work their ways through all shades of scenario questions based on the industry.

The appropriate answer for every scenario question will depend on the position you are being interviewed for. What I mean is this: The effectiveness of your answers has something to do with:

- How you start your answers

- The content of your answers

- Where you finish with your answers

The 'right way' to do this will depend on the position in question. Scenarios may occur in different levels of interviews and different levels of answers will be required. Where as the facts of the subject will remain the same the emphasis must reflect the role/responsibility of the job you are applying for. For example let's look at a scenario on *ensuring compliance with the organisation's health and safety policy/procedures*

Answers
Housing management position (Estate manager –supported housing)
Examples of things to talk about are:
- Ensuring orders meet *standards set by law* and your organisation

11

- Providing *practical support and supervision* to staff around working with agreed systems

- Working to ensure contractors and external visitors *comply with corporate system and procedures*

- Providing *training* and *coaching* to staff around health and safety issues

Housing staff (e.g. Supported Housing Officer)

Your answer may sound like this:

- Assess clients for risks and support them with minimising exposure

- Ensure fire doors are unblocked

- Wear protective clothes where relevant and necessary

- Deal with spillage appropriately and in accordance with manufacturers instructors

- Put up 'wet floor' sign when mopping floors

- Inspect premises at intervals for signs of danger, repairs or maintenance works

WHO IS THIS BOOK SUITABLE FOR? (NOT EXHAUSTIVE LIST)

Tenants/Licensees (service users)
All Housing Staff and Managers
All Care staff and Managers
Wardens and Sheltered Scheme Staff
Researchers of the Housing and Care industry.
Trainers or all Housing/Supported Housing Staff
Writers/authors on the Housing and Care industry,
Community based staff
Refugee advice staff
Youth workers
Housing and Care students
Housing and Care strategists
Tenancy Sustainment Teams

Tenancy Support Officers
Resettlement Officers
Housing Co-ordinators
Housing and Care Students
Housing/Supported Housing Students
Supported Project Managers
Tenancy Liaison Officers
Promoters of equality groups
Facilitators and Project Development staff
Care and Support agency staff
Projects and Hostel assistance
Contact Assessment Teams
Services Managers

HOW TO USE THIS BOOK

EMPLOYEES

Winning Ideas may be used like many ordinary books to acquire and improve knowledge and skill. It is a very instructive material for training, and for refreshing staff on core issues of their day-to-day duties. In all four volumes coverage is made of important changes (e.g. in the law) which affects the way staff operate.

A. Self study

You can read topics from Wining Ideas you find relevant to your job or to your future career. You will appreciate that the industry is a big one. Issues of good practice are constantly under review. Most people specialise in specific areas. The more areas you cover the wider your chances are with career progression and promotions. You may use Winning Ideas as a reference material (reactively) or as a self-development tool (proactively).

B. Group study

a)   Winning Ideas may also be used by teams in group settings. Ideas from them can be generated into quizzes, games, and other forms of group activities. A typical; example is the topic of *Staff Diversity.*

b)   Winning Ideas can be used as a source of training materials. Consider allocating topics to yourselves and each person briefing the team in the first 10 minutes of each team meeting. Staff awareness and motivation will be enhanced. It is an excellent opportunity for developing staff confidence and promoting inclusion.

c)   Using Winning Ideas Managers can draw up various checklists for staff. Checklists are important tools for ensuring consistency and for standardising quality. Similarly an induction pack can be put together for use by all staff who may be involved in starting new employees.

LOOKING FOR A JOB/PROMOTION

It is often said that one 'can hardly find a publication that brings together all the relevant topics needed in this industry'. Winning Ideas makes it easy for you to identify aspects of the industry you find attractive. Furthermore, you get those very materials you need, and in the form you need them, so that you are able to strengthen your ability to get the job, and to develop in your career.

- Check the person specification and the job description for topics you need to cover for your interview

- Try writing out your own questions from the topics (See our publication *Evidence of Performance* for how)

- Try answering the questions

- Check Winning Ideas for those topics and read on them

- You may also want to mark out those questions and topics that conveniently sits in with the nature of the job you are applying for even though they may not be directly reflected in the person specification or job description

- Check how you are doing by referring to Winning Ideas

- Repeat the process all over each time checking your progress

- Test yourself by attempting questions on similar topics found in Winning Ideas

- If there are areas which are uncovered after reading through Winning Ideas:
     Check:
     - our other publications / materials or

     - use other similar publications if you can find one, or

     - contact colleagues, senior staff or any other suitable person for help

- Use the practice question section to practice answering relevant questions in preparation for your interview

COMPLETING APPLICATION TO BE SHORT LISTED

Winning Ideas makes it easy for you to get short listed. However, it is no use turning up at interviews with no 'substance'. You must be able to sell yourself and this means know and owe your answers. You can maximise your benefits by also referring to our publications *Job Winner* and *Evidence of performance*. They will help you with how to actually construct your sentences. To get short listed, a lot depends on what you put in the 'extra/further information' section of your application form.

- Mark out the topics according to the way they appear in the person specification

- Check Winning Ideas for information and read on them

- Make entry in your application form responding to specific topics. Refer to *Job Winner and Evidence of Performance* for best ways to do this. It is advisable to do this on a photo copy version of the application form before transferring to the original one. This will allow you room for relevant corrections and adjustments.

- Photo copy application form before sending it off as you will need it when preparing for your interview

- Find examples of how you must complete the extra/further information section in *Evidence of Performance*.

WANT TO WORK IN THE INDUSTRY

You may be at college, or in training hoping to soon wear the title 'Housing Officer' or 'Supported Housing Officer' or something similar. Winning Ideas provides you with a living experience opportunity of what exactly happens in the industry. This means without previous experience you have the chance to know how to handle most practical issues long before you get into paid employment. In actual fact, you need this if you are to be able to sell yourself well in any serious interview.

Today's employers seek staff with good experience and yet no one seems to want to start with you. This undoubtedly makes it difficult getting an interview in the first place. These are only some few reasons why you will find Wining Ideas indispensable. Some job hunters refer to it as 'bible'. For me, it is a collection of well tested good ideas ready to carry many people into the professional arena of Care, Support, and Housing.

- Check topics covered in class or training e.g. Equal Opportunities.

- Check Winning Ideas for similar topics. Winning Ideas emphasise on practical issues of topics and will help you understand how things work in real situations.

- Now using your knowledge gained on the topics consider how the application can work under different circumstances. Use your imaginations, talk to other people already employed in the industry.

- Consider doing a group discussion on the topic with your mates, this will help you explore the topics further but this time with a more practical touch.

- If you see a job advert you are interested in request for the application pack.

- Compare the information on what is required (for the job) with what you've acquired from Winning Ideas. This will improve your confidence and help you decide whether or not you are ready.

PREPARING TO ATTEND AN INTERVIEW

This probably is one single area that most users of Winning Ideas will highly recommend it for. The presentational style makes it very easy to pick your points. All you need to do is identify the question and then test yourself by remembering the points. We will assume that you have already studied relevant topics in Winning Ideas. Consider the following suggestions:

- Using makers highlight the areas you find containing information relevant to your interview.

- Refer to Winning Ideas: Concentrate on the points (usually used as the key point of paragraphs) in bold writing or italics

- Commit them to memory (not necessarily in the order they appear in Winning Ideas)

- Try reproducing what you have learnt: Write them down on paper or get some one to practice with.

- Compare your answers to those in Winning Ideas to help you assess your readiness for your interview

I will advise that you do not turn down an invitation to attend an interview because you stand to benefit from the experience. Whether or not you feel prepared or ready, give it a go, and use it to help your own experience. This will help improve your confidence for future interviews.

If you require further advice or support on how to maximise your benefits from Winning Ideas do not hesitate to contact us (details provided in early pages of this book).

OTHER PUBLICATIONS FROM S2S

Winning Ideas Volume. 1
By Kenneth Agyekum-Kwatiah

Covers everything one needs, to know to take up a position in Housing or Care. 17 chapters. Covers topics like Project Management; Team Work, Needs Assessment, Quality Management, Health & Safety and Welfare Management

Winning Ideas Volume 2, 3, & 4
By Kenneth Agyekum-Kwatiah

They compliment volume 1 with hundred of most-asked Housing and Care interview questions and answers. Ideal for preparing for interviews and for addressing difficult on-the-job problems.

Job Winner
By Kenneth Agyekum-Kwatiah

All you need for getting job interviews. It contains over 1,000 solid ideas for producing winning application forms, and strategies for capturing the confidence of your interviewers whilst in the interview chair.

Remnants of Accommodation Vol. 1
By Kenneth Agyekum-Kwatiah

Housing Benefit and Council Tax Benefit calculation and regulations, administration, assessment, and how to workout amounts.

Remnants of Accommodation Vol. 2
By Kenneth Agyekum-Kwatiah

Housing Benefit and Council Tax Benefit calculation and regulations. It also covers the future of housing benefit:

Supporting People, profile of all other benefits, worked examples of real cases (calculations), and the management of claims including appeals

Evidence of performance
By Kenneth Agyekum-Kwatiah

Samples of the 'extra information' part of your application forms on various positions in the industry. Over 200 voluntary placements with advice on how to maximise benefits from work placements

CORPORATE TRAINING (TOPICS) AVAILABLE FROM S2S

Client Welfare
- Supporting Mental health clients
- Supporting people with learning difficulties
- Supporting homeless young people

Homelessness legislation
- The role and duties of the local authorities
- Supporting homelessness applicants

Tenants' participation
- Young people and participation
- Best value and Tenants participation compacts
- User empowerment

Team work and team resources
- Building an effective staff team
- Developing a productive staff team

Equal opportunity
- Diversity at work
- Cultural diversity
- Cultural awareness

Care/Support Management
- Assessing Support and care needs
- Care planning
- Support planning

Finance
- Fund raising
- Debt counselling
- Rent arrears management

Housing Benefits calculation and administration
- Housing Benefit in supported Housing
- Housing Benefit for benefit assessors

Resettlement
- Housing and Resettlement with support
- Tenancy/Licences

Staff management
- Supporting and motivating staff
- Promoting diversity at work
- Supervision skills
- Time management
- Managing conflict

Customer service
- Delivering customer Care
- Valuing people
- Ensuring quality on the job
- Assertive communication
- Quality assurance

Drugs and Alcohol
- Supporting people on drugs and alcohol
- Supporting people with history of self-harm

Welfare benefits
- Benefits and resettlement
- Benefits for drug users
- Benefits for elderly people
- Benefits and mental health/learning disability
- Supporting people (the new welfare benefit)
- Welfare Benefits (general)

Project Management
- Tenancy and Licences
- Voids and maintenance management
- Health and Safety for manager
- Health and Safety for staff
- Managing change
- Court proceedings: Rent arrears

Communicable illnesses (Supported Housing)
- Communicable illnesses in supported Housing
- Managing HIV in projects and hostels
- Managing Hepatitis in projects and hostels

TRAINING AVAILABLE FROM S2S

Training on a wide range of topics in this industry is available from S2S. See list in Volume three. Training arrangement may be made by calling S2S on 0207 474 5411.

ONE-DAY WORKSHOPS

(1)   Answered Interview Questions (AIQ): Learn how to anticipate interview questions and how to answer them before your interviews.

(2)   Applications and Interview Strategy (AIS): Learn how to do applications that will get you an interview. Collect samples of good applications for a wide range of positions in the industry and on volunteer opportunities (for job experience). Learn good interview skills.

TIME TO MOVE ON!

You walked into the project's communal lounge and saw two men (homosexuals) kissing and fumbling each other whilst other service users (residents) look on with discomfort. What will you do?

So many answers can emerge with several reasons that may sound right but not necessarily appropriate. Would you walk away quietly? Would you call them by the side and talk to them quietly and sensitively? Would you ignore them and address the matter at a later time/date? Would you challenge them straight away? What place do you give to equal opportunity? What place do you give to the rights of the other residents? What place do you give to customer care or quality service delivery? I will leave you to decide what you would do.

My answer is simple you must stop the already bad situation from becoming worse by challenging the behaviour straight away but at the same time maintain your calm and be professional in your approach. This means being objective, firm, direct, and clear without showing emotions of prejudice. All scenarios must be approached 360 degrees, so there is more to do beyond this point.

This is just to give you a taste of some issues examined in Winning Ideas. It is not all about finding answers to interview questions. More importantly, it is about training, experience, knowledge and growth. *Winning Ideas* aims to equip you with the very best of service competences and thereby help keep you motivated in your job. Using this volume together with the others will give you a most commanding positing in the industry.

Part 1
TENANTS AND RESIDENTS WELFARE ISSUES

SUPPORTING A MENTAL HEALTH CLIENT

Scenario: Whilst on duty in the project a tenant comes to you and complains of hearing voices. What action will you take to address the situation?

Knowing the nature of client needs will help. Initial approach recommendable may vary depending on the client group. On this occasion let us assume we are dealing with a mental health client.

Get more information

'Hearing voices' can mean anything. The extent to which you go depends on the client's ability to communicate clearly and effectively their experience. Establish the following:

- What he hears or heard
- What time(s) the voices occur
- When he heard it last
- How it makes him feel
- Client's own interpretation of the voices and /or what he hear.
- Check if it happened before, when and what form it was experienced
- Check what he has done about similar experience in the past (if applicable)

Record client's comments

Document fully comments as narrated by client (not as interpreted by yourself). You may need to compare them to future experiences in order to establish some useful picture or pattern.

Warm reception

Remember client might consider hearing voices a terrifying experience (especially if it is their first). It is therefore important that your reception is warm and makes them feel that they can talk to you when similar experience raptures in future. Your ability to make a terrified client feel comfortable is fundamental to a good conversation.

Allow opportunities for them to talk freely

Use open-ended questioning that allows them to describe and explain at length how they feel, what they think and the conclusions they hold from their experience.

Further action

Further action will depend on the nature of answers you receive from client. Answers to the following are particularly significant.

- What are the 'voices' demanding of client?

- How does the experience make client feel?

The client may be okay and have no further concerns after chatting to you (perhaps over a cup of tea). This is more likely to be the case if hearing voices is the first experience for him. Voicing out their experience may be their way of getting rid of the problems. If the tenant tells you they are okay after talking to you, you must acknowledge this but also encourage them to;

- Contact you if they have further concerns

- Contact you if they want to talk further about their experience; and to

- Practice any agreed actions e.g. get some rest, or take a nap

Whatever happens ensure the conversation is written down in the right places, e.g.:

- Daybook (containing records of what has happened during your shift)

- Day file (containing full details of conversation)

- Residents file

Ensure you've got down the following:

- Date

- Time

- The mood in which client was

- How contact was established

- Length of time spent with client

- Client's story and concerns

- Your response (making it clear whether it is a temporary solution or not)

- Any action left not completed which other staff members need to know.

If further action is required

Assuming client feels suicidal from their experience e.g. the 'strong voice' asking him to kill himself. If you have further indication that the client might not be able to exercise sufficient control over his experience e.g. he is drunk or drugged and you are unsure of what to do, first of all consider the following:

- Seek the opinion of a colleague (if there is someone else available)

- If you both agree that the situation presents cause for concern, contact professionals (experts) and follow their advice

Prepare yourself before making the contact

Before contacting the professional:

- Have enough information available to give them so that they can make appropriate assessment and judgement of the situation

- Have a pen and paper at hand to write down actions you need to take.

Significant information to provide

When you contact a specialist:

- Inform them of what you've already done

- Most importantly describe what you observed, the mood in which you find the client, their reactions following their experience, etc.

Emergency situations

If tenant approached you having already executed 'voices' instructions e.g. cut themselves or set fire to the flat, then your prior attention must be directed for:

- Taking necessary steps to prevent the situation from becoming worse

- Tackling any life threatening situation

- Ensuring safety for other service users

- Creating a secured atmosphere in the scheme or project

Therefore, implement any agreed emergency procedures which may include:

- Administering first aid (if trained to do so)

- Calling the Fire brigade, ambulance or the police if situation is confirmed)

- Arrange emergency repairs

Post incident checklist

Whatever the situation may be, ensure that:

- The matter is brought to the attention of the team and in particular, the keyworker for the tenant.

- If it turns out to be a major incident ensure that any organisational or project procedures are executed and notified.

- Ensure any information or advice received from specialist professionals regarding the case is professionally passed on to all who need to know.

- Attend to any other person (resident or staff) who may be affected by the incident.

Bring the matter up at team meeting especially if it resulted in a major incident so that further deliberations can be made for an agreed team procedure. Such a case can potentially influence the way risks are assessed for the project and residents.

SCHIZOPHRENIA

It is one of the most common mental illnesses affecting about 1 of every 100 people. It is found throughout the world and can affect men as well as women in equal proportions though men appear to develop schizophrenia earlier than women.

Symptoms

People suffering from schizophrenia turn to behave very strangely and shockingly: Victims cannot tell the difference between what is real and what is not. Such behaviour is called *psychosis* or a *psychotic episode*. Specific symptoms include the following:

Delusions (bizarre, false beliefs)

These beliefs seem real to the person with schizophrenia, but they are not real. An example here is where a person believes that aliens or spies are controlling his or her behaviour, mind and thoughts. Delusions involve fixed irrational ideas such as the belief that your thoughts are being controlled by some malevolent power.

Paranoia

People with paranoia have an unreal fear that someone is 'following or chasing them'. The victim may also come under a firm believe that they are someone important e.g. The queen, Princes Diana, Prince Charles, or the president.

Hallucinations (bizarre, unreal perceptions of the environment)

Hallucination can be:

- Tactile (e.g. feelings that bugs are crawling on or under the skin, or touched by someone)

- Visual (e.g. seeing lights, colours, flying objects, or faces)

- Olfactory (e.g. the person can smell something, though no one else can)

- Auditory(e.g. hearing voices, and sometimes the voices give the patience instructions)

Disorganised Thinking or Speech
It is generally believed that people with schizophrenia speaks very little. Others speak disjointly. Another speech symptom is that some change topics midway through conversations or sentences.

Negative symptoms (this is the absence of normal behaviour)
Negative symptoms include withdrawal, absence of emotion and expression, reduced energy, motivation and activity. Further signs include poor hygiene and grooming. A person may also withdraw from contact with people around them into themselves or into their own fantasy world.

Catatonia (Immobility)
This is a negative symptom where the person becomes frozen in one position for a long period of time.

Inappropriate emotions
Under this symptom include those emotions which appear to be inappropriate to the circumstance. For example, where people ignore differences in sex and behave as if all people are of the same sex.

Types of schizophrenia
Three basic types exist:

- Disorganised schizophrenia

- Catatonic schizophrenia

- Paranoid Schizophrenia

Causes of schizophrenia
Like depression scientist do not know all the factors contributing to cause schizophrenia. The following factors are thought to contribute directly or indirectly to schizophrenia:

- *Genetics:* Schizophrenia appear to run in families

- *Environment:* These are non-genetic factors like family stress, poor social interactions, infections or viruses at an early age, or trauma at an early age. It is believed that genetic and non-genetic factors work together to cause the illness.

Treatment for schizophrenia

Two main forms of treatments can be identified: Medication and Counselling.

Medication: Drugs used in the treatment of schizophrenia are called *antipsychotic* medications. They are used to control states of mind in which contact with reality is severely impaired. They are not thought to be addictive but are focused on reducing symptoms of the disorders. This means that they do not necessarily cure the illness. Examples of antipsychotic drugs are:

Clozapine	Usually only prescribed when a patient cannot tolerate, or his/her symptoms are not relieved by another antipsychotic drug. Thought to cause fatal blood disorders,
Droperidol	Used to calm agitated, manic and psychotic patients. Thought to cause inner agitation, physical restlessness, a mask-like facial appearance, tremors and muscular rigidity.
Loxapine	Use for treatment of schizophrenia, mania and other psychotic states. It is more dangerous in overdose than other antipsychotic drugs and considered 'a high potential for serious neurological and cardiac toxicity'. It is also thought to cause weight gain or weight loss, nausea and vomiting, laboured or difficult breathing, blurred vision, trembling limbs, inner restlessness, flushing and headaches.
Chlorpromazine	Thought to be an effective treatment for symptoms such as hallucinations, thought disorders and delusions ceased by schizophrenia and other psychotic conditions. Prolonged use is thought to lead to development of facial tics and other involuntary movements.
Perphenazine	Known to cause some serious side effects and as a result not recommended for people under 14 or agitated and restless elderly people (by manufacturers).

Counselling: This includes psychological therapy, family therapy and occupational training that may be used along with antipsychotic medication to help people get back into the community to live normal lives.

Question 2   SUICIDE ATTEMPT
How can you tell if a resident/tenant is attempting to commit suicide?

People who attempt suicide may carry with them several motives and the motives turn to reflect in the methods used as well as symptonal actions adopted. The following can provide us with clues.

Writing a suicidal note

This is one of the obvious ones. The note may be left in their rooms, sent to a friend or relative or even to staff. The note may express remorse over an incident or ask for forgiveness for a wrong done to another person. It may also contain news of desperation and frustration leading to the decision to take his life.

Evidence of active or deliberate preparation

Such preparation may include gathering or the collection of things to be used in committing suicide, e.g. obtaining drugs, or asking people about ways of taking one's life.

Other preparations

These involve where the person plans to put things he/she will leave behind in shape. They may not be here but they want to secure a reasonable level of influence over their affairs long after their departure. An example will include putting financial affairs in order, or making a will.

When people are planning to be alone

People who live isolated lives are amongst those thought to be at high suicidal risk. Loneliness can drive people to take their lives. People who turn to want their own space (with no one else nearby) all of a sudden must be checked upon and their concerns established as soon as possible.

Timing of the attempt

This is done so no one would be able to intervene. Some choose the night time and others, isolated moments. Such intentions will normally be preceded with unusual questions, e.g. about who is going to be on duty in the project at specific times, or how the fire alarms gets triggered off.

Previous history

Previous attempts signal need for precautions. Most people who attempt suicide have already been there. The pattern and methods used in the past can provide a clue as to what can be anticipated.

Taking precautions against being discovered

This may take the form of locking of doors, being secretive about activities and hiding of drugs. Such precautions may also manifest as avoidance of questions and unusual quick, sharp and short answers, as if to indicate that the person is not interested.

Not interested in getting help after the attempt
This is where determination takes over. A firm decision to bring the action to an end even where things seem not to go according to plan. The feeling at these times may be that of a belief of being dubbed a 'failure', or an anger about the failure itself.

Telling someone of their intention
A clear example is where the person comes to the office and makes his/her intentions known to a staff member. It's often tempting for staff to brand residents who frequently talk of suicidal feelings as 'attention seekers'. Such attitudes can be very costly.

Showing signs of stress
Stress is a killer. Combined with the problems already carried by for example a mental health resident, the load may be unbearable. If the situation is met with no one to talk to or off load onto, suicide can be considered.

Chains of complaints, and showing frustration
Some people exhibit their consideration of suicide through other ways that won't betray their real intentions. A sudden change from a quiet and contented person to a seemingly genuine constant and bitter complainant can signal the coming of something big.

Constantly talking oneself down
This stems from low self-esteem, and continuous self-deprivation. This may occur where the person has suffered abuse of some kind for a long time.

Acute reaction to loss
This may be loss through death, an accident, or some other forms of tragedies. This is more so for people whose vulnerability has already taken them to suicide attempts in the past.

An escape from intolerable pressures
This may be a fight against addiction such as drugs, gambling, alcohol, or even sex. Often it is the effect of the addiction which results in the intolerable pressures. Such pressures may manifest through deprivation of one's own

family, lack of finance and disgrace. The actual suicide consideration is a direct response to a feeling of hopelessness about the future.

Family history of suicide
It is believed that some individuals may be considered as being more prone to suicide attempts because most people in their families have taken their lives through suicide in the past. Such considerations must be made known to care professionals and relevant precautions provided for in care plans. Refer to notes on *Depression* in other parts of this volume.

A review of one's service agreement or care plan must follow every serious incidence such as a suicide attempt. Below you will find a general framework for assessing and designing a care or support plan.

INDIVIDUAL SERVICE AGREEMENT INDEX

Service agreements are important for assessing quality of work. They provide a framework of agreed specifications by which expectations must be met. Vulnerable people in care or support need to have service level agreements covering their specific needs. The agreements are contained in plans that spell out gaols and objectives and relevant strategies to be engaged. They also show clearly the roles of the parties involved (including residents or tenants) in the implementation of plans. In question two above we saw the need to review clients' support plans after major incidents. This is another occasion where the individual service agreement index in useful.

The index below provides some important areas for assessment as part of the service agreements. This is one area that managers of front line staff must ensure that staff are fully aware of and also that they are able to perform the assessments.

Daily living skills and meaningful occupation issues
Check if clients can do the following on their own.
- Access voluntary or paid jobs.

- Engage in a planned productive activity.

- Explore further interests or developing existing ones around their own hobbies.

- Maintaining own space in a hygienic condition: houvering, dusting, cleaning, brushing, washing, etc.

- Managing own money, able to count and check accuracy of own finances, handling money, able to budget well and pay bills.

- Able to read and write, able to understand visual messages, read and understand official correspondence, communicate with others.

- Able to get out and about, have sufficient knowledge of area, have enough confidence to go to places by himself, no mobility problems, has sufficient travelling skills, shows awareness of safety issues.

- Access college and education centre facilities and services by themselves.

- Have skills for looking for work, if they get a job they can hold it down well.

- Ability to access day centre facilities, therapies, access advice and information locally.

- Able to apply for benefits, manage it and maintaining claims, aware of what is available and also their own entitlements.

- Able to maintain nutrition, plan own menu and meal, do own shopping and cooking.

- Able to maintain personal appearance well, good personal grooming, dressing appropriately, washing and ironing, purchasing clothes themselves.

Physical and mental health issues

You must check the following areas:

- Client's ability to self medicate, able to order, collect, and administer or store prescribed medication.

- Able to access local help from medical professionals, able to gain and maintain contact with a psychiatrists, community psychiatric nurses, counsellors, psychologists, social workers, local support groups etc.

- Able to maintain personal hygiene, able to wash brush teeth, clean dentures, bath safely, respond well to foul smell and investigate, wash hands when it maters, handle waste bins well, identify out-of-date goods, etc.

- Accessing GP service, able to explain difficulties and problems to GP, able to access primary health care service including dentist care, optician service, chiropody service, etc.

- Able to perform activities well without pain or other form of limitations due to physical conditions. Check for any support required for maintaining wellbeing and independence.

Cultural, spiritual and social issues
Check for the following:
- Clients are able to express their wishes according to their own cultural or ethnic backgrounds.

- Able to express any beliefs, values or norms within the boundaries permitted by the service.

- Clients able to exercise their rights of spiritual development by choosing to express any spiritual inclination freely, check if support is required.

- Able to maintain own specific personal identity and choice of gender and sexuality. Check that clients are able to express their wishes without intimidation or harassment.

Emotional issues
Emotional matters affect our self esteem and our ability to achieve desired objectives as well as being who we really want to be. Some important areas to examine are listed below.
- Clients are able to express their emotions or feelings well. For those they are not comfortable with, they are able to cope well managing them. Any support required for helping client express themselves more appropriately or productively?

- Clients are able to communicate effectively, not always misunderstood leading to hurt of feelings, or discouragement. Identify any disability and coping mechanisms required.

- Clients able to establish and maintain personal relationships, able to make their own minds about what sort of friendship suits them, can enter and leave the relationship as and when they deem fit.

- Clients are able to establish contacts with friends and families as and when necessary, also have access for communicating with people who matters in their lives.

- Clients feel comfortable about meeting new people, actively seek to engage in conversation when they want to without help.

- Clients are able to manage stressful situations well. Shows awareness of and try to avoid stressful situations or activities.

- Clients are able to manage well in social environments, able to participate in social activities without limitations.

Tenancy and benefits issues

Check the following:

- Ability to comply with containments of tenancy or licence agreements, able to understand responsibilities and rights

- Clients are able to make application for housing benefit and council tax benefit (if applicable) and are able to manage claims successfully.

- Clients understand their responsibilities around rent and rent payments as well as any service charges that apply. Check that clients are able to make payments accordingly.

- Clients are able to identify repairs and arrangement for maintenance work as appropriate. Check if help is required.

- Check if clients are able to handle neighbour problems competently. Is help required?

- If clients are awaiting resettlements, check that they are able to make their own applications (if this is required) for re-housing.

- Clients are able to access other services or contact other service agencies involved in the re-housing, as well as appropriate information and advice on further support.

- Check that clients are able to relinquish their current tenancy if and when required.

- Check that clients are able to conduct their own transfers of benefits without help.

Check other areas in volume four for more on assessment relating to independent living. Also see Winning Ideas Volume one.

Question 3	VULNERABLE PEOPLE AT RISK OF SUICIDE
Which groups of vulnerable people would usually be considered as being at more risk of suicide?	

In general, everyone can plunge into suicidal thoughts within split seconds but some groups of people are thought to be more at risk. The reasons behind suicide actions are many and complicated. The more-at-risk groups are listed below.

- People who live alone

- People with physical illness

- People who are unemployed, or have lost their job

- Those with psychotic illness, e.g. schizophrenia

- Those with severe depression

- Childless women

- People with history of persistent alcohol or drug misuse

- Those bereaved (especially death of a close relative or a spouse)

- Younger Asian Women (who may be forced to observe certain customs)

- It is a general belief that men are at more risk than women. Men are thought to have a three times suicide rate than women. This is particularly so with those aged over 50, and young men of between 15 and 24.

- Those with history of suicide attempts

- Those with family history of suicide attempts or suicide.

- Single or divorced people are thought to be at higher risk than married people

If you work with any of these groups of people you need to be aware of the driving forces behind their vulnerability and have a team approach for dealing with issues proactively and reactively. *Working with people who are at risk of committing suicide* will be examined further in Winning Ideas volume five.

Question 4   SUPPORTING A SUICIDAL RESIDENT/TENANT
One of our clients has attempted suicide several times. If you are appointed to the post and you become the person's keyworker what practical ways will you consider for supporting the client?

Whereas suicidal thoughts are uncommon they cannot be watered down by any means. Often they signal to staff that something is wrong, and prompts the need for a case review. Consider the following important points.

- It needs a sensitive and cautious approach, in that both the person and those who are affected by his/her condition may need professional support.

- The client must be offered the chance to talk. The listener must be a trusted person (to the resident).

- The environment in which the talking therapy is carried out is equally important. Ensure that client is feeling comfortable and not distracted or uneased by the presence of something else.

- Open ended questions are what is required, the objective being to allow the person to air out their feelings and the reasons in an unrestricted way.

Listen and show that you are listening
It is very important that they know you are listening and that they are believed. Therefore a good listening skill is a must. They must be left feeling that they can come back to you again and again and again.

Decide on your options
Feed on the initial information collected from client when deciding on further action. From the information you receive you may be able to tell changes required or that a better option is to seek professional help.

Immediate access to a professional

If resident is still restless after talking to you check if they will like to talk to a professional. The Samaritans have trained personnel specialised in providing counselling service to people who feel suicidal. It is always handy to have the help line in projects where clients are likely to experience suicidal thoughts.

Other sources of help

Another source of help is the resident's own family friends and advocates. This is not necessarily an all-time good idea, as some people do not particularly see their own people as helpful. You must therefore check with them first.

Support around other problems

These may be those driving clients to commit suicide. Examine reasons behind the attempt. This must also be accommodated in the support or care plan.

Cleaning and clearing of client's room

If client needs support with getting rid of items (e.g. drugs) used in the suicide attempt, inspect them and show them to a professional if necessary. Explain to the clients what you are going to do and why. Make your support available putting their room together and making it safe.

Further professional help

Encourage the resident to see their GP. Professional help in this respect may be very useful in dealing with the underlying issues e.g. depression. Apart from being able to prescribe medication, the GP can facilitate access to further help, e.g. specialist counselling or psychotherapy.

Prioritise

Prioritise any problems that will come in the way of client's ability to control his experience. For mental health client's treatment should be a priority. If client is already engaged in medical services it is important that the care team is informed of the suicide attempt.

Case review

A suicide attempt calls for a case review where the views of relevant professionals are sought. The client is also given the opportunity to air his feelings, views and concerns.

Make care plan clear and circulate it

The new care plan must be well circulated for everyone who needs to know. This is one area where consistency is very important. The plan must identify the following amongst other things:

- What client must do when suicidal thoughts set in.

- What staff must do when clients inform them they are having suicidal thoughts

- Measures for supporting client to minimise the occurrence of suicidal thoughts.

- Roles and the action plan identified for professionals of client's care team.

- New ways for staff to work with client's care professional team.

- New ways for client's care professional team staff to work with him/her.

Compulsory action

If there is evidence of mental disorder, compulsory action under the mental health Act may be considered. Hospitals have protocols for close observation of people who are felt to be actively suicidal, so that they are not left on their own.

Maintain records of events

Any report of suicidal thoughts and events must be recorded in order to keep track of danger signs. Project staff (including locums) must be aware of actions to take when confronted with suicide matters from clients.

Avoidance measures

Support the client to avoid situations, which lead to suicidal thoughts. This may include reducing chances of client being isolated, or being alone for long periods of time. In doing this care must be taken to ensure that client is not being deprived of basic freedom of independence and privacy. This means they must be encouraged (not make to) to do things.

Engage a mental health specialist

Practical ideas for dealing with situations which may lead to suicidal thoughts can be provided by a mental health professional. The leading person in this regard will be the consultant psychiatrist whose views must be sought in all cases.

Rehearse strategies

This is perhaps the most important of all the measures for addressing suicide attempts. This may involve acting up and practising any strategies for acting and seeking help when suicidal thoughts occur.

Also check ideas provided under the topic of *Depression* elsewhere in Winning Ideas

---

Question 5   WELFARE BENEFIT SYSTEM: GOOD PRACTICE
What do you consider a good practice when working with the benefit system or when supporting client with their benefit claim?

The following are some important rules emerging from experience in supporting others in making welfare benefit applications. Like most other things you will understand best when you start practising them. Any attempt to deviate from these rules will only lead to a disservice to clients, and likely to produce unnecessary complications. They are not listed in order of priority or process. See our publication *Remnants of Accommodation* for more information.

Information

Collect as much information as possible about a claim before considering making an application. This saves time and enables you to decide on entitlements. Furthermore, you will be in a good position to explain things to your client.

Involve the client

If it's not your own application ensure that the person you are supporting has good knowledge of what you intend to do. Remember it is their benefit and they reserve the right to know, and to give their consent on how you plan to proceed or what you intend to do.

Rights and obligations

Explain to them their rights and obligation. Claimants need to appreciate that as well as having rights there are some serious obligations that can affect their claim. This is important as welfare benefit represent the only source of income for many people in supported/care schemes.

Application form

Ensure you are using the correct application form. This is very important as delays can occur and a successful backdated payment request will be unlikely.

The right address

Ensure you are sending the form to the right address. Sending it to the wrong address will cause delays and in most cases it will mean no application has been made. If it is at all possible get the form in personally (the client can do this), and obtain a receipt from the benefit agency.

Evidence of postage

Endeavour to collect evidence of postage. If the application form must be posted, always collect a proof of postage at the post office. This may be helpful in future. You must bear in mind that delays in payment can occur all the same especially if claimant is seeking immediate payment. For example, housing benefit is usually paid from the Monday after receipt of claim form.

Avoid false information

Falsification of documents or deliberately giving misleading or false information is a criminal offence. Sometimes you are asked to enter information on a client's form, which you know to be incorrect. It is your responsibility as a Support Worker to advise the client on the consequences and also encourage them to do the right thing. People have been known to let the client him/herself make the relevant entry. At any rate, once you do not sign the form you cannot be held responsible for the content.

If false information appear in your writing it can have serious implication for your professional abilities and for your organisation.

Full participation

Encourage the person you are supporting to participate as fully as possible. This is an essential part of the enablement process. The focus should be to get the client to be able to complete their own benefit forms in future.

Photocopies

Always take a photocopy of application forms before sending them off. This will be useful when doing a renewal application. It can also be used as proof/evidence of application form being submitted in time. Furthermore it confirms that the tenant/resident has taken relevant action in respect of their rent, council tax liability or both.

Send evidence along with HB form

Check for proofs and send them off (i.e. if you are already aware of what is required) together with your application to avoid delays – first time. In most cases however, evidence of IS and JSA or even pay slips may take some time. Send them (all relevant evidence including copies of rent agreement) off all the same as soon as they are available. Do not wait for the council to request for them.

Keep copies of all correspondence

Get into the habit of keeping copies of all correspondence on client's file. This is useful for continuity of service (in your absence). It also puts the clients in control of their own claim at the right moment.

Challenge decisions early

If you spot any inconsistency or problem challenge it fast before they get big. At the very least ask for explanation. Make your request in writing and demand a written response. You may need them for evidence/proof in future.

Change of circumstances

Be aware of possible change of circumstances and encourage the client to notify the benefits agency. Failing to notify them of significant changes can affect payment and possibly loss of benefit. You cannot force the client to oblige but you can encourage them by explaining how their benefits will be affected. In addition, if you work for an organisation you will have the duty to inform the council in writing about certain changes, e.g. when a tenant/resident (for whom your organisation received direct payment) leaves the dwelling. Once aware of a change of circumstance that will affect rent challenge this promptly.

Monitoring systems

Use office diaries to monitor issues affecting rent or vulnerable clients' benefit. At least have a central monitoring system (not claimant's file). For example, enter in a central/project dairy when fresh claim or renewals are due. This will then be part of the daily tasks and an allocated person will ensure they are attended to. This system ensures consistency in a reliable service.

Direct payment

Consider direct payment of housing benefits to your employer. This must be a 'matter of course' with residents and in general with people with support needs. Direct payment can also be set up from IS or JSA to pay service charges or rent arrears (if it falls more than 8 weeks behind, and it is clear that HB will not cover it).

Ineligible rent

Consider direct payment of ineligible rent to your employer if client is incapable of doing this himself or herself. This refers to charges for meals, water, fuel (electricity, gas) etc, which HB won't cover. This arrangement needs to be balanced with the clients' ability to manage payment themselves.

Obtain permission

You need to be prompt with actions on claim matters as delays can sometimes cause irreversible damages. This calls for obtaining client's permission in writing well in advance. This is essential for professional practise and also for dealing with benefits agency staff. It is a requirement under the Data Protect Act 1998.

Appeals

Consider encouraging clients to appeal or ask for revision of decision, but also be sure they feel comfortable with things before starting the process on their behalf. A successful appeal can do a lot for their self esteem but a failed one can be damaging.

Liaison duties

Liaise effectively with other professionals collecting relevant documents where necessary. This is even more important when you have to challenge a benefit decision or support the client with a backdated payment request. Benefit rules put lots of emphasis on evidence. Effective liaison relationship with clients support team members is the best way forward.

Involve other staff

Use staff meetings or similar structures to collect ideas and information about benefit claims, and consider how you can maximise your clients interest.

Keep a clear record of what is happening about client's claims so that other staff can continue providing them with support in your absence.

Question 6   MANAGING PROJECT PROBLEMS
Scenario: Florence has a chiropody appointment. She approached you for £10.00 for cab fares, which she said, was promised to her by another member of staff. Meanwhile there is not enough money in the petty cash tin. Her appointment is clearly confirmed in the staff diary and by her appointment letter. What support will you provide to Florence?

Some good questions to attempt are:

- Is the appointment a life and death situation or can it wait?

- Why didn't the staff notify the rest of the team? Could Florence be telling the truth?

- How do I find £10.00 for Florence when there is not enough in the tin?

Make Florence feel listened to.
Take time to get the clear picture from Florence before assessing the situation for a decision. It is important for Florence to know that you reached your decision only after giving her demands a good hearing and consideration. This will help her to take your answers seriously.

Give Florence the benefit of doubt
Florence may be lying about the promised money but you must not show your disbelief, for the simple reason that she may also be right. It is not the norm for staff to make financial promises to vulnerable clients. However, you can't rule it out all together; some people do. All you can do is to look at how best you can help given the circumstance and whilst acting normal like you would towards any other client. Therefore concentrate on the need not the money.

Explain your situation
Florence needs to know that:
- You have no knowledge of the promise made to her

- As much as you are prepared to assist her there is not enough cash in the tin

- It may be cost effective for her to use an alternative transport

- Given the circumstance you can both examine options and how to address her needs.

Explore options

Take time to explore Florence's options and how you will be able to provide her with support given the resources available and at your disposal.

Assess importance of appointment

Weigh the options against the importance of the appointment. If unsure check with an expert (e.g. GP). If it is a very important appointment and Florence's mobility is restricted check if transport can be arranged for her by the hospital.

Public Transport

Most vulnerable service users will have freedom pass that allows them to use public transport free of change. This is something that can be looked at later on. Meanwhile, suggest to Florence to consider using public transport which cost less than a taxi.

Offer practical support

This may include physically accompanying Florence to her appointment. This may be possible if there is enough staff to cover the project. By this you confirm that you are interested in seeing her needs met.

Support with rescheduling appointment

This may be an option where the appointment is not a matter of 'life or death'. If all offers are declined consider supporting Florence to re-arrange the appointment and communicate this to her keyworker. Staff will then have plenty of time to work on her needs around transport.

Check for a local surgery

Check if a local surgery (NHS) is available for Florence to attend without the need of conventional transport.

Document

Document Florence's reaction to your advice and any obvious effect that the 'disappointment' registered on her.

Question 7   MISSING RESIDENT: PROJECT MANAGEMENT
Scenario: Whilst on duty you received a telephone call from a resident's brother (NOK) informing you that the resident who left the project to visit his brother three days ago did not arrived. Meanwhile the project staff are completely under the impression that the resident is with his brother. What action would you take?

This question has appeared for the third time in our survey of interviews. See Winning Ideas Volume two on actions to take when a client is reported missing and some practice questions.

Question 8   SUPPORTING A HARD-TO-REACH CLIENT
Scenario: David is in serious rent arrears and his landlord has started court action to repossess his flat. You are David's Support Worker with a duty to help prevent David's return into the streets. You have already written to him several times with appointments but he is never around when you call. Meanwhile his neighbours tell you that he still lives in his flat. What further action would you take?

- Consider putting your concerns in writing.
    - Make clear the seriousness of the matter and consequences
    - How you can help
    - How David can benefit from your service

- Suggest meeting at other places other than his home e.g. office, coffee shop, day centre.

- Send messages through neighbours.

- Ensure letters are hand delivered.

- Contact other support agencies associated with David and gain their support in getting him to engage.

- Irregular visits: Early and late visits may help. Also unannounced visits. If you are going to do late or irregular visits make sure you agree this with your duty staff person so that someone is placed in charge of your safety.

- Share difficulties with team members and manager for ideas and try them out.

- If difficulty exists consider getting David's approval or consent (by post) so that you can make representations on his behalf. This means for example you can request for backdated benefits payments or appeal against a decision with his authorisation.

- With David's consent contact HB for payment statement and landlords for rent statement. Comparing the two, check for gaps. Establish reasons for non-payments and take relevant steps toward:
  - Backdated payment request

  - Challenging decisions

  - Supplying relevant information, etc.

Hopefully your actions may lead to a reduction in the rent arrears.

- If you are able to get David to engage, prioritise the need to maintain roof over his head and gain his understanding and co-operation.

- Notify landlord of your contact and progress and request for more time. Also share difficulties and problems confronting you and also David (of course with his consent).

- There may be the need to complete a fresh housing benefit form and arrange for any outstanding information to be forwarded straight away.

- Consider liaising with professionals associated with David's care/support needs for relevant proofs to facilitate backdated payment request of housing benefit (and other benefits).

- If relevant, get David to agree to a direct deduction of payment from his benefits (e.g. JSA).

- Continue to liaise with landlord on matters of courts and agendas for court actions and communicate to David in writing. Freely discuss any concerns arising from this.

- Prepare a report in support of David outlining the progress he is making and arrangement already in place to clear his rent arrears. This will be useful for securing a stay of warrant application.

- Support David at court hearing and verbally explain the efforts he is making to maintain his accommodation.

Street level worker

If David cannot be contacted at all refer the case to the Street Level Worker (SLW). This person has the responsibility for engaging relevant measures to track ex-rough sleepers down and persuade them to return into decent accommodation.

Other support needs

David may have other support needs, which may be preventing him from appreciating the importance of remaining in his own flat. When and if David decides to engage, his entire support needs must be clearly assessed and a priority schedule must be completed. This means that other support needs may receive equal attention than those around his accommodation. The degree of David's vulnerability must be taken into consideration at every stage.

Alternative accommodation

It may be the case that David's accommodation is not suitable for him. He may not be ready enough for independent leaving. In this case an assessment can be made so that a referral is made for him to access an alternative accommodation (more suited to his needs).

Question 9   SUPPORTING CLIENT WITH CCG APPLICATION
Scenario: **You are charged with the responsibility of supporting a fresh tenant to complete a Community Care Grant application. What argument will you support the client to put forward as justification for the grant?**

You will need to discuss the form with the client first and explain what they can expect. It is also best completing the form jointly. You will then have to send the form along with a supporting letter from your organisation confirming your support for the client's application. Your letter must confirm information on how you have prepared the client for resettlement. The areas you need to cover are discussed below.

Eligibility

1.   Show that your client qualifies for CCG.
The client must be in receipt of Income support (IS) or Income based Jobseekers Allowance (JSA) at the time of making the application.

2.   Show that your client has not got too much capital
The amount awarded for CCG is reduced by the amount of capital in excess of £500 (£1,000 if client is 60 and over).
An example of what counts as capital is *Back-to-work bonus*
Examples of what does not count as capital are Payment *made from the family fund* and *Mobility component of DLA (Disability Living Allowance)*.

3.   Show that your client is not involved in a trade dispute.

4.   Show that the application is for help with cost totalling more than £30.00.

5.   State that the application is to help your client set up a home in the community as part of a planned resettlement programme following a period during which he was without a settled way of life.

Excluded Items

Show that the application does not involve excluded items. This is because one can only claim for items that are not excluded by law. Examples of items you can claim include:

- Furniture and household equipment

- Removal expenses, storage and connection charges on moving home

- Clothing and footwear

Examples of excluded items are:

- Expenses in connection with court proceedings e.g. legal/court fees, fines and damages

- Cost of domestic assistance or respite care

- Investments

Priorities

The decision makers are required by law to have regards to all the circumstances of each case. You will need therefore to address the following points;

The nature, extent and urgency of the need
Concentrate on showing how the items identified will help avoid difficulty or ease any form of pressures because of some specific discomfort the client is already experiencing.

The existence of resources which could meet the need
Show that your client has no alternative funding source, or that he can not have access to alternative funding e.g. unable to gain access to charity funds because of lack of local connection.

Whether any other person or body could wholly or partly meet the need
This is about relatives, friends, or other individuals known to the client. Advise that this is not possible e.g. because the client has lost touch with family members and his/her acquaintances are unable to help.

Planned resettlement

The resettlement programme must have started before you set up home. Those who qualify include those who may have been in hostels, night shelters, emergency shelters temporary supported lodging schemes, and rough sleepers.

Remember decision makers are required to pay attention and give priority to those who have for a substantial amount of time been in unsettled lives, and also the impact of being unsettled,

It is usually a requirement that you outline the nature of work you have already done with the client as part of the planned resettlement programme.

The table below is designed as an answer to a section in the Community Care Grant form and shows some specific items you may support your client to apply for: '*About what you need*' section.

WHAT DO YOU NEED?	WHY DO YOU NEED IT?	COST (£)	PRICE SOURCE
Bed and mattress	To sleep on	£99.99	Argos
Duvet	To keep warm at night	£19.99	Index
Duvet cover set	To protect the duvet	£12.99	Index
2 x Sheets and pillow cases for bed	To protect the mattress and pillows	£19.99	Argos
2 x pillows	To rest head at night in bed	£4.99	Argos
Curtains for two rooms	Too keep light, cold and prying eyes out	£25.99	Simmons
Curtain rails	To hold up the curtain	£9.99	Simmons
Wardrobe	To provide hanging space and shelves for clothes	£99.99	MFI
Chest of drawers	To keep my clothes	£34.99	MFI
Easy chairs/sofa	To provide seating	£199.99	MFI
Vacuum cleaner	To keep the floors clean	£33.99	Argos
Fridge with freezer	To keep food cool and fresh	£79.99	Argos
Gas cooker	To cook meals for myself	£144.99	Index
Cooker connection	To connect the cooker	£20.00	Corgi standard
Carpets	To keep place warm and comfortable	£199.99	Carpet land
6 piece saucepan set	To cook meals for myself	£32.95	Argos
4 piece cookware set	To bake and stir food	£14.99	Argos
12 piece crockery set	To have plates to eat off	£4.99	Argos
24 piece cutlery set	To cut up food with	£9.99	Argos
Kitchen knives and tool set	To be able to prepare food	£6.99	Wilkinsons

Kitchen bin. Bowl, cutlery drawer and dish drainer	To be able to prepare food	£7.99	Wilkinsons
Iron and Iron board	To have wrinkle free clothes for job interviews	£15.99	Index
Kettle	To boil water	£9.99	Index
Cleaning equipment set	To clean bath, floors etc	£4.99	Argos
Dining Table and chairs	To sit, write and eat on	£99.99	Sainsburys Homebase
Towels	To dry myself	£9.99	Safeway
Toilet brush	To clean the toilet	£6.99	
Toilet roll holder	To keep toilet paper clean	£4.99	Index
Clothes airer	To hung and dry clothes on	£7.99	Argos
Non slip mat	To use bath without sleeping	£3.99	Argos
Light bulb	To light rooms	£2.50	Staples
Washing machine	To wash clothes	£199.99	Curry's

Table 3.1   List of non-excluded items (Community Care Grant application)

Question 10   EFFECT OF ALCOHOL MISUSE
You have been invited to give a talk on the effect of alcohol misuse. The objective is to discourage individual service users from senseless drinking. What key information will your script contain?

Alcoholism is a disease, but alcohol is not necessarily bad for the body. Alcoholism refers to *alcohol dependency*. It is the stage where the drink controls one's life instead of the other way round. Long term *dependence* on alcohol will register serious consequences on the body.

EFFECT OF ALCOHOL MISUSE

Alcohol is now our third major health hazard, after heart diseases and cancer. Continued alcohol misuse may lead to social, legal, domestic, job and financial problems. It may also cut a life span by ten to fifteen years and lead to overdosing, suicide, and accidents and deaths from drunken driving. The warning is if you choose to drink, drink in moderation.

PART OF THE BODY AFFECTED	EFFECT
Head/brain	Aggressive, irrational behaviour Arguments. Violence Depression, nervousness Chronic anxiety. Unknown fears Hallucinations Serious psychiatric disorder Epilepsy Dementia (wee brain) Blackouts (alcohol amnesia) Serious memory loss Damage to nerves Loss of pain perception Altered sense of time and space
Mouth	Slurred speech Dulled taste and smell, reducing desire to eat
Ears	Diminished ability to distinguish between sound and perceive their direction
Eyes	Distorted vision and ability to adjust to lights. Puffy eyes Impaired visual ability Pinpoint pupils and red eyes
Face	Facial deterioration Looking older (especially women)
Throat	Chronic coughing Throat cancer (Cancer of the Larynx) Difficult swallowing induces severe vomiting

	Hemorrhaging Pain
Chest	Frequent colds Reduced resistance to infection Increased risk of pneumonia and tuberculosis
Food track	Cancer of the Oesophagus
Liver	Liver damage leading to breakdown and cirrhosis and liver cancer
Heart	Weakness of heart muscle Heart failure Anaemia Impaired blood clotting
Stomach	Vitamin deficiency Haemorrhage Severe inflammation of the stomach Vomiting Diarrhoea Malnutrition Duodenal Ulcer
Kidney	Impaired kidney function
Sex organ	Urinary infections **In men:** ▪ Impaired sexual performance. ▪ Impotence **In women:** ▪ Unwanted pregnancies ▪ Risk of giving birth to deformed, retarded babies ▪ or low birth weight babies
Limbs	Trembling hands Tingling fingers Numbness

	Loss of sensation in the fingers Peripheral neuritis
Leg	Impaired sensation leading to falls and numbness causing skin damage Numb, tingling toes peripheral neuritis

Table 3.2   *Effect of alcohol misuse. Source: Alcohol Community centre*

Other effects on the body recorded include the following:

- Gastritis/stomach upsets
- Blood shot eyes
- High blood pressure
- Nausea
- Driving accident
- Loss of balance
- Facial flushing
- Blurred vision
- Dehydration
- Raised pulse
- Trembling
- Blackouts
- Seizures
- Hallucinations
- Mood swings
- Argumentative
- Unrealistic fears
- Poor concentration
- Loss of inhibitions
- Irrational behaviour
- Impaired judgement
- Domestic disturbance
- Disrupted sleep pattern
- Increased nervousness
- Anxiety
- Phobias
- Paranoia
- Depression
- Loss of purpose
- Alcohol psychosis
- Loss of self esteem
- Panic attacks/states
- Korsakoffs/Wernickes
- Confusion/disorientation

▪ Deterioration of nervous system	▪ Premature ageing
▪ Foetal alcohol syndrome	▪ Hypoglycaemia
▪ Menstrual disturbances	▪ Heart disease
▪ Miscarriage	▪ Reduced fertility
▪ Malnutrition	▪ Pancreatitus
	▪ Epilepsy
	▪ Diabetes
	▪ Gout

Table 3.3   *Effect of alcohol misuse on the body*

Question 11   GIVE-AWAY SIGNS OF ALCOHOL MISUSE
What are the give-away signs of alcohol misuse?

The following table explains Alcohol misuse *give away signs*

Physical signs and symptoms	Tingling Looking rough Anaemia/malnutrition or rapid weight Passing blood Not eating Problems sleeping Often drunk Often smelling of alcohol Frequent minor injuries Decline in personal hygiene Seizures

Behavioural signs and symptoms	Projection
	Suicide attempts
	Mood swings
	Problems with keeping appointments
	Changing decisions too frequently
	Irrational fears
	Denial
	Memory loss
	Secretive
	Defensive
	Aggressive
	Sudden change in behaviour
	Forgetfulness
	Low self esteem
	Pathological jealousy
	Personality disturbances
	Delirium tremens
	Anxiety and phobia
Social signs and symptoms	Isolation
	Distancing from good friends
	Disengagement from well established activities
	Spending more money
	Loneliness
	Marital and sexual difficulties
	Family problems
	Child abuse
	Employment problems
	Financial difficulties
	Accidents at home, on the roads, at work
	Delinquency and crime
	Homelessness
Others	Diabetes
	Heart problems
	Blood pressure problems

Table 3.4   Give-away signs of alcohol misuse

Also see the topic on *Alcohol misuse* above.

Question 12   ALCOHOL MISUSE: RELAPSE
How can you tell if one of your clients with a history of alcohol problems and who is engaged in a rehabilitation programme is drifting back into serious alcohol misuse?

This is about how you know that a client needs your help and also when you need to take action. Remember that any major change in a client's situation must call for a comprehensive review of care or support plan. In most cases you will need more than a few signals in order to conclude that intervention is due. The following points are self explanatory. If you work in a team you can put these factors together with tick boxes for staff to use in checking for warning signs. They can also be used as discussion points for identifying areas of difficulties and week points.

The warning signs include the following:
1. Lying about drinking levels.

2. Exhibiting signs of discomfort if there isn't a drink available.

3. Needing a drink to start the day: Priority goes to drinking.

4. Covering up drinking and the amount spent on it.

5. Drinking large quantities without getting drunk or before reaching the buzz level required.

6. Having a desire to increase the amount of alcohol consumed in order to maintain the desired effect.

7. Diminishing withdrawal symptoms. This is especially the case where the person is on a recovery programme.

8. Experience shakes or feeling sweaty when he wakes up.

9. Being drunk more often.

10. Taking days off work/college/well engaged activities because, or for reasons related to drinking.

11. Engaged in disruptive behaviour: Getting into trouble.

12. Having accidents and arguments for reasons of drinking.

13. Informing you that he is drinking more than he planned to.

14. Morning retching and vomiting.

15. Sweating excessively at night.

16. Withdrawal fits.

17. Morning drinking.

18. Decreased tolerance.

19. Hallucinations, frank deliriums tremens.

20. Unable to keep to a drink limit.

21. Difficulty in avoiding getting drunk, calling for more and more drinks in order to get intoxicated.

22. Spending considerable time drinking in bar or pub.

23. Missing meals in preference to being in another place for alcohol.

24. Having memory losses and black outs.

25. Becomes restless without drink.

26. Organises his entire day around drink.

27. Trembling after drinking the day before.

Question 13   SUPPORTING A DRUG ADDICT CLIENT
Scenario: Colin is a heavy drug addict and a tenant of our supported housing scheme. He has been allocated to you as a key client. What practical support will you consider in order to enable him live life as full as possible?

To answer this question you need to show understanding of how drugs affect its victims. Refer to other parts of this book for this. Then look at how you can address the problems using available resources. What is important is your understanding of how those problems affect the victim's abilities to perform normal activities, for example, keeping own space hygienic and clean. Look at the following examples (not exhaustive list):

Domestic and household task

- Cleaning

- Laundering/washing

- Preparing own meals

- Eating well

- Ironing of clothes

Finance

- Budgeting

- Borrowing habits

- Managing debts

- Dealing with creditors

- Managing rent arrears

Work/employment

- Absenteeism

- Inconsistent in progress

- Inability to concentrate

- Short-span memory

- Unable to hold down a job

Dealing with support agencies

- Difficulty in keeping appointment

- Not keeping to agreements/plans

- Breaking of contracts

Behaviour

- Frequently getting into arguments

- Becomes angry quickly and engages in fights

- Trips over and falls

- Other nuisance behaviour e.g. noise, shouting or screaming

Colin will need to know that he can trust you before he co-operates. This may take time and lots of efforts. Meanwhile, it is important for you to bear in mind that Colin may know more about the evils of drug misuse than you do. A swift move to educate and reprimand will rather worsen the situation and you will probably never get him to engage with you. Some practical approach to dealing with this case will include the following:

Check that Colin is ready to quit drugs
No one can do it for him. Until such time the person is ready you will be wasting your time. Help him make the decision by emphasising the way his live is affected by his situation. Better still; the client must be able to come to you with a request for help. Otherwise, he must declare voluntarily his readiness to quit.

Check what support he wants and suggest options available.
A desperate client who wish to quit will open up to just anything, in fact sometimes not being realistic about their decisions. Some end up taking too much than they can 'chew' and when things fail to go as expected hopes are gravely shattered. Guide them through realistic choices.

Harm-minimisation
Support client get educated in sensible use of drugs. This may take several forms and on a wide range of topics. Some important areas to look are listed below:

- Encourage reduction of intake

- Encourage him to eat before taking drugs

- Encourage him not to mix drugs

- Colin must ensure his supply is from a reliable source not just from any dealer as most street drugs are contaminated (bulked up with all sorts of substances)

- Encourage him to avoid sharing needles

- Encourage him to switch to less dangerous drugs

- Encourage him to live on quantities that he can afford

- Stay where people can see them and provide them with support when necessary

Good personal hygiene
Good hygiene is a critical harm minimisation strategy. It can also raise alarm bells for people around you to come to your aid when support is required.

Encourage Colin to see his GP/attend the drug clinic
GP service is usually where many quitters start their journey towards freedom. They will be able to refer Colin to a specialist agency which can help him at different levels and for a smaller no fee at all.

Support with maintaining good eating habit
This is another harm minimisation strategy. Always make sure Colin does his shopping soon after colleting his giro. Also consider the feeding of his metres

Objectives must be specific clear and realistic.
They are best set by the client but you need to guide him away from fantasies. As well as objectives around the drinking habit provide support for him to look at daily skills like cooking, washing, grooming and laundering.

Work closely with professional
Specialist GPs, and drug counsellors provide valuable service in the road to rehabilitation. Be clear in your mind their role of helping Colin to explore further aspects of problem area where their services can be used. You may need to accompany Colin to appointments if necessary.

Assess suitability of accommodation
Check if the area is suitable for someone who wish to recover from addiction. It will be hard work supporting Colin if he is surrounded by alcohol addicts all the time. Assess whether or not the domestic atmosphere is right for the programme.

Support with engaging in group therapy
Group Therapies have been known to be very effective for many people. The Alcohol Anonymous for example works by learning from successful quitters. They become mentors for new addicts and through encouragement and support help others to drive their determination through and quitting alcohol.

Relaxation

Support in accessing services that will enable Colin to relax e.g. Yoga, and acupuncture. Massage service is now available free of charge in some day centres and sports centres.

Help with budgeting

Reach agreement over a budgeting plan allocating money for food, household items cloths as well as any debts. Other areas to consider are rent, service charges, debts, utility bills, and personal items like toiletries. You need to prepare for a real 'fight' on this one as less money available to an alcoholic means less alcohol. In effect your good intentions may be perceived as a deliberate attempt to sabotage his 'successful life'.

Shopping and cooking

Another important area for support is shopping and the preparation of healthy meal. This has already been mentioned but let me place emphasis on safe method of cooking and safe shopping. Because of the obvious risks in these areas support must be proactive. Encourage client to reduce number of cooking time, avoid dinking when cooking, or where he is planning to cook. Furthermore, he must consider shopping locally in order to reduce the travelling distances (especially when he is drinking).

Relative and family connection

Support with efforts made to contact and maintain relationship with friends and family. The vulnerable alcoholic is often isolated from decent members of his own family. On the other hand this is not exactly what the client wants. Discuss any problems he has and include this in the support plan.

Assistance with dealing with neighbour dispute

Serious alcoholics are more than likely to create serious neighbour problems. The banging, shouting, falls, noise, braking and smashing of items all leads to aggravation. Neighbours will register their complaints with the landlord and demand action.

Detox programme

Should Colin be required to go on a detox programme consider ways of supporting him. This may include the following:

- He is aware of what the programme entails and what will be required of him

- The benefit he stands to gain

- Checking that Housing benefit and council tax will not be affected. Otherwise, what needs doing?

- Liaise with his landlord to ensure that his licence or tenancy won't be affected

- He is able to continue to receive his Income Support or JSA without interference. Otherwise, what needs doing?

Question 14   DRUG ADDICTION: WHY PEOPLE DO DRUGS
Working with drug users takes understanding, patience, and tolerance. This means staff needs a firm understanding of circumstances that drives people into 'doing' drugs. Why do people 'do' drugs?

A *Drug* can be defined as:
'Any substance with the ability to alter the function within a living organism'.

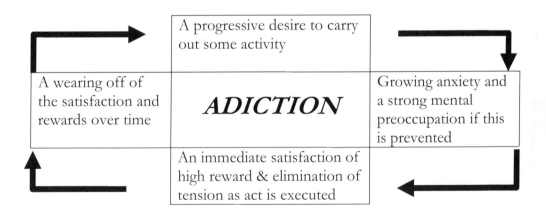

We all use drugs e.g. caffeine, alcohol and tobacco, but we do not abuse them, in that it does not take over our lives and prevent us from doing what we want to do. We are not interested in drug doing as a business venture, but how people make themselves vulnerable because of the choices they make around their drug lives.

Statistics on drug abusers:
- 95% of people use alcohol by 16 years of age (UK)

- 41% of UK students use Cannabis

- Young people are most at risk.

Drug or alcohol misuse occurs when addiction has taken over a person's ability to live a normal life and perform normal activities as and when they wish to.

MAIN REASONS FOR 'DOING DRUGS'

Domestic influence
Some one may do drugs because both parents do drugs. It could also be that they have access to drugs prescribed for other people living in the same household.

Friends/colleagues pressure
This is how most smokers start. This stems from the social factor that demands 'join us' or 'leave us'. Most young people believe one must participant in group norms in order to prove belongingness.

Curiosity
A desire to establish for yourself reasons why others take to the habit. The curious mind will try anything in order to gain a first hand assessment of its own suspicions.

Strong desire to prove a point (e.g. not daft)
This is the 'macho syndrome'. Young men especially like to prove their manhood by taking up all sorts of challenges. It is also about the 'gang thing' where acceptance is based on a specific mark, or sign, or some other form of identity. Members are expected to pass 'the test' to proof how hardened they are, and to justify their inclusion.

Genetic
It is argued by some people that drug dependency runs in some families. Whether or not this is a fact is yet to be fully established. The fact still remains however, that you are more likely to find a long chain of people doing drugs in the same family. Research shows that the risk for developing for instance alcoholism does indeed run in families.

What warning signs in a client's behaviour or attitude can indicate signs of drug/alcohol misuse?

Warning signs for drugs misuse has a lot to say about altered patterns; how individuals spend their time, present themselves or even conduct their own small spaces. Some pointers that may suggest that something is wrong are explained below.

WARNING SIGNS

Change in behaviour e.g. quick temper
This may include quick temperedness and unprovoked aggression. It may also include switching of groups and a change in the way the person spends his/her time.

Sleepless nights
Typical with shared rooms; complaints may be received from room mates. Night staff patrolling the project may also register concerns about the person. Drug effect can make a person enjoy nocturnal activities more with pounds around especially communal areas or looking for something to eat in kitchen areas.

Petty clashes with rules (e.g. in hostels)
Usually such breaches are not too serious to warrant a warning letter, and yet can't be ignored. For example a drug user will be usually reluctant to respond to an alarm clock, then shows up too late for his breakfast. Instead of realising his fault the agonising pain of anger may push the person to ignore staff orders. The person helps himself to some food, and in the extreme he takes his anger upon staff, becomes rude or presents all sorts of disruptive behaviours.

Loss of appetite
Drug cravings can displace a good appetite leading to weight loss. The other side of this is that mounds of food will be crammed away (for 'future reference'). In projects or hostels where food is served a recent user will be seen hanging around for as long as it takes to get that 'seconds' which is consumed at night when options for accessing food will be limited. Such

people will also be found complaining about food portions and about staff serving the food.

Unpredictable moods
This may manifest in several ways. Some examples are listed below:

- Short giggles
- Extreme quietness
- Negative facial expressions
- Irritability and restlessness
- Suspicious and secretive or cagey

A resident known to be calm and composed will all of a sudden turn out as agitated and disturbed. For example when the person's giro fail to arrive on time, he or she will be seen swearing and desperately finding someone to blame. Thoughts that may run through the person's mind include;

- How to get his /her next fix (of drugs)
- How to pay back money he/she already owes to friends and colleagues
- What he/she is going to do about the cravings

Short span concentration (forgetfulness)
Forgetfulness or diminished concentration span is an important warning sign. This may show as missed appointments, missed rent or service charge payments or failure to comply with rent agreements. A significant deviation from the person's agreed support or care plan will also be apparent. During keywork sessions staff will notice a marked change in the resident's ability to hold information and also voice out issues discussed few moments earlier. Coupled with this behaviour it will be very obvious that they are not premeditating or acting up their actions.

Sores/rashes around mouth and nose
This is more true for those who sniff drugs. They turn to cover up these areas. Some choose not o look straight at you when talking to you.

Complaints of tiredness

'Freshers', or new users especially go very pale and wear all signs of tiredness during their first few weeks of exposure to drugs. Some people go white or chalky in their faces, and also light or washed-out on their feet. A constant complaint of tiredness from a known to be healthy and ruddy (healthy-looking) resident should trigger concern.

Loss of interest in physical appearance

The person directs loyalty and attention to their new drug love life, and nothing else will do except the next fix. As soon as the last one has dried out of his system all resources are diverted to finding the next fix. Physical appearance as well as other important issues in life are brushed aside.

Disengagement from well established activity

Lack of concentration coupled with a careless attitude may lead to a sack from work, or the person may simply decide to pack it in himself. Diminished academic performance is also possible. Many drugs are very potent in addiction. Drugs have the power to make dependants loyal to them by whatever shape or form. In their addictive grips they share no loyalty with nothing. A serious drug addict will stop at nothing in securing his next fix. The strong cravings and the effects of the drugs pulls down any good thing built over the years: Relationships with loved ones break down, day centre attendance gets pushed aside, hospital treatment appointments are treated as having trivial importance, and project/hostel rules as obsolete.

Stealing money, goods and prescribed medicines.

Stealing money to buy drugs, goods to sell or exchange for drugs, and medicines to misuse. It's about anything to lay hands on 'that drug'.

Long unexplained absence from the project/hostel/home

This may be because of a new company the person has found or chased away because of money he owes to others in the project or in the area. It could also be that the person is hiding away from other drug dealers because of failed promises. Another reason may be that he had an accident and got hospitalised, or detained by the police for some wrong doing.

Isolation

A preference of being aloof and staying away from public areas or the reception) area (where he can be seen by staff). This is usually the case where there are strong rules on drug abuse.

Unusual guests

Receiving unusual guests who might be perhaps 'much older' or 'too young' to be the person's friend. Their guests usually have strange or care-free appearance. Most of them will only pop in, then pop out - frequent short visits. This may suggest that the person is dealing in drugs.

Use of street language

Sudden use of street language by someone who is usually considered to be careful and respectful with words. The new words would be those found common amongst drug users.

CAUTION

A caution here is for all staff to remember that most of these behavioural symptoms are common with young people and a hasty conclusion can prove rather costly to the staff team. What may initially appear to be a danger sign may really end up as an over reaction.

Question 16   PHYSICAL SIGNS OF DRUGS DOING
Scenario: The staff team has received several reports that one of your key clients does drugs. Meanwhile he has denied any drug use. You decided to check out the truth by looking for clues yourself. What are some physical signs that may confirm your suspicions when you visit the client's room?

We now turn our attention to signs that will emerge from contact with a user's room or private space. News of physical signs may reach staff through different routes:

- The person's room mate would have brought some of these to the attention of staff long before they emerge fully.

- Cleaners working in the resident's room are also likely to report some strange findings.

- Periodic health and safety checks or hostel risk assessment activities may also bring some issues to light.

- Hostel staff on patrol may spot strange items/deposits in the person's corner.

- Contractors or maintenance men carrying out repairs in the resident's room may report concerns.

Trade marks (physical signs) of 'doing drugs'

- Peculiar looking cigarette ends
- Powder or plant material in twists of paper
- Small plastic bags
- Tablets or capsules
- Cans or metal tins
- Pill boxes
- Metal foil wrappers
- Twists of paper
- Spill marks on clothes or bedding
- Faded sleeves
- Straws
- Spots or sores around the nose or mouth

- Very dry lips appearing cracked
- Chronic cough and cold
- Plastic bags with traces of glue
- Used match sticks
- Bottles
- Rags (in waste bins)
- Butane gas cylinder
- Trail of odd smells from:
  - Bedroom
  - Persons breathe
  - Person's clothes
- Needles, syringes or ampoules
- Sugar lumps

Solvent Users trade marks

Other signs that may be visible or detectable include a highly visible trail of odd smell originating from:

- Bedroom
- On the person's breath

- The person's clothes

Such a person may be a regular solvent inhaler, and in addition there will be:

- Spill marks on clothes, or bedding
- Faded sleeves (as a result of regular secret inhaling)
- Spots or sores around the nose or mouth
- Very dry lips which appear cracked
- Chronic cough and cold

Drug Injectors Trade marks
Groups of items forming apparatus for a person injecting drug include the following:

- Needles
- Water
- Citric acid
- Pieces of tampon

- Syringes
- Lemon juice
- A rubber tube/strap
- Spoons

On the bodies of the person will be marks made by the needles. More on this will be covered in Winning Ideas volume five.

CAUTION

You must bear in mind that most of these items can easily be associated with collections of an average young person. For example spoons and lemon juice are very much of everyday items. The line between a definite abuse and a normal use should be a mater of experience.

Question 17   SUPPORTING A DRUG ADDICT CLIENT
Some of our residents have serious drug addiction problems. What steps would you take in providing support for them?

Support provision
The reaction to a new case by staff should not be one of shock, anger or aggression. Problems with drugs should always be anticipated and for this

reason staff must prepare themselves for eventualities through training, risk management and support resource management.

A calm and composed approach is the answer

This is because in most cases drug abusers are very much aware of the harm they are inflicting upon their bodies. The problem is at the addictions stage they have lost control. Do not approach them hailing guilt and shame. Do not be too harsh, show understanding, stick to facts. Use open ended questions to get them to do the talking rather than you lecturing them on what is right or wrong.

Focus on developing a collaborative approach

You need your client to work with you. Focus on gaining his co-operation. Do not think of doing things for him especially if he himself is not consenting. A lot has to come from him. It doesn't matter how long it takes, you need his co-operation or the entire support work will suffer terrible frustrations.

Get more information

Go beyond suspicions and speculations. You need facts. If you have succeeded in getting his co-operation you must go a step further collecting more information from him. Every drug user carries his/her own baggage of problems and support needs. Check for the following.

- What is being taken?

- How much is being taken?

- How it is taken?

- How long the client has been taking the drugs?

- Where and when the drugs are taken?

- How the habit is funded?

- How the habit is sustained and what are the main sustaining factors?

- Who are the client's close friends or form his close companions?

- Have there been previous attempts to quit drugs?

- Has he suffered relapse and what were the triggers?

- How long was the client able to stay without drugs and what was the coping mechanism?

Questions like these will put you in a better position to understand the problems of your client and therefore resource your ability to organise help.

Listen

Be prepared to listen, bearing in mind that the client himself may be going through difficulties. Good listening skills are what you need to advance your relationship. It is true to say that most drug victims may know more about drugs than you do. You will be surprised how much information your client has about the harmful effect of drugs. The fact that he has chosen to share the knowledge at a time of asking for support requires that you concentrate on facts and not emotions.

Establish exact nature of client's problems

Do not assume that your client's core problem is 'drug addiction'. It may be something of a distanced nature. Get him to be specific, and concentrate on those problems before you concern yourself with the secondary cause (drug addiction). Any attempt to ignore the client is likely to induce a rebellion and reduce chances of gaining his co-operation.

Help client to gain deeper understanding of consequences

This follows good listening and comes after you have succeeded in allowing client to anchor his confidence in you. Help him to analyse the issues using the information you have gathered. Here you must concentrate on effects, and consequences. You also need to look at this at different angles of client's life (e.g. college, domestic, employment, etc).

Client must accept help

At this stage hopefully, the client will understand realistic implications of doing drugs and hopefully this will reinforce his willingness to obtain help.

Client must be prepared to take a key role

More importantly the client must be ready to take on a lead role in the quest for help around the drug habit. Make it clear that you will be available to provide support but only if he is ready to take steps towards recovery. This helps to determine the client's seriousness. On the other hand you need to make careful assessment of client's abilities and match this to the support method.

Assist client to examine suitable options
This is where you discuss alternative ways the identified problems can be dealt with. Use you expert knowledge to bring hope to a desperate and frustrated client who is ready to fight addiction.

Action plan
This may actually come from the client. It is more or less the basic idea the client has for dealing with the problems. Assist him to guide against unrealistic ideas and goals.

Agree on service plan
After considering relevant details of the matter you can support client through a working document which must be agreed by himself and your organisation. Such a document is called Service Level Agreement. Essentially, you are agreeing the type of service that must be provided to the client in order to meet his specific needs. Communicate the plan to people who need to know, making sure that client has given his consent over confidentiality.

Check for involvement of needles
This is where you concern yourself with a harm minimisation strategy. If needle is involved check the following:

- What type or kind is used?

- Where does client gets them?

- Does client share needles with others?

- How does he dispose of used needles?

- How does client use needles?

- What part of the body is involved in the needle use?

- What drug(s) is/are involved in the needle use?

- Where is the needle used (public areas, clients flats, project premises etc)?

If needles are involved, advise client to do a test for communicable diseases like HIV and hepatitis. Then liaise with experts to help him minimise harm. If your work involve going into the client's flat you need to put in place your own strategy for reducing risk towards yourself.

Client must keep a dairy

Keeping a diary helps with progress monitoring. Failures can also be recorded as well as the triggers. Any specific days of success can be a source of important motivation. Use keywork sessions to discuss notes and help client examine alternative ways of approaching problems and difficulties.

Assess risk (to client and others)

Risk assessment will help you to plan ahead, removing likely obstacles long before they arrive. Access the environment in which you are delivering support. Look at neighbours, friends, budgeting skills, etc. and ask if anything needs dealing with in the recovery plan. Plan for them as well.

Involve expects

Consider specific problem areas identified and fish out local resources for addressing them. Check with your colleagues, partners, etc. for details of good services that can be easily accessed by client. Refer him on for further help. Some services you may wish to consider are:

- Drug specialist in health centres or specialist projects

- GP service

- Drug clinic service

- Drug Rehab organisations

- Self help groups

Continuous needs assessment

Continue to assess needs against resources of the project. Check if needs are growing beyond margins that can be accommodated within the project. Where a more suitable accommodation will be appropriate do a planned transfer making sure that a comprehensive support or care package is put together and implemented at the same time.

More topics on *Drugs and Drug misuse* and *Support for the drug addicted* will be featured in Winning Ideas Volume five. Also see other parts of volume four for ideas on *Drug laws*.

Question 18   VIEWING A PROPERTY CHECKLISTS

A significant part of this position is about accompanying (prospective) clients on viewing after successful interviews. What sort of things will you support the client to check during the viewing?

You must first check if the offer is a reasonable or suitable one using the list below.

SUITABLE OFFER CHECKLIST

Structurally sound
Building not showing any sign of weakness both internally and externally in the form of e.g. cracks in beams, walls or columns.

Health and Safety
There must be no serious health and safety issues. This covers areas like ventilation, lighting, moulds, exposed electrical cables.

Water supply
Supplied with clean water, hot water facility and plumbing facilities.

Electrics
Electrics are working and are safe.

Within chosen area
Is property in client's chosen area? Client may decide to go ahead with the offer even though the area was not chosen by him/her. However, they have every right to refuse the offer on this ground alone and for the same reason why the area was not chosen in the first place. This will usually not count as a 'reasonable offer'.

Support needs
Offer agrees with client's support needs (e.g. not in 'drug' areas if client is recovering from drug addiction).

Abilities

Accommodation sympathises with client's specific abilities (e.g. disabled client not restricted in movement due to too many steps).

VIEWING A PROPERTY CHECKLIST

In general you must support the client to decide whether or not they wish to accept the offer by going through the following list. It must be noted that the content will vary depending on the property in question, and also client's own preferences. For this reason it is important to ensure that what is priority for the client in respect of their own flat is discussed well in advance of the interview and viewing.

Check for the following:

- *State of repairs*

- *Decoration in good condition*

- *Size and location of flat*

- *Location of functional areas suitable*

- *Room sizes*

- *Location of fuse box*

- *Structurally sound*

- *Electrics are working and are safe*

- *Cistern in toilet flushes*

- *Plumbing works and is safe*

    - Taps running

    - Hot & cold water available from sink and bath

    - Any pipe work corroded?

    - Any pipe work leaking?

- *It is secured (especially doors and windows)*

- *Heating and hot water*

- *Operation manual for heating system*

- *Walls and ceiling*
  - Any cracks or holes?
  - Any damp or mould?
  - Signs of crumbling?
  - Any hazardous material used (e.g. polystyrene tiles)?

- *Kitchen*
  - Walls, ceiling and floors easy to clean?
  - Wall socket for a cooker present?
  - Gas supply point for a cooker (if applicable) present?

- *Bathroom and WC*
  - Toilet bowls, shower trays free from cracks?
  - Sealant in reasonable condition?
  - Windows can be opened with ease?
  - An extractor fan that works?

- *Concrete floors*
  - Lifting?
  - Damp?

- *Pests*
  - Signs of rats, mice, or cockroach infestation?

- *Toxic material*
  - Any strong fumes from timber preservatives?
  - Any decaying asbestos?
  - Any loose or damaged mineral fibre (outside loft)?

- *Security doors*
    - Entry phone working?
    - Key fob or token for operating main entrance door working?
- *Stairs and banisters safe?*
- *Balconies secured?*
- *Railing and fencing secured?*

Also assist clients to locate and familiarise themselves with the facilities and issues discussed in the answers to the next question.

Question 19   SUCCEEDING IN TENANCY SUPPORT

It is believed that most tenancies of ex-rough sleepers collapse within the first six months. What initial support will you provide to clients to enable them take up tenancies successfully?

Meet with the client

A three way meeting with the client and another person already familiar to the client, (prior to signing the tenancy) is very important. The meeting must be used to discuss roles and provide answers to any questions and concerns client may have about the working relationship.

Familiarise yourself with needs indicators

Ensure you are familiar with the needs of the clients and any work done with him by previous support staff/agencies. It is also important that you are aware of methods and approaches that works well with him as well as any current issues.

Familiarise yourself with risk issues

This is about risk to client (with special reference to accommodation, or having to live alone), as well as any risk that client might present to others. Another important side of the risk information is that it will help you make important decisions about expectations and where to place emphasis when working with client.

Dealing with emergencies

Discuss client's ability to deal with emergency situations. Emergencies must be judged within the light of clients needs and assessed risks. This means not all clients will have the same things on their emergency list. Nonetheless issues around security flood, fire, gas, and electricity must always be covered.

Reporting repairs

The need to report repairs may be necessary as early as the first day of moving into the property. This is down to the fact that some minor maintenance works may not be obvious during the viewing.

Garden: Who has access to it

This is an area that can easily become a 'headache' at a later date. Issues around gardens are often ignored during the signing up. Sometimes it's a matter of other tenants exerting control or the tenant failing to maintain the garden (considering it to be the responsibility of the housing provider). Though most clients would like accommodation with a garden maintaining them is not what they think deep about.

Location of hot water storage tank

Check that client can use it safely as and when necessary. This may require actually letting them having a go under your supervision. Depending on the needs of the client you may have to put up some reminders on the wall (next to the storage tank) to help them.

Location of cold water storage tank

Not just about the location. Check that client can also use it as and when necessary. This may require actually letting them having a go under your supervision. Depending on the needs of the client you may have to put up some reminders on the wall (next to the storage tank) to remind them with how to work it.

Also locate the following:

- Gas meter

- Gas lever to turn on or off

- Electric meter

- Main water stop cock (normally located under kitchen sink, or in airing cupboard, or in cellar)

- Electricity fuse box and on or off switch

Support client to arrange connection of relevant utility services to flat.

Telephone numbers:
- Emergency gas number for gas leakage

- Emergency telephone number for electrical problems

Provide information on:
- Benefit application and transfer request

- Accessing local facilities

- Furnishing flat

- Local support services. If for instance client has mental health they should be linked into local support as soon as possible

- Housing officer's details

- Local Tenancy Sustainment Team

Question 20   SUSTAINING INTEREST IN THE COMMUNITY
The person appointed to this position will have the responsibility of providing on-going support to clients with a view to sustaining their interest in the community. What considerations will you make in order to ensure that such interests are met?

Local facilities and services that client may need support to use include the following:
- *Job Centre;* for help with looking for employment, JSA, advice, job placement, etc.

- *Community centres;* for advice, social activities, etc.

- *Doctor (GP) and or Health Centre;* health service

- *Post Office(s);* correspondence, TV licence, rent payments, etc.

- *Sports Centre;* sports activities, keeping fit, advice etc.

- *Leisure Centres and Parks;* for relaxation, games, other recreationary activities

- *Police station;* reporting emergencies, crime, problems with neighbours

- *Hospitals (A& E Service):* for accessing health service in emergency

- *Libraries;* feed interests and hobbies, support academic exercises, get information, etc.

- *Adult Education College;* Basic English, basic skills, further education, etc.

- *Housing office and allocated Housing officer;* to report problems with neighbours, repairs, etc.

- *Advice centres;* to obtain advice on a wide range of issues including housing

- *Benefits Agency (DSS);* to claim benefits, follow up claims, etc.

- *Careers office;* get advice and support with career development

- *Local shopping centre;* do shopping

- *Local market;* do shopping or sell things

- *Local church/mosque;* feed spiritual interests

- *Local ethnic minority support group;* Information, advice and practical support on specific issues relating to the person's cultural needs.

ACTIVITIES ASSOCIATED WITH THE CLIENT MOVING INTO NEW FLATS

Community Care Grant (CCG) application

This is social welfare help for people with unsettled life acquire things like furniture, carpet, cooking utensils, etc.

Crisis loan application

Like CCG this is a social fund loan available to clients who are in crisis. This may be the only source of financial assistance for people on Incapacity Benefit who cannot access CCG.

Housing benefit application

Assist them to complete and send off their Housing Benefit application to prevent rent arrears problem from the start.

Others include the following:

- JSA: Change of address notification and transfer of claim.

- Decoration voucher (from the landlord if available).

- Furniture acquisition arrangement.

- Electricity connection or supply to flat.

- Water connection or supply to flat.

- Gas connection or supply to flat.

- Electric and Gas meter reading. The reading must be taken and passed on to the companies involved.

- Provide client with contact details (for contacting your organisation).

- Obtain copy of tenancy (agreement) for client's file (optional). This enables you to assist them to establish their rights and responsibilities when it matters.

- Check that tenancy agreement content is read and explained to client before signing.

- Check client has relevant emergency numbers (for all the support teams).

- Emergency phone numbers for client to keep:
    - Electricity, gas, and water services

    - Gas leakage

    - Your landlord (emergency service)

    - Water company

    - Electricity company

- Police, flood, accident (phone 999)

Explain that the following must be completed for your organisation's files & indicate a time scale for doing this.

Summary contact Information

This contains summary profile of client and will provide the support agency with information like National Insurance number, date of birth, next of kin, referral agency details, GP and other support agencies working with the client.

Individual Service Agreement (ISA)

This form will contain the agreed support plan between the client and the agency providing the support. It will also reflect support need indicators identified by previous service providers.

Risk assessment

This will contain any identified risk towards client and from others in respect of his new accommodation.

Correspondence

Explain that the client is welcomed to keep copies of important correspondence on your organisation's file & access them when necessary. The invitation will depend on the level of client's needs. Where a client seems capable of maintaining and managing their correspondence independently, they must be encouraged to continue to do so.

New tenants pack

Not all the information due to client may be available at the signing upor booking in stage. You must check for any outstanding documents. Check if client can obtain the landlord's new tenants pack, which will normally include:

- Complaints procedure
- Equal Opportunities Statement
- Tenant's Guarantee and insurance arrangments
- Policy on Tenant's Participation
- Procedures for dealing with repairs

Financial implications of new accommodation

Check client understands the financial implications with

- Decoration of flat
- TV licence
- Rent
- Council tax
- Utility (water, electricity, gas,) bills
- Furniture replacement

Next appointment

Agree on next meeting and ensure client is clear on how to contact you.

<hr>

Question 21   PROBLEMS FACING CLEINTS
What problems do people with long history of rough sleeping face?

Abilities and disabilities

For example mental health, drug and alcohol related problems affecting their ability to look after themselves or manage their own affairs.

Criminal records,

Some have criminal records, making it difficult to get into employment or engage in some form of meaningful occupation.

Negative experiences

For example, evicted from previous tenancies and carrying with them the negative experience of having to observe strict tenancy agreements. There is a preference for living free of such restrictions. Tenancy-related problems are received badly and dealt with badly. Others may be living with scares from some form of social exclusion experience.

Illiteracy

This makes it difficult for people to deal with tenancy matters with the required level of confidence. Completing benefit application forms for instance can be a problem. Another example is doing job applications.

Self esteem

Loss of self esteem perhaps through chains of failures and rejections by the so-called 'decent society' which controls jobs, education, and accommodation.

Access to advice and information.
For many people it is hard enough finding the need for such a service let alone accessing it. On the other hand those who wish to use the service are put off by long queues, long holding times during telephone calls, etc.

Lacking basic living skills.
Some people lack the ability to budget, prepare a meal, clean and keep a tidy environment, or doing washing up. Others find it difficult to live mutually with their neighbours by observing boundaries (as per tenancy agreements).

A way of live
Long history of homelessness, which for some people becomes a way of life. The people in this group find it difficult to accept other ways of life and will keep returning to the streets where they feel more secured.

Rent and other charges
Rent and service charges are the usual responsibilities that come with tenancy agreements. Most people find this a daunting experience. The management of rents and remembering to honour payment obligations may not be a welcoming experience for some people.

Budgeting skills
Budgeting well, especially where some lifestyles, e.g. drug addiction keeps taking tolls on financial resources. Most of them cannot cope with the change.

Social skills
There is lack of social skills, which include the ability to get on with people. It is also about showing respect for other peoples' rights whilst exercising their own.

Access to decent accommodation
Lack of access to decent accommodation. Most rough sleepers are single males who have very little help through the conventional Homeless Persons Unit (HPU) of local authorities.

Hygiene problems
Housework and hygiene problems may occur where street life is carried into decent flats where no one but themselves must clean up any mess.

Drug and alcohol addiction
Unable to manage drug & alcohol use well and this most often interfere with their ability to manage their tenancies.

Ability to access services.
This may be restricted because of one's illness, communication problems or simply, lack of knowledge.

Loneliness
Loneliness is a problem for many single ex-rough sleepers who are unable to keep dogs or share needles, or jokes with their 'buddies'. Taking someone away from the street and putting him/her into an accommodation is certainly not an entire solution to a complicated problem.

Anger management
Anger management sometimes affects people's ability to get on with others or to hold down employment. Some are unable to work with their support workers or housing officers over problems associated with their tenancies.

Other problems that can be identified include:

- Completing forms e.g. application (benefits and jobs applications)

- Anti-social behaviour/self harm

- Accessing specialist support for addressing health problems, e.g. mental health

- Low confidence/low self esteem affecting independent living

- Ability and willingness to engage in services available

- Difficulty furnishing flat: getting access to low cost furniture

- Connection of utility services to the new flat

- Finding employment and being able to hold down a job

- Getting trained, going to college or learning a new skill

- Getting help with health problems and engaging in service delivered by relevant professionals or experts

- Lack of interview skills and failing to get jobs

- Lack of employment experience and failing to meet job criteria

Question 22   CLIENT ABILITY CHECKLISTS
If you are successful you will be providing support for clients with long history of rough sleeping, some of whom also have mental health and living skill problems. If you are to draw a checklist for ensuring that they will be safe and reasonably independent in their new flat, what will it look like?

CHECKING ABILITIES OF CLIENTS

TICK	AREAS OF ASSESSMENT	SUPPORT REQUIRED?	
		YES	NO
	Ability to:-		
	Cook		
	Shop		
	Do DIY (e.g. changing bulbs fuses)		
	Paying rent, utility bills & council tax		
	Making friends and socialising		
	Reporting repairs		
	Dealing with emergency e.g. flood		
	To read, understand and act on correspondence		
	Register with a GP		
	Manage tenancy, understand and accept responsibilities		
	Engage in local support services if required		
	Get on with neighbours		
	Do own washing (e.g. use public washing machines)		
	Manage issues of health and safety in flat and take appropriate action		
	Look for employment		
	Engage in training/college programmes		

Use the phone in emergency			
To chase up benefit applications			
Make benefit applications			
Budget well on low income			
To eat well			
Keep clean and tidy flat			
To arrange or acquire TV licence			

Table 3.5   *Initial checklist for assessing tenants' level of independence*

Question 23   CLIENTS: RISK OF LOSING TENANCY
In what ways can you tell if the tenancy of a person with long history of rough sleeping is at risk of breaking down?

Neighbour problems
If people do not get on with their neighbours they feel isolated and begin to think that they belong somewhere else. A case in point would be where a neighbour is constantly threatening you or making you feel unsafe because of their activities.

Reaction to maintenance
Where the property itself is not maintained to a good standard it would be easily concluded that the tenant is better off and in some cases safer outside than inside. Some people find it too much having to chase up repairs and deal with irresponsive workmen and landlords. They may care less about reporting faults and in the end lose interest in the property all together.

Health problems (e.g. Mental Health)
Many homelessness results from mental health problems either directly or indirectly. Health difficulties deprive people the ability to make rational decisions about their own security. To this extent someone with e.g. mental health problems may find good reasons for being outside than inside a home.

Change of interest
When one's interest changes such that they want to pursue other objectives other than the one associated with their accommodation, they may want to give up their flat. Other times, change in interest is unplanned. For example,

one may drift into a habit, which in turn competes with resources for paying due attention to the containment of the tenancy agreement.

Disengagement from meaningful occupation
Some tenancies are created because of a desire to be meaningfully occupied. Others are associated with a desire to be close to relatives, support, or some special facilities or services. Once the fundamental reason is effaced or cease to exist, the tenancy can be thrown into risk. Being meaningfully occupied is a key to stability, which strengthens one's attitude in a responsible direction. Such an attitude is then a vital asset for maintaining a tenancy.

Rent arrears
Rent arrear is the one big 'monster' that robs thousands of people the ability to keep roof over their heads. Rent arrears may result from poor budgeting skills, mental health problems, learning difficulty, mismanagement of welfare benefits, as well as addiction problems.

Not settling down
Some tenancies fail because the tenants fail to accept their tenancy roles and responsibilities. In fact to some people (with long history of homelessness), it's difficult to accept the reality of a formal tenancy. Hence many use their new home as an extension of their street life; drinking, smoking drugging, prostituting, etc. While this is going on, it becomes difficult for them to settle down and get organised. Many tenancies that end within 6 months of commencement hardly get furnished with beds, chairs, or wardrobes. Monies received from the Social fund (e.g. Community Care Grant) are squandered on drugs, drinks and the like.

Continuous use of street facilities
People with long history of homelessness may find it all too difficult to disengage totally from using street facilities like day centres, soon after signing their new tenancies. People in this category continue to rely on others and hardly find the need to be independent. If this continues for too long (perhaps beyond the six month mark) it is very unlikely that the person will fully accept their new status (as a tenant) and commit resources to maintaining his tenancy appropriately.

Development of negative interests

People who are caught up in bad habits like drug misuse and become addicted, find their finances highly disturbed. Service charges (e.g. water bills, electricity bills, and gas bills) do not get paid. Services may become disconnected and this will in turn drive their interest away from that particular property.

Evasion of trouble

This may result from association with gangs, or credit purchases, or even getting into trouble with the police over some criminal act. The first thought is to go away. The flat is abandoned, rent arrears accrue and the landlord takes possession eventually.

Risk assessments

By checking referral notes you can pick up warnings of possible difficulties around tenancies. Risk assessment documents usually provide warning signs. For example:

- Breakdown of previous tenancies

- Budgeting difficulties

- Criminal records especially over drugs, and assault

Under 25s

A good percentage of people under 25 years (with history of rough sleeping) are thought to have problems around basic living skills. This may include lack of ability to budget effectively, establish and maintain relationship, as well as living with neighbours peacefully.

Disengagement from support

If a person with serious and obvious problems (e.g. mental health) disengages from service, it could represent a sign of relapse and therefore a warning that something could go wrong with the tenancy.

First 6 months

The first six months of most tenancies are thought to be the most critical. Beyond this point it is believed that one can tell if a tenancy will succeed. The success rate is expected to be higher after the first six months.

Mismanagement of benefits

This may result from illiteracy problems, or learning difficulties. The welfare benefit system itself is not exactly easy to use. Most users are only able to do so with some help. Most people with homelessness background face the problem of first finding help, then secondly, managing their claims beyond the initial contact. Issues of changes in circumstances, entitlements and backdated payments (amongst others), can all be too complicated for someone who had nothing to worry about out there in the street. A state of neglect is easily reached which then results in breakdown of claims and therefore rent arrears.

Breaches of tenancy agreement

This may include the following:

- Nuisance towards other tenants

- Misuse of equipment or furniture provided by the landlord

- Harassment towards other tenants

- Using the property for illegal activities or for other purpose inconsistent with tenancy agreement

- Persistent refusal to allow access for landlord or his agents to carry out activities required by law

Breakdown in communication

Communication breakdown can also put tenancies at risk. This may occur between client and the welfare benefit office; client and landlord; client and support agency, etc. When communication fails, assumptions are made, actions are taken on those assumptions and things go wrong. A case in point is when HB office refuse to make backdated payment because according to them no application form was received from the client. The landlord failed to contact the tenant about non payment of rent and after 52 weeks, the landlord now realises the seriousness of the arrears and writes to tenant. The tenant is unable to find the 52 weeks old receipt/proof of his Housing Benefit application.

Information from other agencies

Warnings received from agencies (especially ex-service providers) either at case conferences or handover meetings can provide some useful pointers as to whether or not a particular tenancy may be at risk.

Suffering harassment

People may suffer harassment because of their colour, nationality, sex or race. Whatever form it takes, harassment can lead to all sorts of discomfort and insecurity. Abandonment is one usual response.

Others

- Talking about difficulties, showing signs of dissatisfaction, increasing frequency of complaints.

- Showing signs of disinterest in community.

- Major incident: Some people are not able to deal with tragedies well. For some it's the end of the world and this could mean relapsing.

Question 24   PREVENTING HOMELESSNESS

What general support can you provide to vulnerable people to enable them maintain their tenancies for as long as possible and to prevent a return into the street/ homelessness?

I have no doubt there is a big clue in your job description. If you know it well you will probably be able to answer this question with ease. As the support required will always be related to identified needs and problems you will find it useful to also refer to the problems covered above.

Pre-tenancy stage

The work of tenancy support workers starts at the pre-tenancy stage. It is a good practice for you to be involved in the clients preparation work leading to the resettlement. I am not referring to the work itself. Gaining information on what is going on; the client's specific needs and the plan of action leading to the resettlement programme will resource your ability to start well. Look at the protocol covered below.

Tenancy stage

This stage is covered in more details elsewhere in this book. As a brief explanation consider the following steps:

- Collect information (including Support Needs Indicators and Risk Assessment) from referral agency, analyse, and obtain clarification where necessary.

- Do an Individual Service Agreement with client

- Complete forms designed to collect information on client profile (including special needs). Similarly, collect basic information on client history including ex-service providers.

- Draw up action plan to include;
  o   support with furnishing flat,

  o   connection of utility services, and

  o   information and advice on accessing local services.

- Draw action plan around any identified support needs and agree on strategies for achieving gaols and objectives

- Identify external services and plan for engaging them

- Use progress meetings to assess and monitor progress

- Provide practical support where ever necessary

- Budget for and respond well to crisis, emergencies, relapse, etc.

- Evaluate progress and review plans periodically using impute of your team and those of specialists to maximise quality service for client.

I am sure you will find lots of information in this book that will be relevant to this topic. You are encouraged to combine them so you can have the right cocktail for your situation. Some specific considerations are as follows:

Support plan
Have a clear, well explained support plan for supporting clients. The plan must take into consideration all of the factors above. You may Check Winning Ideas volume one for how to plan support and care.

Liaising with others
Continue to liaise with referral agencies and ex-service providers (where necessary). Also liaise with external agencies and professionals identified in clients' support plan in order to maximise his benefit from your service.

Rent arrears prevention

Keep an eye on this and provide appropriate support. Ways of supporting client with rent arrears are covered in Winning Ideas volume two. You will need to emphasise on prevention rather than recovery.

Debt counselling

This may be relevant if client has serious budgeting problems and ends up with debts. Consider an external support where necessary. This topic will be covered in detail in volume five. Debt counselling must take into consideration client's culture and spiritual needs, as well as health problems which might exert demands on his finances. Be careful not to over react to huge debts. Realistic assessment is very important.

HB and other benefits

Once again being proactive is the answer. Good practice for supporting clients with their claims is covered elsewhere in Winning Ideas. The nature of support will include the following:

- Making claims, and completing forms the right way

- Chasing up application forms and ensuring payment is made

- Claiming full entitlements

- Accessing and sending off relevant proofs

- Reporting change of circumstance

- Applying for backdated payments

Meaningful occupation

This is about going to college, training, or engaging in some form of productive activity. This kills boredom, improves future opportunities, and gives more reason to be in a secured accommodation.

Health

Pay attention to any health problems identified, making appropriate referrals and engaging specialist agencies in the service.

Post tenancy stage

Ensure that client does not return into the streets without first equipping him with relevant information and also ensuring that he can access an alternative service.

Rehabilitation programmes

Rehabilitation programmes provides options for some clients. They may be for example around drugs, or anger management. Support clients to access relevant service specific to their key problems. The Alcohol Anonymous (AA) for instance is available for people who wish to quit drinking.

Advice and advocacy

The use of advisory service available within the community as well as your own input paves a way for accessing further services.

Maintenance problems

This is another key factor leading to abandonment and tenancy loss. Support tenants with reporting repairs and chasing them up. This is also about empowering them to exercise their rights.

Encourage use of local facilities and services

This will help sustain client's interest in the community. Sometimes you need to physically accompany then to meetings or appointments. The few initial experiences may be hard but they are usually okay after a while.

Making representations at court hearing

This may be necessary if client is facing a court action for example because of rent arrears. Support client with application for stay of warrant, and also justifying such an application by making representations in court.

Question 25   MAINTAINING TENANCIES SUCCESSFULLY
What practical support will you consider in your working relationship with your clients in order to help them maintain successful tenancies?

Appointments

Support with attending appointment:

- Accompanying them

- Encourage use of diaries, calendars and planners

- Maintain a central dairy for your team so that staff can remind client

- Maintaining telephone contact (with service providers)

Challenging behaviour

Prompt challenge on actions that might threaten their tenancies. Examples are listed below:

- Theft (stealing from neighbours)
- Noise (e.g. loud music)
- Use and dealings of drugs
- Nuisance towards neighbours
- Not exercising control over guests' or friends' behaviour

Health

Support them with getting registered with GP (transfer from old one). The NFHA (National Family Health Authority) will be able to provide you with details of medical professionals in client's area. Also, facilitate access to other medical specialists, e.g. counsellors, psychiatrists, psychologists.

Provide information on alternative therapy, especially for those with ethnic minority origin. Furthermore, take time to explain practical support they can obtain from you and your service.

Basic living skills

Once the needs in this area are identified you may find it necessary to provide some supervision, directions and advice. This will be done whilst following an agreed plan.

Encourage outings and support to improve social life

Meeting new people and trying new ways of occupying one's time can lead to a positive change. Clients learn from others' experience and they become more willing to accept help from others.

Support with budgeting

This includes debt counselling service accessed through referrals. Also provide practical support with how client spends his money, backing this up with discussions at progress meetings.

Intervene during arrears problems and provide support

Liaise with the housing officer and the benefits office so that problems confronting your clients are clear. You will need the client's written consent for this. The housing officer can allow your client more time to make an arrangement to clear rent arrears: The benefits office may agree to backdate payments which will lead to arrears being cleared.

Support with meaningful occupation (e.g. training, employment).
The idea is to give clients a productive way of spending their time and reducing chances of returning into the street through the acquisition of non-productive habits.

Court action
Provide support during court actions taken against client by landlords. See answer to previous question.

Welfare benefit application and claims management.
This will include the following:

- Help with making applications, e.g. JSA, Housing benefit, CCG, etc.

- Information on what is available

- Writing supporting letters

- Support with challenging decisions; appeals and reviews

- Support with backdated payment request

Support with reporting maintenance
Like in other areas of support, emphasis must be on empowerment. Support will range from bringing maintenance work to landlord's attention, chasing up outstanding repairs, to claiming compensation on behalf of client.

Supporting with furnishing flat
Provide client with information on where to go and advice on how to get the best out of their limited financial resources. Sometimes this means making referrals and accompanying them to furniture projects.

Tenancy management
Support with understanding tenancy agreement, their rights and responsibilities. This is especially relevant when client needs to exercise some rights, challenge landlord's decision, or challenge their own behaviour. On the

proactive side, this is also necessary for client to create the right balance between their rights and responsibilities.

Support with neighbour problems
Liaise with housing officers to ensure that client is able to occupy their home without harassment or any unwanted acts of discrimination against him.

Accessing information and advice
Support with accessing information and advice on what they need (especially from their local area). It is always useful to provide a list of local services and facilities to clients when they first move in. More importantly let them know how they can update the list themselves. A checklist of local facilities is provided elsewhere in this book.

Dealing with external agencies
Support with dealing with other agencies especially when problems arise. Such agencies may include utility companies (e.g. London electricity) and rehabilitation projects.

Anger management
Encouraging positive ways of managing anger, and helping them to channel that energy into productive ends. Professionals to be involved will include counsellors and psychologists. Self–help group therapy is known to have produced some good results in anger management. Liaise with other specialists (internal and external) to enhance quality of life for client.

Question 26   SUPPORTING A TRANSFER APPLICATION
Scenario: A client has approached you asking that you support his application for a transfer he is no longer interested in his present accommodation. As a Tenancy Support Officer what do you consider to be justifiable grounds for supporting such an application?

Racial and other forms of harassment
Many homes are abandoned because of this. It is better to engage a planned resettlement in good time (especially if this is what the victim wants).

Violent attacks

Either on the person's body or property. The logical and immediate answer is either to remove the danger from the victim or remove the victim from the danger.

Neighbour dispute

Constant neighbour dispute which may not necessarily originate from the client, especially if this means that the person's interest in his accommodation has faded away completely.

Needing more support

This may result from deteriorated health condition or some other area of support.

Support not required

Opposite to the point above, this point refers to where changes in needs makes it necessary to move someone on as part of a planned resettlement programme.

Medical needs

Where clients need to move in order to benefit from a medical service relevant to their particular health problems.

Meaningful Occupation

Where clients want to move in order to engage in some more productive occupation. This may be to attend college, take up employment, or undergo some training.

Clients support needs versus services received from the RSL

It may be the case that the service provided in the Residential Social Landlord's (RSL) scheme is not needed by the client. On the other hand the client may require much greater level of support than what is provided in the scheme.

Others

Other acceptable reasons are:

- Change in household size creating congestion where client lives

- Change in income status so the e.g. client can no longer afford the rent

- Job transfer leading to long journeys to and from work.

Question 27   SUPPORTING A MULTIPLE NEEDS CLIENT
Scenario: George is a heavy drinker. He also smokes heavily and doesn't care for food. The staff are now concerned that his situation is not helping his incontinence problems especially as his hygiene has reached a very low level. George has now been assigned to you as your latest key client. How would you go about addressing this case?

Assess George's situation
Start by collecting facts (information) surrounding the case. Check for the following:

- Input from staff in general.

- Input from George's former keyworker.

- Input from advocates, friends or befrienders who have known him for a long time and are familiar with his problems.

- Input from his family members.

- Input from professional bodies who are also ex-service providers of George.

Look at the following example.

DRINKING	FOOD	INCONTINENCE AND HYGIENE
What he drinks	What George eats and why	History of incontinence
Frequency of drinking		What drives it or sustains it
Pattern of drinking	When he eats and why	Pattern of incontinence
Expenses made on drinking	How much he eats and why	George's management of the incontinence (methods already tried which worked well)
What motivates	Identify the problem from not eating	Professional help already

drinking History of drinking, etc.	Expenses on food and why, etc.	obtained Any professional perspective on George's incontinence
What does Gorge wants from drinking?	*What does Gorge wants from this situation?*	*What does George wants from this?*

Formulate a care plan

See Wining Ideas volume one for how to formulate a care plan. The plan must take the following into consideration:

- What George wants from each situation

- Problems or difficulties that might impede George's progress

- Opportunities (external resources) and strengths available to George.

- Realistic goals and objectives

- Realistic time scales for achieving objectives and monitoring progress

- How achievements will be measured

- Clearly identified support team

- Strategies for working with the support team (including staff in your own staff)

- Clear methods for implementing plan and how George will receive support with his part

- Monitoring processes and methods to be used

- Evaluation and review of plan (including time scales and lead persons) and methods to be used.

Practical support

The actual support will depend on the outcome of the assessment, which may include:

- George is a heavy alcohol addict, and will need professional help straight away.

- George lacks budgeting skills which may explain why he fails to eat well.

- George has an inherent health condition affecting his ability to control his bladder or bowel.

- George's incontinence has a lot to do with his eating and drinking patterns.

- George's drinking habit is boosted by his social life (e.g. friends he associates with).

- George has lost any hope of winning and has collapsed into hopelessness and not ready to work on his problems.

All the above are possibilities and in fact the list can go on and on. So can the following practical support. The emphasis will depend on the precise outcome of the assessment.

The following suggestions may apply only if George himself has agreed to confront his problems. Again whether or not there will be any support will depend on the outcome of the assessment. Furthermore, the nature of support and the emphasis will depend on a combination of factors including:

- The nature of project (care or low support project)

- The resources of project e.g. availability of qualified staff

- Staff working culture e.g. emphasis placed on teamwork

- The availability of local professional support if this is required

Should it be the case that none of the above is available, consideration must be made to refer George to a more suitable project where his needs can be better met. However, good practice requires that whilst further referral may be a possibility, temporary care or support arrangements are put in place to ease up life for George as far as possible. See the examples below.

Drinking

- Reduce money at George's disposal gradually. This can only be done with his full consent and co-operation.

- Provide support with shopping and keep an eye on amount of alcohol consumed.

- Encourage social drinking in preference to discrete ones. At least if someone saw him drink, staff can assess appropriately what measure of support must be provided to him. They can also be able to tell whether or not George is following his care plan. Secret drinking can lead to all sorts of problems (e.g. suicide) especially if Gorge also suffers from depression.

- Consider harm minimisation strategies. Use checklists on alcohol abuse available elsewhere in this book.

- Consider referral to specialists & befriending service

Food

- Acquire food coupons so that real cash for alcohol is limited.

- Provide support with shopping.

- Discourage late eating and drinking (especially soon after collecting his benefit money).

- Support with cooking and preparing quick, easy and simple meals.

- George can keep notes of what he eats in diary for discussions at keywork sessions. Use such sessions to recognise positive efforts.

Incontinence and hygiene

- Ensure Gorge has the right bed, bed covers and there is a suitable arrangement for washing covers.

- Encourage or support George to clean up and wash bedding after each incident. Check for external agency support if possible.

- Arrange clean or sufficient supply of clean linen and show him how, where and when to obtain them.

- Support him with room cleaning and personal hygiene.

All the above must be grafted into the support or care plan. The issues in the plan must be prioritised and goals must be graded into short, medium and long term ones. More importantly, they must be realistic and achievable.

Note the following important strategic considerations

Confidence
Your style of working with George must emphasise on building trust and confidence. Incontinence can be embarrassing and George may feel inclined to be understandably cagey and secretive.

Sensitivity
Be sensitive when involving people in George's care. This will imply getting his approval first. Equally, when feeding back you need to do this tactfully leaving him feeling not discouraged but full of a desire to keep the drive on towards total rehabilitation.

Involve professionals
Follow the advice from the appropriate specialists consistently and work closely with people George confides in and feels comfortable with.

Involve people George is already familiar with
They may include advocates, previous keyworkers, social workers, and befrienders. The more he is placed under the impression that people empathise and understands his problems the more he is likely to co-operate.

Difficult times
Show empathy and understanding freely, especially when George is confronted with additional difficulties e.g. bereavement. Relapse may occur and this must not be seen as lack of co-operation.

Consider self help group activities
Self-help group activities are usually a source of empowerment. However, not many people feel comfortable sharing their intimate problems in public. It may take some getting used to, but it is no doubt an important and resourceful option for alcohol addicts.

Involve the team
Consistency is of extreme importance if progress is to be measured well. George's care or support plan must be shared and regular discussions must be

held to give everyone involved a clear picture of what is being achieved, changes, and what else needs doing.

So that you can gain deeper understanding of alcoholism, I have devoted the following lines for further ideas that will increase your ability to provide professional help for your residents or tenants.

ALCOHOLISM

Understanding Alcoholism

This is also known as alcohol dependency. Alcoholism is the stage of addiction where the client loses control of the relationship they have with alcohol. In fact Alcoholism is a disease that involves the following:

Craving
This is a strong desire, feeling of need or urgency for accessing and drinking alcohol.

Loss of control
The inability to stop or control the drinking once it has started until one has reached levels dictated by the drink itself.

Physical dependence
This is about withdrawal symptoms such as nausea, sweating, shakiness, and anxiety after stopping drinking.

Tolerance
It refers to the need to drink greater amounts of alcohol in order to get the level of buzz sought for.

With every drop of alcohol on the tongue there is a crave for another one. Cravings lead to more drinking, then loss of control. Over time tolerance levels increase leading to much higher levels of cravings. As the cycles push forward it becomes more and more difficult for the person to withdraw. When there are prolonged periods of cravings withdrawal symptoms begin to show, and the person becomes very uncomfortable until the next drink. With such cravings an alcoholic will continue to drink despite serious family, health or legal problems.

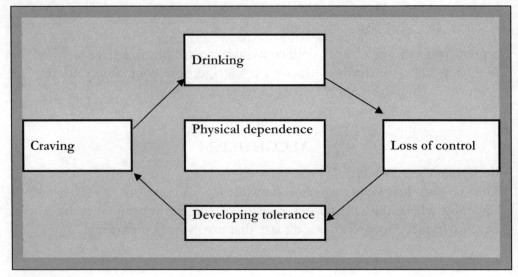

Fig3.1   Alcoholism cycle

Alcoholism is chronic. It lasts a person's lifetime and usually follows a predictable course. It is believed that the risk for developing alcoholism is influenced both by a person's genes and by his/her lifestyle.

Checking for alcoholism
To find out if a person needs help with his alcohol consumption try asking the following questions:

- Have you ever felt you should cut down on your drinking?

- Have people annoyed you by criticising your drinking?

- Have you ever felt bad or guilty about your drinking?

- Have you ever had a drink first thing in the morning to steady your nerves or to get rid of hangovers?

One *yes*   = possible alcoholic problem
More than one *yes*   = Alcoholism problem is very likely

Cure for alcoholism
Alcoholism unfortunately has no cure (clinically) what so ever. Even where an alcoholic has been dry for a long time, relapse is possible. A lot depends on the person himself as well as the support he or she receives.

Treatment for alcoholism

Alcoholism is treatable. Such programmes normally combines counselling and medications to help a person stop drinking. With support and treatment it is possible for an alcohol dependant to stop drinking and rebuild their lives.

Benzodiazepines (Valium, Librium) are sometimes used during the first days after a person stops drinking to help him safely withdraw from alcohol. Because they are very addictive they are not used for prolonged periods.

Naltrexone (ReVia- TM) is used for helping people to keep sober. Combined with counselling it can reduce the craving for alcohol and help prevent a person from returning, or relapsing, to heavy drinking.

Disulfiram (Antabuse) is used to discourage drinking. When the person drinks alcohol he will feel sick and will want to stay away from it.

SUPPORTING A PERSON WITH ALCOHOLISM

Do not ignore the problem. Don't take the opinion that the person is finished and can't be helped, even if it is the case that he/she has already been in therapy.

Time your intervention

Intervene at the right time. The best time is usually soon after an incident. Choose a time when the person is sober. Make sure the concern is presented to the person in private and respectfully.

Be specific

Don't beat about the bush as if you fear rejection. There is also no need to speculate. Use specific examples of the ways in which the drinking has caused problems, including most recent ones.

Analyse the results

Help the person to see the seriousness of the outcome of their behaviour. Avoid making threats. Instead make the person willing and desiring to seek help and give up. At the same time inform him of what help is available or what you can do to help.

Getting help

The next step is to facilitate the process of getting help. Gather information in advance about treatment options in your community. Hands-on support can be easily arranged from the local areas than from distant locations. Arrange an appointment for initial visit and an assessment. The treatment counsellor or alcohol specialist using a series of questionnaires will establish the level and amount of help the person needs and will be able to decide the type of recovery programme suitable for the person.

If help is refused

Try and engage advocates, friends and close relatives if the person refuses to get help. Also consider other specialists in the person's care team, especially those with whom he enjoys good relationship. A friend who is recovering alcoholic may be particularly persuasive, but any person who is caring and non-judgemental may be able to help. You may need several attempts to coax an alcoholic to seek help so do not give in after a few trails.

Look at the wider picture

Check if there is anyone in the client's live who is suffering because of the problems associated with the alcoholism. And see how you can include the person in the entire programme. They may include family members, children, spouse or partner. Also consider the effect registered on other people outside the person's immediate domestic environment (e.g. work).

Drinking safely

A standard drink is:

- One 12 ounce bottle of beer or wine cooler

- One 5 ounce glass of wine

- 1.5 ounces of 80 proof distilled spirits

Note that beer varies considerably in its alcohol content. Malt liquor is also higher in its alcohol content than most other brewed beverages.

People who can't drink

Certain people must not drink at all. They include:

- Women who are pregnant or trying to become pregnant. Alcohol can have a number of harmful effects on the baby. The most serious of birth defects caused by alcohol is Fetal Alcohol

Syndromes (FAS). Children born with FAS have physical abnormalities, mental illness or with learning and behavioural problems.

- People who plan to drive or engage in other activities that require alertness and skill. They include those using high-speed machinery.

- People taking certain (prescribed) medication. More than 155 medications interact harmfully with alcohol. For e.g. alcohol's effects are heightened by medicines that depress the central nervous system (including sleeping pills, antidepressants, anti-anxiety drugs, and some pain killers). If a person is taking large doses of certain pain killers and drinking alcohol he is risking serious liver damage.

- People with medical conditions that can be made worse by drinking.

- Recovering alcoholics.

- People prevented by the law.

See other parts of this book for more information on the *Effect of alcohol* on it's victims.

Question 28   JOB SEARCH SKILLS
What skills do residents need for looking for and remaining in employment?

LOOKING FOR A JOB

- Reading and writing

- Completing application forms

- Doing own CVs

- Preparing for and attending an interview

- Acquiring or collecting information on what is available

- Organising and co-ordinating information

- To be self motivated

- Being focused and determined

- Working independently

- Prioritising and processing needs associated with looking for a job

Other problems (not skills)

- Not having bank account where wages can be paid into

- Not having identification

- Not favouring police checks due to criminal records

- Lack of access to photo copiers, computers, stationary, stamps, etc.

- Too drunk or drugged to attend interviews

- Lack of decent clothes

- Not knowing where to look

- Lack of money for transport

- Finding a decent accommodation to support work life

REMAINING IN THE JOB

- Working with authority, rules and boundaries

- Inability to learn on the job

- To be motivated

- Using complex and technical information at work

- Processing skills

- Taking job seriously (e.g. reporting to work on time)

- Staying focused (e.g. working well with targets and objectives)

- Dealing or coping with difficulties on the job

- Getting on with people

- Dealing or coping with complex situations

- Patience and tolerance for handling problems

- Responding to training and development

- Working well within a team

Others (not skills)

- Anger management problems

- Decent clothes

- Criminal records

See Winning Ideas Volume two for more on this topic.

Question 29   PROMOTING TENANTS PARTICIPATION
A resident is refusing to participate in social activities. He is one of your key residents. What action will you take?

Note that the need for action will depend on whether or not the situation presents cause for concern. A one off situation is not likely to raise concern. The answers provided below assume a cause for concern situation. Otherwise, if someone does not want to engage in social activities it is simply a matter of choice and should normally not attract criticisms.

Find out why
Establish his reasons. The action to take will depend on the answers you receive or indeed his reactions. It could be that he would prefer some other form of social activities, or he is unable to take any interest. Whatever the case may be you will need to balance the situation with respect for the client's own social preferences. Other reasons may be associated with:

- Shyness

- Culture

- Disabilities

- Intimidation

- Harassment and discrimination

- Not knowing which part to play

- Being foreign to the activities

- Not able to see the importance

- Crippled by some previous bad experience(s)

Your concerns should not be so much about these reasons. The key question is what negative effect is presented because of the situation?

Discuss, alternatives and offer options
Check if he would prefer something else and make some offers to facilitate choice. In doing this you need to be sensitive to the client's own opinions and tastes as well as values, and in some cases gender. You must also remember that peoples' social affiliations say a lot about their beliefs, and customs.

Offer to accompany or check time convenience
Go a step further by offering to make things a lot easier. You do this by practically exploring how structural problems can be removed: If the timing, location, or span of activities is unsuitable check how this can be altered. Those who feel very isolated or shy may need someone's company to help ease into social activities. This is about confidence and again about helping to boost one's interest up.

Discuss benefits of social activities to client, and defuse myths client may have
Help the client to examine positive outcomes from social activities and also how they can benefit. This is more relevant if you are able to relate matters to their specific circumstances establishing clearly any therapeutic effect on their mental and physical state. The use of success stories (of similar client groups) can be effective in matters like these.

Check abilities and agree a plan
This is more the case where a client is prevented from taking part in social activities because of e.g. some health or behavioural reasons. If it is the case, that the client is denied abilities because of some difficulties, you must agree on a plan for supporting him to get around them. The plan will take into consideration how the identified problems work to prevent benefits from

social activities. Also identify relevant specialists input over specific time scales.

Identify local resources and discuss how he can be supported
Look in-house for support. Resources here will include staff, rooms and spaces, communal facilitates, and money from project's petty cash tin. Practical support may range from anything as trivial as reminding him of appointments to physically engaging him in a specific activity.

Consider a slow start from the beginning
Depending on individual's circumstances consider a slow start. It is very important you assess one's abilities carefully before exposing them to experiences that could shatter their confidence and interest altogether. Encouraging meetings with own relatives and friends can be a starting point. People feel more secured with their own groups. Then, joining a befriending scheme can offer further exposure to the social arena.

Pitch expectations according to abilities
Realistic expectations are important. As noted earlier failures can be more costly. Money can easily be a hard to reach resource for many people seeking to benefit from social activities. It is always important that necessary steps are taken to remove the 'money blockage'. Another matter to consider is the case of language barrier and physical access to location of activities.

Consider proactive measures
This will include having good induction for all clients, and also using management styles that emphasise on client involvement. E.g. there must be an open support for and commitment to the project's social activities and Equal Opportunity policy. Such measures will reduce incidents of non-participation.

Publicise achievements e.g. in news letters
This helps send the message of acceptance. It leaves people feeling valued and provides solid foundation for improved confidence. Newsletters, notice boards and residents meetings are examples of media that can be used. Recognise and praise positive efforts no matter how small.

Get other staff involved for purpose of continuity

Continuous support is important if the client is to be able to maintain momentum and stay focused. This will also allow him to make substantial assessment of his own progress and be motivated by the results.

Offer participation in project groups

This is even more relevant if the client found social activities unsuitable. Give him the opportunity to contribute to decisions and to be part of the organising team.

Question 30   SUPPORTING CLIENTS: ANGER MANAGEMENT
How would you work with a resident who do not get on with other residents because of anger management problem?

Show understanding and invite him to deal with anger

Most people with anger management problems are very much aware of it. The problem is they find it difficult to control themselves. A most effective approach is showing understanding. At the same time invite the person to talk through his feelings.

Listening skills must be used effectively

This involves helping client to analyse the effect of their own behaviour. This may be contrasted with what the client really wants. Using their own experiences help the client to analyse alternative actions that he could have taken.

Agree a plan

A plan will be in place depending on whether or not client accepts help. Starting with the problems, agree clear goals and strategies for achieving them. It may be worth looking at short and easy-to-achieve goals to start with rather than being too enthusiastic. Ensure that the client is involved in deciding what exactly is to be achieved.

If client refuses help

You need to remember that no offence has been committed simply by not getting on with others. There is no trouble and as such no action is required other than perhaps simply expressing your concern about the client's attitude.

110

You must also make him aware of any action that could be taken against him (in line with project rule/organisation's procedure) if he gets into trouble. You need to be specific. If possible, sight a few examples. In doing this be careful not to suggest that client's behaviour is imperfect. No one is perfect and no one must be expected to get on with everybody. Make the client aware of consequences of actions in respect of the rules of the project.

In case of a relapse
Use moments of relapse to explore alternative ways of venting anger. Also assist the client to analyse the effect of his own anger on himself. The client can be encouraged to keep records of his own progress or performance which can be discussed at meetings. You get opportunity to praise good efforts and the client can be motivated from his own achievements. Failures must be seen as a norm not necessarily as weakness of client: It is normal for any one to make mistakes when doing something new.

Referral to specialist help
Refer to a specialist if client consents and support him to attend appointments. Use progress meetings to assess progress and the need to alter support plan so that it remains relevant at all times Discuss benefits and difficulties and agree on measures for addressing problems.

Practical support in-house
Examine further ways in which the unit can help. This may include
- Reminding client of appointments

- Accompanying him to appointments

- Absorbing transport cost (e.g. using petty cash)

- Arranging late dinners (where necessary) on days of his appointments

- Making meeting rooms available for client's sessions if they are to take place on project's premises

- Providing client with pen, dairy, file, etc. (stationary) needed for his programme

- Provide practical support around any rehabilitation programme the client is placed on

Progress meetings
Discuss triggers and discuss alternative ways of working around them; remember it is best to assist client to deal with situations than to avoid them. Keep notes so that both of you can maintain a clear picture of progress.

Recognise good behaviours to reinforce desired actions
If you observe any positive behaviour no matter how small, you must let client know how helpful it is. You need not wait to do this in a structured meeting. If you discover any relevant information in your staff logbooks follow it up immediately. Make contact with client if you can and reinforce his positive behaviour. On the other hand, show your disapproval tactfully where necessary.

Inform your team
Bring concerning matters to team leader's attention – so that you can obtain support yourself. The agreed plan can also be implemented even in your absence if the rest of your team members are aware of what is happening.

Risk assessment
Your client will not only be presenting risk to others, he will also be putting himself at risk if he is getting into trouble all the time. The risk assessment should also cover issues around working with staff and others (in and outside the project). Staff team must establish safe ways of working with the client and be clear on measures in place for supporting him to behave well around other people.

Consider meaningful occupation activity
Support resident to engage in a meaningful occupation programme that helps to improve his anger management. Whilst on such a programme client may be allocated mentors who themselves were once mentees in similar programmes. Meaningful occupations provide the additional benefit of helping client to direct energies into something more productive.

THE ANGER TRAP

Anger

It is a completely normal, usually healthy, human emotion. But when it gets out of control and becomes destructive, it can lead to serious problems in the overall quality of one's life. According to Dr. Spielberger anger is 'an emotional state that varies in intensity from mild irritation to intense fury and rage'. It is accompanied by physiological and biological changes. When one gets angry their heart rates and blood pressure go up as do the levels of their energy, hormones, adrenaline, and noradrenaline.

According to Susan Kramer (in her book Dealing with Anger from a Spiritual Point of View, 1998), 'anger is an emotion arising in our mind triggered when we are faced with a problem we cannot easily resolve or when our desires are thwarted'. She stressed that 'people do actions but that people are not their actions, people may create unpleasant situations but people themselves are not the unpleasant situation'. With this understanding it becomes easier to conclude that there is an answer to anger management problem.

Damaging misleading beliefs

Perhaps the most powerful of all the forces that drives anger is the misleading beliefs or assumptions held by its victims. Look at what the person with anger management problem is saying to himself:

- I am a fire cracker nothing can touch me.

- I am king or queen of denial and I feel great

- I am stuck, I cannot get out, It's part of me. I was made that way

- I am a volcano ready to go off anytime

- There is a strong me within me, no one can tell me anything different

- There are flames inside me consuming me but I cannot help it

- I am at my breaking point, this is me

- I'd rather be right than be happy

- I know I am right when I am right

- I am an emotional train, can't stop now, got to prove my point at all cost

- I have an uncontrollable temper. I cannot help it

- I am a prisoner of my anger

- That's me I have a short fuse

- I know I am a danger to myself, but that is who I am

- I must win because I always do

HOW TO MANAGE ANGER

The goal of anger management is to reduce both one's emotional feelings and the physiological arousal that anger causes. Help your client to understand that they cannot get rid of, or avoid, the things or the people that enrage them, neither can they change them, but they can learn to control their own reactions. The client can start by finding out what it is that triggers his anger, and then develop strategies to keep those triggers from pushing them beyond limits.

Anger management strategies
Strategies for managing anger include the following:

Controlling stress
This is covered more extensively below. Stress is identified as one of the major sources of anger. Keeping it under control will reduce incidents of trigger.

Relaxations
This may include practicing breathing techniques, using imagery or non-strenuous slow yoga-like exercises.

Cognitive restructuring (changing the way one thinks)
Instead of cursing and swearing when angry, one can consider trying to find reasons behind the anger. Consider this example: 'though it is understandable that I am upset about this, it's not the end of the world, and getting angry will not solve the problem anyway'. You will see there is no substantial reason for the size of your anger.

Problem solving

Consider how you handle and face the problem. Decide to give it your best but also not to punish yourself if an answer doesn't exist or doesn't come right away. Approach problems with your best intentions and efforts.

Better communication

One must not jump to and act on conclusions hastily. Slowing down and thinking through one's responses, and not saying the first things that come into mind. One must also listen carefully to what the other person is saying and take time before answering.

Using humour

Humours can help you get a balanced perspective of things. Let's say you call someone 'silly cow' in your anger. Stop and for a moment or two, imagine what a silly cow would literally look like. If you can draw a picture of what the actual thing might look like, it will take a lot off the furry.

Changing ones environment

Our immediate environments can be a source of irritation. It may be problems or some form of responsibilities. It may be lighting levels or not having immediate access to something. Consider gathering together or identifying your resources before you start work. Also, consider planning for breaks. Have time for caring for yourself.

Using timing techniques

If you discover that doing a particular thing at a particular time always leads to friction consider doing it other times. It could be for instance that you are not successful because you are too tired at that time of the day.

Using voidance techniques

Try and avoid things or situations that make you angry. Sometimes it comes down to choice. The things we choose ourselves comes back to hunt us. Choose to avoid unhealthy debates and arguments.

Using alternative techniques

Try looking at different ways of doing things especially when the one method you know becomes your source of rage and frustration. This may for instance be about the route you take to college, shopping or work. Try finding alternative routes.

Taking counselling

You may choose to see a psychologist or other trained and licensed mental health professionals who can work with you in developing a range of techniques for changing your thinking and your behaviour.

Assertive training

Assertiveness is not a usual lacking quality of a person with anger management problem. However, it is true that angry people need to learn to become assertive rather than aggressive. It should be more about channelling energies more constructively in frustrating situations.

Controlling your stress levels

The secret to successfully controlling anger lies in one's ability to be a gentle, loving person even when they are mad (according to Lynne Namka, 1997). There are mainly five steps in controlling anger. These are:

- Recognising that there is a problem

- Accepting that you need to do something about it

- Choosing to take control and taking control

- Monitoring progress

- Learning from progress and making relevant adjustments

Stress control methods

Anger is more likely when one is stressed. Successful anger management keeps the stress at a minimum. Consider the following positive things one can do about stress:

- Taking deep breathes

- Being progressive with relaxation

- Taking lots of exercises

- Listening to a relaxation tape

- Talking to friends about areas of interest

- Praying and meditating

- Sharing your feelings and concerns with others

- Doing something different (a hobby) or developing new interests

- Get out and about; go walking in the greens, trees, mountains etc.

- Working on the triggers, identifying them and either dealing with them or avoiding them

- Be aware of your own limits and try and avoid things beyond you

- Always try and find humour in situation

- Seek social support; from friends, family members, support groups, etc.

- Participate in self-help group activities

- Take plenty of rest

- Take vacation

- Read journals

- Avoid self-negative verbal statements

- Avoid self angering thoughts

- Take stock of the problems you are confronted with and cancel those you cannot realistically deal with and put them behind you

- Consider writing. Write on things that interest you that will take you into a new experience

- Be clear about what you can and what you cannot take from others and set your boundaries

- Opt out when you think its getting too much for you

See Winning Ideas Volume one for more on *Coping with stress*.

Empowering statements

Empowerment statements must be encouraged especially during stressful times. Examples of these are listed bellow:

- I will survive

- I can do it

- I am in charge here, not my anger

- If I stop and think I can begin to take control

- I am going to take a moment or two, and then I am going to take care of myself

- I am going to make it

- I will do my breathing until I can figure out what to do next

- I won't allow my anger to take charge

- I will concentrate on the situation not the person

- I will try and look at the facts of the case before reacting

- I will give myself plenty of time to ponder over details before I react

Things to avoid

Encourage your client to avoid the following: You may photo copy the page for him to keep in a diary or on a wall as a rule to refer to daily.

- Eating excessively (binge)

- Entertaining negative thoughts over and over

- Overworking their bodies

- Indulge in excessive alcohol or drugs

- Exploding their anger on others or things

- Deny problems (as if they do not exist)

- Dwelling on intrusive negative thoughts

- Personalise or internalise anger

- Being trapped in excessive violent TV programmes/films

- Ignoring problems and confronting the person involved

- Hanging out with negative people

- Withdraw into self with hope that silence will provide answers

Skills for dealing with stress

Apart from being able to dealing with one's stress, six areas of skills are relevant to successful anger management. These are:

- Skills for releasing anger (current or old) effectively

- Skills for learning assertive ways of dealing with threats

- Skills for learning to contain excessive anger

- Skills for observing instead of over reacting to threatening events

- Skills for channelling anger into something constructive

- Skills for learning to feel empathy and respect for others

These skills will be examined further in future volumes of Winning Ideas. If you are supporting someone with anger management problems achieving these skills must be central to the support objectives.

Part 2

STAFF MANAGEMENT & TEAM MANAGEMENT ISSUES

Question 31 SOLVING WORK-RELATED PROBLEMS
What problems have you experienced in your previous employment and how did you solve them?

This is usually one of the first questions you get at Housing and Supported Housing interviews. You must see it as a huge opportunity to

- Establish a firm grip on the interview and take control

- Impress upon the interviewers your understanding of the roles involved in the position

- Your ability to embrace problems as a positive experience

- Make known your knowledge of important issues of the trade e.g. issues o professional expectations like 'confidentiality'

This question is similar to:

- Tell us your experience of dealing with problems in your job

- What problems can one experience in this job?

- How do you overcome problems which you are likely to encounter in thi job?

- How do you handle problems you encounter in your job?

Note that this question is about your job description. It is important that what yo choose to talk about is firmly within the job description for the job/position you ar applying for. Choose specific areas you believe your interviewers will be interested ir You can do this by considering topics like:

- The needs of the particular client group e.g. Mental Health Clients an Medication

- The organisation or project objectives e.g. customer care or customer satisfaction

- Issues of professional practice e.g. confidentiality

- Issues of legal requirement e.g. equal opportunity

It is important to make your points clear and also interesting. Make it easy to remember and for your interviewers to relate to. One way of doing this is to talk about a common or well-known behaviour of e.g. service users around their medication, residents being abusive, disruptive or difficult.

Set the problem
Start by setting the problem. It is important you clearly indicate why it is a problem. You can do this by for example, relating the situation with your own weaknesses (at the time) or that of the team, or some failed professional duties.

Make problem real
You can make the problem real by stating clearly what the consequences of the incident was and how it impacted on e.g. staff, organisation and the team, your health, professional duties etc. If you remember the date, or where the incident took place mention it.

Relate problem to the job
If you decide to talk about client issues you must choose a problem related to the client group you are applying to work with. If this is not possible use one related to 'vulnerable clients' or an experience in a similar setting.

When stating how you overcame the problem(s) consider the following:

Do not emphasise on your weaknesses
1.   Do not give the impression that you were completely incapacitated by the problem in a way that made you very vulnerable. This is because you are expected to budget for difficulties and complications that may arise in your job and therefore expected to show resilience.

Look at problems as a positive thing

2.   Clearly identify to your interviewers that you see every problem in a positive way – as an opportunity to learn, and this helps in your determination and ability to:

- Learn from your experiences

- Embrace new experiences (difficulties) and confront them

- Emerge with minimum effect on the quality of your work

These are what your interviewers are interested in. Not in you as an individual but in how you are able to remain on course and achieve your job objectives when confronted with difficulties and complications.

Say how you dealt with problems

The next step is to consider how you overcame the difficulties in practice. Other considerations your interviewers want to hear from you include an indication that:

- You are able to think fast on your feet.

- You are able to work using your own initiatives and creative abilities.

- You give due respect for professional issues in the job.

- You have genuine considerations of your work colleagues in your choice of solution.

- You have due regards for your employment contract and organisation's policies and procedures.

- You are mindful of and also able to work within legal boundaries.

- You are able to identify and use opportunities e.g. identify high-risk situation, emergencies, harassments, etc.

- You are able to maintain control of your actions throughout your solutional process e.g. not panic, remaining calm, being composed, and staying focused.

- Methodical in your approach e.g. using any team agreed procedures

- Creative about using resources at your disposal meaningfully.

- Able to progress a difficult process to a safe end. This involves not just about solutions for today but for the future as well.

Anything standing in opposition to any of the above is not acceptable

Make clear how you use available resources
This brings us to the next stage. Remember the question is about you and your experience and abilities so clearly state how your own role and actions was instrumental to the eradication of the problem. Interviewers are interested in how you use your own strengths or that of your team, or your organisation's.

Consider the period after the solution
The final stage is a consideration for the period after the solution and what your learnt from your experience.

Good enough solution
A solution is not good enough unless it is able to avoid or contain similar problems in future. Therefore, look for immediate solution, a short term one and also a long term one. Examples of these are covered below.

An immediate solution
- An example of an immediate solution may be using your first aid skills to prevent a (an unconscious) client from choking to death by clearing his/her airway. Also, calling the ambulance and having the person taken away for immediate specialist treatment.

A short term solution
- A short term solution may be to inform the victim's key worker and other relevant agency personnel accurately about the incident. Then, write an incident report so that appropriate measures are put in place to safeguard the client's welfare and prevent similar incidents.

A long term solution
- A long term solution could be following up documentation of the incident (in staff communication book, incident report etc.) by bringing the matter up to the team for further discussions. The idea being for the team to learn from the experience and take proactive

measures to prevent or minimise similar incidents in future. From here an addition may be made to the project's risk assessment checklists.

All answers to scenario questions must follow this pattern. Refer to our publication Evidence of Performance for a complete coverage on how to answer interview questions.

Support your choice of solution with reasons
When you talk about your solutions make sure that you support them with reasons. I mean reasons which your interviewers can subscribe to. Such reasons must be consistent with the following examples:

- To 'help the resident maintain his/her self esteem'

- 'This way I was sure to maintain confidentiality'

- 'By this I managed to send a clear massage that harassment is a breach of the organisation's policy and cannot be tolerated under any circumstances'

- 'The changes I made increased choice for our service users and made them feel respected and valued.'

- 'By this I was able to operate within the organisation's policies and procedures, and keep our service users happy at the same time.'

Consider a sense of humour
If you can make your story humorous it sometimes pays well. A caution here though is that not everyone may find your comments that 'relaxing'. On the other hand if it goes down well it could get every one involved and attract significant interest from your interviewers. Another benefit is that it will help you to relax and improve your confidence as your interview progresses. If you are very observant you can tell if your interviewers will entertain humour or not.

Get your interviewers involved
An important key to your success at interviews lies in your ability to take control and get interviewers involved. You are the one telling the storey. It is what you say and how you say it that will capture the interest you need to attract. As we saw earlier a sense of humour can be helpful. Other ways of doing this is as follows:

- Use clear speech

- Speak a little slower than usual

- Right pace of speech

- Use correct jargons (if you can)

- Use good eye contact

- Use stories that interviewers can relate to

- Show knowledge of interviewer's own service users

- Be orderly and sequential with your storey

Questions of this nature must be anticipated in any interview even outside Housing and Supported Housing or Care. You must therefore cover this as part of your preparation for interviews. Carefully design your storey taking into considerations all the ideas above. Rehearse them well and practice telling them to yourself over and over long in advance before your interview.

Question 32   OVERCOMING WORK-RELATED PROBELMS
What area did you have problems in your previous jobs and how did you overcome them?

Important consideration about this question is whether interviewers are referring to

- Your job description/responsibility of your job, or

- Your job itself

If you can get this clarified, do, otherwise you must assume the question refers to your job description. What you need to think of therefore is a problem that prevented you from following the requirements of your job. They may involve issues like:

- Administration duties (e.g. computer literacy)

- Clients needs assessment and welfare (e.g. welfare benefit)

- Dealing with emergencies (e.g. fire, flood, injuries)

- Working with health and safety legislation

- Project management (e.g. void control)

- Rent and rent arrears monitoring (e.g. payment agreement, evictions)

Essentially the question is about a short fall in your own ability and therefore what will become your responsibilities in the post you are applying for. Let's say you had problems monitoring rent arrears because you were not very computer literate when you started your job.

Chose the problem carefully
Whatever you decide to choose as the problem you need to consider the following:

- They must not undermine the confidence of the team or your work colleagues.

- They must not be a serious one that attracted or could have attracted disciplinary actions.

The right problem
Choose problems:

- That are common and can occur under reasonable circumstances

- That your interviewers can easily relate to

- That relate to the job you are applying for

- That are usually identified with new staff

- That you were able to resolve conclusively

Examples of problems you can consider talking about are:

- Not very literate with computer, which slowed down your work

- It took you some time to adjust to shift work. You ended up with lots of unfinished work which got you stressed out.

- Not used to working with lots of people in the past and was unable to understand importance of team dynamics when your housing or supported housing career started.

Significant solutions

An important thing to bear in mind is that the problems you choose to talk about must have very significant solutions. The way you choose to address the problems is very important and your interviewers will be waiting very anxiously to hear them.

Looking at the examples of problems above you can establish a clear pattern. They are all referring to very important issues about your job description. This tells your interviewers about your awareness of significant values required in the industry:

- Computer literacy

- Slowed down work

- Stress effecting quality of work

- Team dynamics

Problems to avoid

Avoid problems involving the following:

- Breach of confidentiality

- Inability to work with health and safety rules

- Conflicts with organisational policies and procedures

- Personal problems with your manager or working with a difficult manager

- Problem around equal opportunity issues (especially whilst dealing with service users)

- Difficult agency (partner organisation) staff because you were at fault

Show knowledge and value

For the suggested problems use your solutions to show how knowledgeable you are and how much value you placed on the issues involved. When talking about the solution be careful to project the following:

- Your own initiative

- Willingness to accept help from others

- Flexibility

- Use of planning skills

- Co-operating with other staff (in finding solutions)

- Willingness and readiness to use   or consult organisational policy

- Professional knowledge and awareness about your job

- Effective use of time

- Willingness to share problems and difficulties

- Methodical and creative in approach

Look at the following example:
'...... *from my previous experience in the industry I have learnt to view problems as opportunities to learn something new. With this attitude I am able to remain calm, flexible and open to ideas. So I shared my problems with the team during one of our meetings and an experienced member of the team volunteered to spend an hour each day with me addressing my problems with computers. Within four weeks I became pleased with my progress. With this motivation I willingly accepted an external training/ course (organised by my manger following discussions in supervision sections). I now represent my team at the regional level on Information Technology network programmes.'*

Constructive solutions
Your solutions in this case must be a constructive one. You must begin by showing you were unhappy or uncomfortable about the situation and finish with the overall benefits. We have already seen where you can start with the solutions. Let's now look at some possible overall benefits. They will include the following:

- Improvement in quality of work

- Able to organise own work load with confidence

- Able to work longer hours which was a relief not just to me but also to my colleagues

Link benefits to values
Always link the overall benefits to other values not just personal ones. Example of this is provided below.

'When I was finally able to work the computer, my arrears monitoring skills improved. I was able to send letters out in time, and generate clients' statements with ease. This reduced complaints from clients and improved my relationship with them.'

Similarly you can talk about overall benefits. Let's look at the following examples:

- Benefits to the team and colleagues

- Improving self esteem and confidence of service users

- Improvements of the atmosphere in hostel or project

- Deeper understanding of and better ways of working with organisation's procedures

- Time saving through e.g. avoidance of reworking

- Enhancement of organisational image or gaining an improved profile

- Effect on team work

- Safer workplace or better work atmosphere

- Improved liaison skills and better or more effective ways of working together with external agency staff

A striking significance in the above examples is that they are all important objectives that your employers expected from you then. It is equally true with your potential employers. This is exactly what they want to hear and you must tell them just that.

Focus on old problems
When answering questions of this type, focus on an old problem (whether real or fabricated). It does not matter which angle it's coming from as long as it fits in with your previous employment experience and job description of the post you are applying for. There is no use talking about an existing problem because there won't be time enough to get you out of it and get you fit for the job you are applying for.

Use dates to communicate your old problems
Put the problem at the start of the position concern. Also, the further the date of the problem the better. Thus when you start with *'I had an important experience in 1985 when my Supported Housing career began as a Supported Housing Officer in a small hostel run by CentrePoint...'* you immediately imply that your problem occurred long time ago when you were new in the industry. Your interviewers can relate well to this because of the following reasons:

- The year 1985 (More than 15 years ago).

- Almost every one (if not everyone) go through learning processes at first start: 'Rough rides' are common.

- You managed to set the scene as a remote one, which has no reflection on or of your present abilities.

Communicate your experience
Additionally, a remote date has the benefit of communicating a message about your experience and possible competence (e.g. in 1985). In our example it is very clear that the interviewee is well experienced (over 15 years).

Learning from your experience
Another area of your story needing highlighting is what you learnt from your experience. Talking about this brings further opportunities for winning points with your interviewers. Interviewers are pleased to hear about how much you added to your knowledge, awareness or experience.

Complimenting this must also be comments on how you felt after your experience. Interviewers want to hear you say things like the following (examples):

- Heightened confidence

- Better motivated

- More focused

- Enthusiastic

- Methodical in my approach

- More creative and innovative

- Setting realistic targets

- Remaining calm and composed in emergency

- Encouraged and challenged

Question 33 WORKING WITH DIFFICULT COLLEAGUES
You will be working as part of a staff team if appointed. How would you deal with your colleagues who have a different approach to dealing with tenants?

Different approaches to things can be a good asset for the team. This is on account of the diverse client needs and also the fast changing market, which we serve. Different approaches using different skills make for flexibility and can also be instrumental to a good change management process and therefore create learning opportunities for the team as well as the organisation at large.

Where different approaches lead to desired fruits it must be embraced as a positive experience. Positive fruits (examples) include:

- Professional in nature

- Working within the law

- Working well with organisational policy and procedures

- Able to produce client satisfaction and also instrumental in achieving organisational objectives on clients welfare

- Not destructive in the way the staff team operates

On the other hand, different approaches to dealing with clients may have consequences standing at the opposite end of all the advantages listed above. Characteristics of a destructive working style include the following:

- It attracts too many complaints (from especially clients).

- It brings confusion amongst members of the staff team.

- It is disruptive and hampers progress.

- Makes the service and its delivery inconsistent and therefore confuses clients.

- Generates poor relationship with other partners or agencies.

- Make other team members defensive and therefore self-centred. Every aspect of teamwork is affected (negatively).

- Service standard get compromised and not achieved.

- Professional boundaries, the law and organisational policies and procedures get ignored or breached and organisations get punished by all forms of external sanctions.

As a team member and an employee (with a contract of employment) your loyalty is first of all towards

- Your organisation, and then
- Your team,
- Your colleague, then
- Yourself

Put team interest first
Loyalty to team mates must be conducted in harmony of team interests. Therefore, though there is the need to seek individual colleague's interest, the method engaged must have team interest as a focus. A good team must be able to address individual needs as well as those of the team. One cannot be done at the expense of the other even though in varying times emphasis and priorities may differ.

Conflicts
Where conflicts emerge between the two (team interest and individual staff interest), the interest of the team must be paramount. The only exception is where such conflicts have arisen because the team's decision conflicts with provisions of the organisation or the law, or some well-documented professional practice.

Don't be too quick to criticise
You must give people the benefit of doubt especially if the issue is not a serious one. Good team members must be accommodating and tolerant. However, if blunders are of very serious nature (e.g. a breach of health and safety law) a much quicker action may be required.

Tell them and be specific
The best way to deal with colleagues with disruptive working styles is to let them know in a tactful way. Tell them if you disapprove of any specific action. Emphasis must be on 'specific' actions. It will be meaningless not to be specific, as you cannot despise them outright without reasons they can relate to.

Be sensitive
It must also be done sensitively. This means you must chose:

- Your words carefully (e.g. not premeditatedly or angrily)

- Your time carefully (e.g. not when the person is preoccupied with other things)

- Suitable atmosphere (e.g. not in the presence of other colleagues or clients)

Make them aware of your concerns
Don't miss this one. Make them aware what you think but more importantly establish the effect it will register on the team as a whole. The conclusion you draw over the correctness of your colleague's actions must be weighted against, for example:

- Team objectives

- Organisational procedures

- Other colleagues' interests or views

- Agreed service standards

This way criticism is likely to be seen as constructive.

Pitch your criticism
It is important you come across as a colleague and not as a supervisor or manager. People are more likely to listen if you are able to assure them that you yourself can equally make similar mistakes. Informality is important for achieving this.

Mind how you start
Sometimes it's best to start by making the person aware that you can see the reason why he/she is doing things in that particular style, then finish with e.g.

'... but I am concerned about the effect it will have on team efforts'. This approach should be preferred to one that lashes out accusations straight away.

Do not put your interest first
Another important strategy is not to put your own interest first i.e. before the team's, or for that matter anything corporate. Your concerns must e.g. be about the overall team agreed standards and achievements. Therefore avoid using 'I' 'mine', 'my' etc. Go for w*e, our, us,* etc.

Be tolerant and understanding
We saw this point earlier but it is worth further clarification. As a team player you need to be able to demonstrate sufficient patience, tolerance, understanding and flexibility to allow your colleague to change. This is even more so where the person realises the value of your concerns and is willing to change.

Offer your assistance
If you believe the condition is right offer to help out. This will probably be the case where your colleague is willing to change but doesn't know how. Many staff will say nothing to colleagues with disruptive behaviours because of fear of how they might react. It's better to let them know what you think than backbiting them before others. If you are rejected you will at least know where you stand and then consider other alternatives for yourself.

If the colleague agrees with you and changes his/her habit, the matter is finished and nothing more must be done. However if the situation persists you must consider further action.

Tell them what you intend to do
Make the person aware that you still have difficulties with his /her style and you wish to bring this to the attention of his manager. The manager can address the matter through structures like:

- Supervision

- Appraisal

- Walking management and coaching

- Team meetings

- Disciplinary interview (if necessary)

Tell them what you intend to do anyway if on your first approach you were snubbed.

Bring it to the attention of the team members
This will be the case if the disruptive behaviour is experienced by more than one person. Where this was the case you would have heard other team members share your views. If the negative behaviour has reached an 'epidemic' scale it needs to be addressed as a team problem.

Openness is important
Good teamwork thrives on openness. It is better to let him/her know what is coming than for them to discover your secret endeavour later on. Once you have aired your views you can get on with your job stress-free. Even if you fail to get support from managers you will at least know your position.

Talk to someone who can help
If for some reason you are unsure about what to do though disturbed, make sure you share your concerns with someone who is in a position to help. No, not in a *gossipy* way. I am referring to doing something with a view to avoid being stressed out. Talk to someone who knows more about your organisation's policy. Someone you can trust. The support you receive may help you maintain your concentration and get on with your job with much ease.

DIVERSITY IN WORK FORCE

Diversity in the work place includes all differences that define each person as unique individuals. Such differences include those of the following:

- Culture
- Ethnicity
- Gender
- Age
- Sexual orientation
- Abilities or disability
- Nationality
- Skills
- Education
- Race
- Religion
- Opinion
- Experience
- Belief
- Colour

135

These qualities make us who we are and what we bring to the workplace. Valuing diversity creates better working relationships with customers, partners, suppliers, and the communities where we work. Diversity does not refer to individuals who are different from the majority, it covers all differences. It refers to physical differences, how people think, their beliefs, values, life and choices they make. These differences make us who we are as individuals and are a resource to providing new insights, different perspectives, and ways of doing things, all of which if brought together, can help creativity, problem solving and growth.

IDEAS ON STRATEGIES FOR PROMOTING DIVERSITY

Diversity programmes must be taken one step at a time: Taking on too much and succeeding at very little will lead to despair. Start by conducting a solid needs assessment of your situation and identify gaols. Some important gaols for consideration are:

- All executive staff as well as operational managers must be aware of issues of diversity.
- Using intranet system to promote diversity in the work place.
- Designing and implementing a diversity newsletter or diversity column in an existing corporate publication.

It is important that the goals are clear and are able to communicate clear objectives. They must provide hints on processes as well as what diversity is. At the heart of the diversity programme must be the idea that we are all equal.

A wide target
Diversity is for everyone and the programme must be designed to help every one. Everyone must have the opportunity to be the best they can be in the organisation. It is essential that this idea is central to the entire programme to reduce friction amongst staff. You need to carefully balance the needs of individual groups and the needs of the workforce as a whole.

Pay attention to groups with more pressing needs

Certain groups of the workforce may have more pressing needs and these must be budgeted for. It could be those of the women workforce, the disabled workforce, or the black workforce. This will very much depend on what is revealed by the initial workforce survey results.

Pay special attention to information

Facilitate communication between employees' different heritage with a goal of breaking down the walls of ignorance and assumptions. This can be done using group activities or staff training programmes.

Be mindful of lowering standards

Lower standards are one of the causes of failures in diversity programmes. Diversity programmes must emphasise quality, productivity and success. Therefore all corporate programmes must communicate the right massage. Diversity programmes must not be implemented at the expense of good customer service.

Direct a focus on managers

Managers of frontline teams are perhaps the most influential figures and through whom the organisation's values can be promoted. Train managers so that they understand the human and legal impact of discrimination.

Prompt action and investigation

Prompt response is necessary. Investigation must be impartial and must lead to actions deigned to stop the undesired conducts and prevent them from reoccurring.

Displays

Use displays in your work place such as books, posters that demonstrate corporate acceptance and awareness of inclusiveness.

Internal outreach strategy

The organisation must do everything possible to encourage participation by all types of people in the organisation. There must be a safe environment where for instance closed-gay people can come out or participate at any level they deem safe.

Outreach programmes

Outreach programmes for the community may include supporting local organisations which are established for the sole purpose of promoting awareness of specific ideas, needs, groups, or relationships. Similarly, employees can be allowed to represent the organisation in specific promotional functions organised by these groups.

Commit resources to the course

Ensure there are sufficient resources to sustain the course. You may have a resource room, shelf, corner, or kiosk. List of literature may be made available on subjects on diversity, and names and phone numbers of organisation's of all kinds especially those offering support. Also consider designating a person with deep practical knowledge on the issue of diversity to co-ordinate affairs. It's important that the workforce have ready-access to information.

External resources

Diversity programmes can also be significantly resourced through for instance, external counselling service organisations. Staff who feel distressed or are experiencing diversity-related difficulties in the work place can be encouraged to access such services: This represents additional evidence of the organisation's support for such victims.

Have a hot line

Encourage staff to report all forms of harassment and discrimination. There must be scope for people to talk privately or in confidence. This means the organisation must be flexible on means of collecting information.

Award performance

Consider sending clear messages on acceptable behaviours. This can be part of some annual corporate celebration where awards (e.g. in the form of certificates) are presented to individuals or groups.

Punishment for bad behaviours

Organisational policies must make clear behaviours that are not acceptable and if encouraged will defuse benefits from diversity programmes. Managers must be supported to implement the policies and quick action must be taken in the event of breaches.

Human resources

Consider a non-discriminatory policy on taking references and making background checks for every new employee and using such methods to prevent the inclusion of people who can potentially destroy diversity programmes. This must be conducted in a non-discriminatory manner.

Managers must provide leadership in diversity

Managers must work to clear objectives and aim at using initiatives which create the right work environment where people can be constantly reminded of the diversity mission. Some positive objectives to consider for achieving diversity at the work place include the following:

- Attract, retain and develop good people with the best talents.

- Creating cultural acceptance within the work environment.

- Attracting and maintaining customers and partners with the right business attitudes.

- Creating opportunities for maximising use of corporate human resources.

- Creating the most motivated and competitive workforce possible.

AN INDIVIDUAL'S RESPONSIBILITIES

Educate yourself

Encourage staff to educate themselves about sexual orientation. This will help individuals to express a position that balances their own opinions with the change agent behaviour which their organisation seek to encourage.

Laws and organisation's policies

Staff must take time to understand the relevant legislation that governs issues of diversity especially those affecting their work places. They must also consider the organisation's own policies on anti-discrimination practices. This can be made part of team training exercises, perhaps in the form of quizzes. See Winning Ideas volume one for ideas on equal opportunity and it's laws.

Social functions

Gay and lesbian co-workers must be encouraged to be part of social groups formed at work. When appropriate, encourage them to bring their partners to functions.

Mind your language
The use of Inclusive language must be encouraged when ever possible. For instance *partner* can be used instead of *husband* or *wife*. Also discourage class language like *you* instead of *us*.

Share your knowledge
Share your knowledge from training programmes that may help promote diversity at the work place: Share anything you've learnt about human sexuality and homophobia that might encourage others to adopt productive behaviours.

Avoid living under false assumptions
Living under false assumption may lead to acting falsely. Do not assume that everyone you come into contact with at the work place is heterosexual. This must be avoided as it may lead to offensive comments and behaviours.

Ask questions
If you do not know, ask. It's better to ask than make assumptions and act on them. For instance, if you wish to know someone's orientation or origin, ask them politely. Don't be too quick to guess or pronounce other people's names if you are unsure: *How do you pronounce your name*? Consider this first.

Displays
Show what you believe through the way you customise your small little places at work. What about a little sticker or poster on the wall communicating to everyone that you value diversity at work?

Don't entertain discrimination
Refuse to take part in any act of discrimination. For example, refuse to laugh at anti-gay 'humour'. Instead, and if possible point out the negative effect this may register on the team and the organisation as a whole. If you are unable to do this simply walk away, and refuse to be part of it. This advice would equally apply to those who find it difficult to publicly subscribe to a pro-gay campaign because of their religious believes.

Refer to your organisation's policy
When reacting to anti-gay or anti-lesbian humour you will find it useful to refer to the organisation's policy about non-discrimination. If you are able

to do this it will help you to dissociate yourself from groups that indulge in verbal discrimination.

Be a sign poster
If you are aware of anyone who is troubled about topics on diversity, encourage them to read books or attend education sessions on orientation. Also advise colleagues from ethnic minority groups to involve themselves in working party activities in order to influence service outcomes.

SOME USEFUL TERMS ON DIVERSITY

As noted earlier, access to information is critical to the killing of ignorance. Staff must be mindful of the destructive effects of those terms they sometimes use without many thoughts or without knowing their full meanings. Which of these terms applies to you or your work place practices?

Stereotypes *(an idea)*	▪ Oversimplified conception or belief about an entire group of people which ignores specific associations or qualities of individuals within that group.
Sexism	▪ Discrimination by members of one sex against the other based on the assumption that one sex is superior.
Heterosexsim	▪ Prejudice against or open display of dislike for gay, lesbian or bisexual people.
Homophobia	▪ This is about fear. Homophobians have a fear of homosexuals or people believed to be lesbians, gays or bisexuals.
Prejudice *(a feeling)*	▪ Irrational hostility towards members of a particular race, religious, or group. It is about making judgments based in scanty information.
Discrimination *(action)*	▪ Action taken on the basis of prejudice. Treating people unjustly or unfairly because of some pre-

141

conceived ideas or beliefs you hold about them.

Scapegoating	- It is the act of blaming someone or a group of people for a fault because of their identity. Scapegoating is based on prejudice not on any material facts, conclusions are hastily drawn, and blames are levelled against someone or some group just because of their identity.
Ableism	- Comes from the word *Able'* (having the skill, power, or resources to do something). It is a term used when people exhibit prejudice against people with mental illness or learning disabilities.
Anti-semitism	- This is based on negative ideas about Jews. It is a form of religious hatred directed at Jews because of their religious belief.
Bigotry	- Comes from the word *Bigot* (a person who is intolerant). Bigotry is prejudice founded on negative perceptions (about beliefs or practices) directed towards a person or a group of people.
Hate incident	- These are incidents cause by behaviours which constitutes an expression of hostility against a person or the person's property on grounds of race, religion, disability gender, etc.
Racism	- Discrimination based on race. Expressed prejudice against people because of their race, colour, nationality, or ethnic origin.
Classism	- Discrimination based on people social and economic status in the society or place of work.
Ageism	- Discrimination based on age. Treating someone less favourably because of the person's age.

CHECKLIST FOR DIVERSITY AND CLASSISM

Where as race and gender are more visible differences, class can be a bit harder to identify by sight alone. Power differences and the presence of hierarchy manifest themselves in the workplace. Below is a checklist to help you decide whether or not your diversity programme is succeeding. The leadership of every organisation must set an example by making sure that members at all levels within the organisation are recognised. All employees regardless of their positions must be treated with dignity.

If you wish to audit the diversity programme in your organisation or work place try answering the following questions. Ask what can be done about the areas you have concerns in.

- From what background are most of the managers in your organisation?

- From what background are most of your senior management team members?

- Who (or which group of people) in your organisation is treated with more respect?

- Who (or which group of people) in your organisation has more power and opportunity to gain more money or increment?

- Does educational, training and development opportunities vary by level or groups of people?

- Does your organisation seek to recruit from particular groups of people or area?

- How fair are your recruitment procedures?

- Do interview panels always have a balanced mix of people?

- Is any project or department dominated by particular groups of people?

- Does your organisation use alternative recruitment channels to give more people equal opportunities?

- Are old staffs given preference over new staff (joining from outside organisations)?

- Do all staff have access to organisation policy?

- Do all staff use the same cafeteria, or kitchen for their break?

- Where notices are displayed in your organisation: Do all staff have access to them?

- When meetings are organised to seek employees views on issues affecting them do they all have the opportunity to attend?

- Are there provisions for people with little English or those who use English as second language?

- Do your organisation use uniforms to differentiate between people unnecessarily?

- Are there certain meetings classified 'members' only?

- Are some people asked to use their own resources when doing their jobs whilst others are provided with organisational resources?

- Do you always have to write your concerns on paper before you receive attention?

- Are there some areas in the workplace with restricted access to only some type of people?

- Are team-building, team meetings or training events scheduled during off-hours?

- Are some people allowed to arrive late to work and others disallowed?

- Are there any special activities reserved for 'members only'?

- Do you find that you get results quicker when you use your manager than going to head office yourself?

- Amongst your staff team: Do you think you all have equal access to your manager?

- During functions, do managers have reserved seats?

- During functions, are invitees required to appear in special outfits (e.g. tuxedos)?

- Do employees use classist terms or comments in the work place?

- Are people who work long hours or overtime favoured over those who restrict themselves to regular hours?

- Does it feel as if your organisation has different rules for people at higher levels in the organisation?

- Are perks offered only at certain levels?

- Does the manager of the project always say 'good morning' or 'how are you today' to cleaners or porters, or caretakers?

- Do people only speak to or know the names of important people?

Question 34   HOME VISITS: PRECAUTIONARY MEASURES
If successful your job will include visiting clients (tenants) in their homes on your own. What precautionary measures will you take to ensure your own safety?

Notify office when you are doing visits in clients' home.
Your team must have a central system for collecting and monitoring such information. Provide information on how long your meeting will be and phone in to say that you are OK. If you have not phoned in after the estimated time the duty staff must contact you to see if you are OK.

Use the dairy
Enter in the diary your movement ensuring that date, time, and the correct address is known to the duty staff. Also include the addresses and any relevant telephone numbers.

Mobile phone and mobile phone battery

Use a mobile phone so that you can be easily connected with the rest of your team when necessary. Furthermore, check that your phone battery is working and test your phone before each visit.

Emergency details

Check that other members of your team have your telephone number and you theirs.

Provide your manager with emergency telephone numbers for yourself and next of kin so they can be contacted where necessary. You may be able to contact someone else besides your team members e.g. if you lose your phone (in which is stored all work-related numbers). Also provide telephone numbers for close friends with at least one of them likely to know your where about.

Policy and procedures

Follow any laid down policy or procedures of the team or organisation or project. Take active part in any rehearsals arranged by your team.

Let someone know you are 'alive'

Call the office when you finish your appointment so your team knows you are safe, and information can be updated.

Good assessment

Assess clients well before making a decision to visit them in their flats. Always make sure you are familiar with the risk issues around the client. Speak to referral agency or ex-service providers for details if necessary. Remember, the information you obtain on the person's past is not as important as your current assessment of him.

Alternative meeting places

If you have concerns about your safety, consider meeting at alternative places which may include a public place (e.g. coffee shop), your office or day centres.

Stick to planned visits

This must be preferred to unannounced ones though this is not always possible. Planned visits allow you time to make the relevant backup arrangements and to take the necessary pre-cautions. Should you need to do an unplanned visit, phone in and inform someone about the change.

Drinking or drugging clients

Avoid meeting alone with client when they are drunk or acting under the influence of drugs. Similarly it is not a good advice meeting with clients when they have their visitors present, unless this was agreed before hand.

Dogs and wild animals (used as pets)

Consider the dangers of visiting clients with dogs or wild pets. If you have any doubts agree another venue for meeting instead of the client's home.

Encourage meeting with clients outside their homes

I am talking about actually planning towards discouraging home meetings. Meeting outside in many ways brings life out of people. It encourages many vulnerable people to improve their confidence, acquire interests, and regenerate old ones.

Learn from experience

This may be your own or others shared at team meetings and use them to modify your own methods.

Question 35 QUALITIES OF A GOOD TEAM
What do you expect from your team?

Most employers are aware of the value of a good team. You will normally be expected to show awareness of this even where you were not asked a direct question on the topic. Team work must focus on team approach and team assets.

Your expectations must include the following. Specific expectations are also explained below.

- Things that are reasonable and realistic.
- What will enable you to deliver the package outlined in your job description
- What will make you a good team player (e.g. show needs of a good team)
- What will contribute to achieving the objectives of your organisation

That you will be treated equally and with respect
Equality of opportunities is not reserved for just employers. Every one must observe it, customers as well. Individuals may have preferences as to which member of staff they will like to receive service from. This is natural and nothing is wrong about it. However, it will be wrong for anyone to compare staff against each other in a manner that amounts to humiliation or disrespect. You must be respected for who you are not what someone else wants you to be.

Your contribution will be valued no matter how small
This is about recognition and appreciation. They must be anchored on the fact that you are a member of the team rather than the size of your contribution. This is basically because you won't be able to satisfy every one but you can satisfy the overall objective of the team with that bit of your own contribution. No matter how small your contribution is you want to feel valued and motivated by it.

You must receive co-operation and support of team members
Team work must be alive, organic and 'human'. It is like dealing with one human being instead of the many bodies involved. You need people to understand your circumstance and to take appropriate act and make you feel you are not alone.

There will be trust and honesty
You also want people to trust you to the extent that they can open up to you. Transparency and sharing is the key to involvement and participation. Team loyalty thrives on consultation, respect and clarity of issues.

Understanding of your specific problems and needs
Team needs must by all means be on the 'table', but without sound bodies there will not be a sound team. You want people to understand that you are a specific individual with specific needs and can be confronted with specific problems and difficulties. The team must allow you resources with which to deal with things that are of personal nature.

Consistency in work approach (e.g. when executing agreed plans)
'Team members with disruptive working styles are a pain'. Consistency is one of the positive hallmarks of a good team. This can happen if members are

focusing on one objective, strategies are clear and there are systems in place to ensure control with guidance and appropriate support.

Function as a team – in unity and strength

No apathy. No neutral grounds. No undecided fellows, you are either in or out! Social activities which fuel the 'gossip' life of the team can help. Never think gossip is a bad thing. It's a very important part human that cannot be taken out. With good management healthy social activities can be one valuable source of unity and strength for the team. I have no doubt some management fanatics will object to this. Try opening up a *gossip line* for staff to collect more information about 'rumours' within the organisation. You will be surprised how this will increase corporate awareness, in the right direction.

To work with organisational policies and procedures

The good team must show business awareness in its functions. This is one of the ways of staying consistent with operations. There must be opportunities for strategies to be tested with corporate objectives and priorities as well as policies and procedures.

Times of conflicts used to achieve best results

Conflicts are bound to occur. They must be seen as natural and in fact they must be planned for well in advance before their arrival. All plans must for instance have contingencies. Whatever happens the team must stay focused always working hard to sustain mutual interest, and advancing it's course.

Clear team objectives

Team objectives must remain clear at all times. Equally, strategies must be clear and also laid out according to priorities, so that every member of the team is aware of what is happening. Effective communication holds a serious role here to ensure that members are aware of team actions at all times.

Practical support

Not just words, works are even more important. For instance, if you have to attend to an emergency and cannot cover your duty, you expect a volunteer (colleague) to help out.

Openness

There must be openness and transparency in all matters affecting the team and it's operations. Way of achieving this can include the following:

- Having a structured agenda for team meetings to include matters being speculated, those unclear, and those about the future of the team

- Discuss the way external operations may affect team operations

- Any changes anticipated in the near future that will affect the team and the way it operates

- Issues about members of the team which staff should know

- Involving team members frequently when deciding on team strategies for dealing with problems

Learn from it's own experience and growth

You expect the team to keep records of its operations, and to be able to learn from mistakes and take such experiences into consideration when addressing problems and strategies in future. Just like an individual, the team must be able to learn, develop and grow.

Corporate environment of the team

The core function of the team must work to a plan which is consistent with corporate values and business objectives.

Staff development

Members must place value on staff and their development and this must be reflected in team priorities. The needs of individual staff member must be carefully balanced into those of the team. Decisions on strategies and priorities must especially take this into consideration.

Evaluate and Review performance

This is always a source of important learning for the team as a whole. This function is everybody's business, and must be done jointly through e.g. team meetings, quarterly or annually appraisal functions, depending on what is suitable and appropriate.

Pro-activity, not re-activity

This is about strategic awareness, working towards taking advantage of situations long before they arrive. Lots of re-active work means the team is not learning and developing. Proactive work approach leads to confidence and self value.

Flexibility in operations

There must be flexibility in operations, enough to easily accommodate change and respond well to changing needs. Such needs may be those of clients, individual members of the team or indeed those of the team.

Democratic approach

Due recognition must be given to consultation and democratic procedures in reaching most decisions. Remember however that this cannot always be available. The team must be able to work well under its leader, and where consensus cannot be reached forge forward with respect for the leader's decisions. Being sensitive to confidentiality issues means not every thing can be discussed openly.

Best use of diversity

Scope must exist for recognising diversity in the team and this must be used to achieve best results. The topic of team diversity is treated in more detail elsewhere in this book. Diversity must be embraced by good teams as an asset not a liability. In fact it is one of the major requirements of team formations. Differences in experience, skill, language, ability, etc. makes the team more able in its operations.

Opportunities

Opportunities must exist for team members to exercise and practice their skills, knowledge and abilities. This starts by knowing what is available, then having ways for improving team's activities using what is available. The team gets motivated and clients are able to receive quality service. Remember no contribution is too small

Change management

The team must have a positive attitude towards change. Change must be handled effectively and seen as an opportunity to learn and grow. Members of a good team look forward to 'change' and do not get intimidated, become anxious, or stressed because of change.

CHARACTERISTICS OF A GOOD TEAM

We have already seen how diversity if managed effectively can lead to the creation of a good team. Let's look at some characteristics of a good team.

Consider the list below and see if you can add some more ideas. Hopefully you can create your own list that will suit your specific situation. Also look at Winning Ideas Volumes one and two for more on *Team work*.

- Team members receive supervision regularly.
- Team members trust and support each other.
- Members have real sense of achievements in their jobs.
- Work is well planned before executed.
- People in the team work well together.
- People are pretty open with each other.
- Generally, members pull in the same direction.
- Regular feedback is provided to all members on how the team is doing.
- People know what they are expected to achieve in any given time.
- Close supervision and support is given to new members.
- Staff feel that they have been involved in setting their targets.
- Problems are discussed openly and freely.
- Team members have sensible workload most of the time.
- Members often feel that they have accomplished something.
- Members have control over the way they do their jobs.
- Staff are encouraged to contribute ideas and suggestions.
- People feel they are able to rely on each other.
- Staff show understanding of the purpose of their jobs.
- Room is given to social activities outside work.

- People can feel that their contributions really matters.

- Team leader values opinions of staff and shows this openly.

- Members feel that they are working to clear objectives at all times.

- Lots of discussions prevail in the team.

- Members are constantly seeking ways to motivate themselves.

- The team is well resourced for doing the work they need to do.

- There is a real feeling of satisfaction from the jobs that people do.

- Team leader and members of the team make people feel welcomed.

- Opportunities exist for everyone to take active part in team activities.

- People are aware of their priorities.

- There is respect for time and it is used wisely.

- There is enough controls and boundaries to ensure compliance but these are hardly implemented.

- People are aware of the resources of the team and take this into consideration when executing their tasks.

- People set themselves high standards because they receive the encouragement for doing so.

- People are able to have open disagreements in the team without resulting to destructive arguments.

- People feel proud to belong to the team, and show this by defending it at every opportunity.

- Team members get praised for positive efforts, and they spend quality time exploring further avenues to repeat performance.

- People are treated as responsible adults not as confused infants who must be told what to do, say, or see.

Question 36   MANAGERIAL SKILLS CHECKLIST
What managerial skills do you expect from your line manager?

This question is already covered in Winning Ideas volume two

Consider the following two important points. Managers must be:

- Professional in practice (e.g. not disruptive or controversial)

- Corporate minded (e.g. work well with policy and procedure)

Managers also need to be flexible in their expectations and make room for change. Some specific examples of management skills are listed below.

- Planning
- Negotiation
- Communication
- Organisational
- Co-ordinating
- Supervision
- Appraisal
- Problems solving
- Financial management
- People management
- Interview

- Investigation
- Interpersonal
- Decision making
- Accountability
- Training and coaching
- Presentational
- Observational
- Report writing
- Liaison
- Records management

- Entrepreneurial
- Monitoring
- Creative
- Innovative
- Initiative
- leadership
- Processing
- Analytical
- Administration
- Interpersonal
- Evaluation and reviewing

See Winning Ideas Volume two for more on this question. Also see *good qualities of a manager* below.

Question 37   STAFF COMMITMENT TO AN ORGANISATION
What can we expect from you?

This question is very much about your job description and the person specification. You need to bear in mind that the reason you are being interviewed is that there is a specific job to be done. If you fail to take a good look at what your job entails you might blow this one.

Focus on the job description and the person specification

You prospective employer is looking for a specific person for a specific job. Using the person specification, show how your skills, experience, abilities, commitments and knowledge will enable you to deliver the job requirements as outline in the job description.

Show how your contribution can make a difference

You do this by examining your own strengths, giving examples freely of how others have already benefited from them. Your strengths may include the following examples:

- Computer literacy e.g. in a particular package that will benefit specific areas of the job.

- Knowledge on specific aspects of the job e.g. asylum and immigration issues, health and safety, or welfare benefits.

- A natural ability in working with figures e.g. giving you absolute control over rent arrears, and other forms of accounting procedures.

- Interpersonal abilities e.g. able to build relationship easily, work with a wide range of people effectively, or showing understanding and empathy easily.

Consider the end result

You must always bear in mind that the end result of the job itself is important. In other words you need to show that you understand the purpose of the job. You do this by relating the benefits to:

- The organisation's clients (to show that you are customer focused

- The organisation's own interests (e.g. enhanced image). Matters of professionalism and quality are usually seen as a big corporate asset.

- The staff team. For example, observing confidentiality, and being flexible are seen as qualities of a good team player.

Establish benefits from your contribution

The important question here is how can the organisation benefit from your contribution? This will probably be obvious after showing how you can use your strengths to make a difference, but just to be sure consider highlighting the benefits. Let's look at some specific examples of what every organisation wants from staff.

- To embrace and work well with change
- To learn and grow
- To bring to the attention of the organisation things that will affect it's interest regularly
- Show understanding of the purpose of the job
- Good team player and contribute to team efforts
- Be able to carry out your duties to levels expected by the organisation
- Motivated and enthusiastic
- Adhere to organisation's policies and procedures
- Be aware of corporate priorities and reflect this in your work
- Contribute idea, experience, and knowledge for the purpose of achieving overall corporate objectives
- Represent the organisation (externally) professionally
- To present your organisation highly through the quality of your work when working with outside agencies
- To show awareness of legal matters affecting your work and comply with them

- Treat organisation's customers with respect and courtesy and aim to keep them happy at all times
- To make your skills knowledge and experience available to other staff who might need them
- Motivate yourself
- Show awareness of own development needs and contribute to self improvement
- To be loyal, trustworthy, and honest in all undertakings involving your work
- To be professional and stay professional at all times in the course of your work
- To show commitment to equal opportunity openly and freely
- To use organisational resources wisely and thoughtfully
- To partake in sensible discussions leading to change in the work place and in processes
- To receive supervision from your line manager and follow directions, advice and instructions given
- To be productive in your job through the meeting of work objectives and department targets

Your conclusion

Say how your earlier comments fit in into any priorities of the organisation, e.g. customer satisfaction or tenant involvement. Clearly indicate how your presence in the organisation and your skills will be instrumental in achieving current key objectives.

Question 38   QUALITIES OF A MANAGER

This organisation seeks to maintain a professional image amongst its competitors. In many ways we rely on our managers for effectiveness in service. It is therefore important that our managers are of good quality. What qualities would you bring into the job?

The topic of G*ood management qualities* is covered in other parts of this book as well as Winning Ideas volume two. Using these ideas you can draw out a wider picture of what can be expected. This will help you put together a list to suit your specific situation. In other areas the qualities are explained in more detail.

Good social and human relations qualities
Works well with people. Thinks of others' interest. Willing to share and to receive from others.

Technical competence
Possesses enough experience, skills, abilities, and knowledge for doing the work he does effectively.

Reliability and loyalty
Can be trusted to do things. He is consistent in his ways and does not easily give in when confronted with problems.

Leadership qualities
Provides a source of life to the team. Advises, instructs, guides and directs well.

Conceptual ability
Able to think and work with ideas as though they are tangible. Shows strategic awareness.

Emotional resilience
Not rendered useless by serious incidents. Able to get soft with people but also applies the organisation's disciplinary policy effectively. Very serviceable even in times of problems and difficulties.

Negotiation skills

Able to achieve balanced results from deals. Understands the effect of pursuing different objectives.

Understanding the environment

He updates his knowledge of the business environment continuously. Able to take advantage of opportunities and takes appropriate steps to minimise threats.

Continuing sensitivity to events

Responds well to events. Does not procrastinate. Able to make good assessment of situations and their effects. Engages the right resources for dealing with events.

Proactive

Thinks ahead of time. Good anticipation. Projects sensibly into the future and plans for things long before they arrive.

Decision making

Makes up his mind on what he wants. Looks at options and priorities before reaching conclusions.

Interested in facts

Does not surround himself with gossipers. Have a desire to collect information from root sources. Spends quality time building networks with good agencies.

Flexibility

Willing to accommodate other people's view. Wiling to go out of his way to make others feel supported. Works well with change and sees it as a learning opportunity.

Effective communication

Speaks clearly, listens well and responds to comments made by others. He is sensitive to problems around communication and he makes genuine efforts to be understood.

Willingness to learn new skills and Ideas

Shows understanding of the value of learning. Ceases every opportunity to add to his knowledge no matter the source. Learns from own failures as well as others.

Say *sorry/ thank you*
Ready to show that he is human. Expresses remorse and appreciation when they are due. Does not command respect, he earns it by doing the right things.

Approachable
Makes himself available. Initiates conversation willingly and also easy to engage in one. Has good listening skills, and a genuine desire to assist others.

Creative and innovative
Good at confronting and dealing with problems. Able to look at issues from different angles and to find solutions through creative thinking.

Motivate and support staff
Understands the value of staff as a factor of production. Interested in individuals as well as his team. Takes time to find out ways for improving team performance, and for sustaining a happy 'crew'.

Objective and honest
Interested in facts not rumours. Does not make promises he can't keep and keeps promises he makes. Transparent, positive and resourceful.

Role model: Enthusiastic and dynamic
He is confident in himself. He likes his job and portrays this at every opportunity. Always looking for new and exciting ways of achieving objectives.

Organisational, methodical and sequential
Considers all factors carefully before reaching decisions. Takes time to plan work, collect resources and make sure work progress along lines of approved designs.

Quality minded
He thinks, and acts quality in every aspect of his work. Interested in customer feedback and prepared to take sensible risk for the purpose of meeting quality standards.

Ability to supervise and appraise staff

Has the relevant skills for exercising control, providing directions and guidance towards achieving desired work objectives. Able to support staff with analysing their performances and planning their developments.

Firm and fair

Treats people with equality and respect. Once he makes a decision he sticks to it. Does not allow himself to be bullied.

Resourceful

Knowledgeable and being available to help when it matters. Able to provide support, advice and information about job and on matters outside the immediate job environment.

Question 39 MOTIVATING QUALITIES OF MANAGERS
What qualities in a leader/manager motivate you?

You are advised to combine the information here with other good management qualities covered elsewhere in this book.

Managers should:

- Be adaptive in their approach

- Show respect for their staff

- Appreciate the good work of staff

- Be fair and just

- Be genuinely interested in their staff

- Show good examples

- Be honest

  - Say *thank you* to show appreciation

  - Say *sorry* to show that he/she is human

- Provide healthy, safe and good working environment

- Endeavour to train staff

- Demonstrate professional skills and abilities, and superior knowledge.

- Show enthusiasm and motivation freely.

- A 'we' approach management to make me feel that he/she understands my concerns and difficulties.

- Listens and responds to my needs concerning my job as well as issues affecting my performance at work.

- Encourages progress in my work and interested in my personal and professional development.

- Values my contribution to the team's aggregate performance, and shows this openly.

Check for more on motivating qualities of a manager in other sections of this book and also Winning Ideas volume two and four.

Question 40   BENEFITS OF DELEGATION
As a manager you will need to delegate some of your duties in order to meet tight deadlines. In what ways will delegation benefit your staff and the organisation at large?

Customer care
Customers are more likely to feel cared for because of quick responses to queries and more staff are able to make decisions without hesitations. The waiting time for consultation with 'the manager' is eliminated, and customers will begin to feel that staff are competent in their jobs.

Staff development
Delegation develops staff through acting-up opportunities, and those associated with a feeling of greater responsibility and accountability. Above all, it provides necessary scope for the release of creativity, innovations and creative thinking, all of which are elements of staff developments.

Job motivation: Variety

Doing something different does not simply create variety, it also provides a mechanism for avoiding boredom, being repetitive in the way you work and therefore helps sustain interest. This way one is able to work longer hours and also hold position for long periods of time. Delegation therefore has a long term positive effect of staff retention.

Ensures continuity of work

Work must not cease or freeze simply because 'the manager' is 'off sick' or 'not available'. What maters is this: Customers are always on duty. They will keep coming for everything you have promised them and even more! Remember that. Delegation strengthened by good flow of information will facilitate service continuity which will mean service reliability for your customers.

Education: e.g. Org. Policies & procedures

Delegation educates, and education initiates change, a vital component of corporate growth and productivity. The exposure to corporate files, important statistical data, budget information, personnel files as well as the benefits of liaising with other managers of other departments and outside agencies –all bring solid education that can hardly be found in the classroom. Another obvious source of education comes from the failures and mistakes we make as a result of taking risks in our jobs.

Encourage involvement

If people can experience what managers encounter, the chances are that they would show understanding and cooperate especially in times of change. In such cases people are more willing to volunteer their services, show interest and be more patriotic and loyal.

Enhance team work

This point hails from the one above in that common problems lead to common solutions. The staff team is likely to grow stronger in pursuing strategies towards common objectives. Team work is likely to be stronger.

Facilitate supervision

This point stems from the fact of shared knowledge around difficult problems. A typical example is the bureaucracy and the negative culture of poor communication amongst internal staff. It must be said that supervision can only be facilitated through delegation if a good level of respect for each other exist.

Facilitate change

If there is any time when more hands can be a necessity in a corporate body, it must be times of change. Flexibility is a key ingredient for change and delegation makes this very possible. The taking of quick decisions and sharing of information are all extremely important for making a good change.

Releases creativity and innovativeness

Delegation helps bring out the very best out of people as they are confronted with challenges. They will want to demonstrate that they are capable by working much harder.

Essential information flows more easily

Delegation also paves way for accessing information that was previously classified 'managers only'. Using the relationship already enjoyed by staff of lower ranks information is easily zipped through the 'gossip' network.

Saves time

More hands will be available to perform a comparatively less job, leading to time saving.

Training

Delegation provides a very important source of information. Knowledge and opportunities to experiment on the job.

Staff motivation

The motivation comes from the challenges presented by the new position. As one sees positive outcome from his own efforts he starts to believe in himself more. Before long he is volunteering to do more work. The staff feels more trusted and becomes more loyal.

Aggregate effectiveness

From the forgoing it is obvious that delegation will lead to an over all improvement in productivity.

Creation of specialist staff
Delegation can lead to specialisation as people are put in charge of specific tasks they are believed to be good at.

Staff feel more confident
This may come from a sense of job security or the actual experience of making decisions and seeing them implemented.

Question 41   BENEFITS OF STAFF TRAINING
In what ways can this organisation benefit from training its staff?
What are the benefits of staff training?

Meeting Corporate objectives
Enables organisations to meet objectives. New goals and objectives are set all the time each one requiring specific strategies. Training and refresher courses are inevitable for meeting desired objectives.

Competition and efficiency
This is about business survival. To be able to maintain an organisations competitive edge you need knowledgeable and skilled staff.

Effective change management
Training is required so that change can be managed effectively. Change is inevitable in business operations. New systems, methods, and procedures are put in place all the time and people must be trained on them.

Reduces absenteeism and illness
This must be balanced with motivation and adequate staff support. Training on stress management for instance may lead to an improvement in attendance.

Reduces mistakes, errors
This is likely to lead to more positive results from work, and motivation, as re-work time is eliminated or reduced drastically. Additionally the work place will be safer for staff as accident rate will fall.

Reduce staff frustration and stress
Replacing this with more support for each other. Knowing what to do but not knowing how to do it is a pain, not just frustrating.

Improved organisation's reputation
An organisation which trains its staff may acquire Investors In People (IIP) status. Furthermore, the positive effects of training enjoyed by staff will be told to your competitors by your customers as they experience the results.

Produce confident staff
Training brings awareness and technical knowledge which also improves staff confidence.

Improve customer service
Following on from above, customers prefer staff who deliver service with confidence, after all you've got to believe in what you are selling.

Motivation
There is nothing demotivating as not knowing much about your job or how to do it. With training staff can begin to see results and be motivated by the positive outcome.

Job satisfaction
Continuous enjoyment of motivational experiences will lead to loyalty to your job. You feel content where you are.

Job security
If the management wants to spend money training you they must have plans to continue to employ you. There is also the feeling that you might get promoted sooner or later.

Innovation and creativity
Training improves our ability to find creative solutions to problems. It also resources our ability to look at things from different angles and be innovative.

Benefits to clients
Most clients have no problem telling a trained staff from an untrained one. This is because of the quality of service they receive. The trained staff knows how to put him/herself in clients' 'shoes'.

Feeling more part of your organisation
From the above it is clear that both staff and customers will feel a sense of loyalty towards the organisation: 'This is how we treat our customers', or 'this is why I enjoy being a tenant of Family Housing Association'.

Opportunities to share with others
Training gives people something to share. It opens up debates, and creates further opportunities for development.

Improved social life, association and working together
With improved interaction comes enhance social life, support, respect, and the need to accommodate each other's views.

Question 42   IDENTIFYING TRAINING NEEDS OF STAFF
How will you identify the training needs of your staff?

Supervision and performance appraisal
This is the one-to-one setting meant for identifying and responding to needs of individual staff. See Winning Ideas volume one for more on *staff supervision.*

Analysis of job requirements
Check if job description matches with the actual requirements of the job and the way it should be done.

Changes in legislation
Check if this affects the way the job is done and if staff needs more awareness.

Professional body's requirements
A professional body of which your organisation is a member may require that your operations or staff categories meet certain criteria or standards.

Business objectives
This is also about business priorities. Check if operational priorities harmonise with skills, abilities and knowledge of the post holder.

Feedback
This may be from other departments, external agencies, or your customers. Check if any aspect of your service can be improved.

New staff induction
Every new staff must be inducted whether or not he/she has previous experience in a similar job. Induction is another form of training.

Innovative programme activities (e.g. pilot schemes like mentoring for BME staff)

These offer development opportunities. It starts by identifying gaps in knowledge, skills, abilities etc. Training is this case would involve being able to establish and maintain contact with specialist organisations.

Corporate audits (staff survey)

Audits are carried out mostly by regulatory bodies. They normally send in an inspection report outlining areas that need to be improved. This helps to identify training needs.   Such third party recommendations usually carry mandatory requests.

Local or project targets

The department or project itself may set its own targets from time to time either to respond to some emerging issues or as proactive/strategic measures. The usual approach will be to prepare staff before the time.

Organisational analysis

Sometimes it becomes necessary to perform a complete analysis of the way the organisation operates and look at ways to make it more competitive. Such an exercise can lead to gaps in training being revealed.

Changes in needs of clients

One of the hallmarks of a good quality service is *responsiveness*. Clients' needs keep changing and so must be the response in the service they receive. Any such change will mean a shift in training needs.

Observation: Walking management

Sometimes it is not about what is said about staff or by staff: It is what you see. This could for example be about sensible use of resources, correctness of filling systems, safe use of equipment, etc.

Survey of human resources

Survey of human resources and indeed training attendance can reveal isolated or disadvantaged groups that need more attention.

Accidents and major incidents

This is probably the most dramatic of times when training becomes a matter of course.

Complaints
We are not talking about once, or twice, but when they reach a proportion that they become a cause for concern. The organisation must act or loose clients.

Aggregate performance
Where there is drastic fall in aggregate performance an investigation may lead to the identification of training needs.

Training due to corporate strategic planning
Certain training programmes are designed to enable the organisation to take advantage of some future opportunities.

Social or community pressures
Pressures from the environment in which businesses operate sometimes levies a duty to train staff. For example where an organisation operates in an area noted for drug dealing, vandalism and graffiti, they would ensure that their staff are trained to deal with emerging problems.

Responding to actions of consumer groups
Consumer groups like 'WHICH' put lots of pressure on organisations to force changes in operations, and design specifications, hence triggering a need for training.

Transfers
The effect of transfers is similar to the need to induct new employees. There may be aspects of the new job you will need help with before settling down well.

Question 43   TRAINING OPPORTUNITIES
What types of training programmes or training activities can you make available to your staff as part of the staff development function?

On-the-job training

- Coaching (advising, guiding & instructing)
- Planned work (towards e.g. NVQ)

- Job rotation
- Job tasters

168

- Training positions
- Job expansion

- Secondments
- Job enrichment

Off-the –job training

- Attending one day or short training courses
- Full-time courses
- Part-time courses (evenings, weekends, etc.)

- Short courses (seminars, workshops, etc.)
- Distance learning (e.g. via internet)
- Simulation (e.g. training for air pilots)

Informal methods

- Conferences
- Forums
- Open days
- Quality circles
- Seminars
- Service Improvement Groups
- Heading working parties
- Chairing meetings
- Participating in employment interviews
- Visiting other departments within the same organisation
- Attending progress meetings with funders or stakeholders

- Doing presentations
- Business fairs
- Joint working
- Link work
- Net working
- Mentoring
- Staff duty systems
- Leading project functions (e.g. organising project anniversary party)
- Inviting specialist to attend team meetings
- Drills, rehearsals and role plays

The coverage here is meant to be brief as this topic is already covered in Winning Ideas volume two. What you need to bear in mind is that training methods must relate to the following:

- Team's interest and objectives
- Organisational benefits and priorities
- Individual's vocational developments

You also need to pay particular attention to:

Your budget
In most cases staff training requires an extra expense either by way of providing cover or that of paying for the training itself. What ever the case, you need to be sure that the training is necessary, and justified in terms of the overall cost. The timing or duration of the training is also significant and may have cost implications.

The type and quality of training
Training must be relevant to the business of the organisation and preferably has direct benefits for the department or project. Furthermore, the quality of training must be consistent with the problems, difficulties, and challenges encountered in the practical aspects of the job.

Practice opportunities
Opportunities for the trainee to experiment and practice what is acquired on training. Without this it is unlikely the staff will develop. This may mean reviewing the job description and clearly identifying opportunity areas.

Continuous supervision
Provide continuous supervision to ensure that you understand any difficulties confronting staff and helping them on with advice, directions, and guidance.

Practical support
Provide practical support so that they do not feel alone. They must also have confidence that they will not only receive promises but also action. Make sure staff will be equipped with time, equipment, and other facilities necessary for progress.

Motivation
Motivation, without which no tangible results can be achieved from training. A motivated staff will share his/her knowledge and experience with the team and everyone can benefit from that person's training.

Question 44   MAKING TRAINING AND DEVELOPMENT EFFECTIVE
This organisation is committed to training and development of its staff. As a manager you will have a key role to play in this. What suggestions do you have for making this (training and development) effective?

Organisation to show full commitment
The staff need to know that the organisation is serious about it's commitment to train them. This can be done by e.g. committing funds to it, openly reassuring staff, and taking appraisals and staff supervision seriously.

Training needs assessment based on organisation's vision
The training must be anchored on the organisation's business and priorities so that staff can be able to establish the relevance of training and how they can use the acquired Knowledge in their jobs.

Staff should feel real sense of involvement
This will happen of staff are involved in establishing the type of training. They must be made to own the idea so they can work with it.

Clear objectives
Clear objectives must be appreciated by staff as having direct reflections on task required in their jobs. If people do not know where they are going they cannot tell if they get there.

Planned and staggered over a period of time
Training programmes must be prioritised, and the timing for delivery must be relevant to the jobs that needs doing. Furthermore, too many training programmes must not be delivered within a short space of time or staff may find it difficult to absorb the information no matter how useful they are.

Use appropriate methods
Not all staff can stand the traditional blackboard and chalk approach. Multiple methods must be used. The right methods must be chosen for the right programme.

Consideration for disadvantage groups

The organisation needs to consider and encourage involvement of those groups of staff who may be 'hidden' and therefore easily 'forgotten'. This may include Cleaners, Night staff, and people with disabilities.

Review and evaluation

Evaluation methods used must be relevant to the objectives sought for. Any procedures that are inconsistent with desired objectives must be replaced, new targets set, new strategies identified and further training programmes commenced. Staff must be involved in the evaluation exercise.

Ensure training is delivered at right pace

Staff must be given opportunity to comment on each training programme at the end, and fed back to trainers. Approved trainers list must be reviewed periodically as well. This will ensure you have the right people to provide the right stuff.

Training must be delivered in the right atmosphere

Training facilities must be right environmentally. Lighting, safety and security, access, comfort, proximity, etc. These must all be looked at.

Resources

Allow people time and other resources. For example, travelling expenses for attending training can be absorbed by the organisation. Similarly, managers can arrange suitable covers for staff who wish to attend training.

A coordinator, and a SIG (*Service Improvement Group*) to support coordinators work

A named person must be put in charge of training activities to co-ordinate programmes. A working party made up of people from all shades of the organisation can also resource the coordinators efforts through e.g. improvement and exploration meetings.

Training audits performed periodically

This will reveal what is available and what is not. This will help give reasons to failures and also identify areas needing improvements.

Training for unity

Training and its processes must look at how to unit organisation staff by developing a strong sense of togetherness through a common culture and purpose. One way of doing this is to have core training for all staff. Core training on, e.g. customer care, and cultural awareness, stress the corporate value placed on issues that are central to the service and image of the organisation.

Question 45 MANAGING AN EXCEPTIONAL STAFF PROBLEM
Scenario: You are a manager of one of our housing schemes. You receive a call from the police informing you that one of your staff has been arrested for shoplifting. What measures would you take?

What you need to remember is that you have a duty to support your staff as long as their contract with your organisation is live. Your approach must therefore be one of a 'desire to support'. Remember that a person arrested by the police is innocent until proven otherwise. This is of course not to say that there is no need for action. Action is required but it must be the sensitive type.

You need to remain calm.
If you dislike that particular staff, it is not the right time to show this by capitalising on the incident and actively seeking to terminate his or her contract with the organisation.

Public knowledge
Another important consideration is the fact that when the police are involved it could mean the beginning of public knowledge. You do not want the public and for that matter the media to toy with your organisation. Remember you won't just be dealing with a member of staff, but also the public. Therefore you need to be sensitive and work hard towards containing matters in-house.

Look at the wider interest
The police is only an institution. You must understand that they are doing their job. Remember you are a professional and your organisation, other managers and staff will judge you on how you react to the incident. Your first move must be to check whether or not the person arrested is truly one of your staff.

More information
Get more information. For example, establish:
- The full name of the person
- Date and time of incident

- Date of birth
- Full description
- Time of incident
- Which branch of police station
- What items were involved

- Place where incident took place
- Name of the police officer you are speaking to (or in charge)
- Whether or not the person is to be charged

Do not be hasty in concluding that the person is your staff until you have spoken to him. Even after this you can only conclude by saying 'I *believe* one of my staff has been arrested by the police'. Remember, the police may not release very detailed information about the person.

Speak to the person
The idea behind speaking to your staff is not about querying. It's not the time to cast blames. In fact the best approach is to focus on the person's well-being. Things you might want to check include the following:

- Establish that is the one the police have already informed you about. This can be done by checking voice, last shift or next shift

- Whether he is okay

- Is he being treated well by the police?

- Whether or not he is able to exercise any rights

- What the police are planning to do with his case

- Whether or not he needs anything whilst in police custody

- Whether he wants someone to visit him e.g. a solicitor, friend, relative

Action requests made
After talking to the staff, action requests made. It is important that you allow the staff to tell you what he wants and not what you think is good for him. Though, there is no reason why you cannot suggest. The staff may not want to make the matter known to relatives for some good reason, e.g. a vulnerable mother who may have a heart attack upon hearing the news.

Provide support

Your immediate concern must be to work to make sure that staff is receiving fair treatment and can access any support relevant to his situation. You may want to consider visiting the staff at the police station to satisfy yourself that he is okay and to make him aware that the organisation is not taking any hasty decisions against him. This would especially be the case if there are doubts surrounding the matter or the staff is protesting against police action.

Confidentiality

Whilst doing all these you need to observe confidentiality. This however is restricted by your duty as a manager and your responsibility towards your organisation. Beyond this you cannot devolve the information you have received to any third party without the expressed consent of the staff concern.

Keep records

Ensure that you have documented clearly any information you have received as well as action taken on the matter.

Contact with personnel department

Do not be too quick to contact your personnel department unless this is what your organisation's policy says. As a manager you are expected to consider every appropriate action within your own authority before looking elsewhere for advice. In other words you must not be seen as deflecting major incidents without first assessing the situation and/or taking immediate professional actions within your powers and job description. However your organisation's policy and procedures come first. You may be required to relate such matters to a designated person within 24hours or immediately. If you are unsure of what to do never hesitate to contact your manager so you can work together on this.

Further assessment

In the absence of a clear organisational procedure, your next move will be to assess the situation. Assess the matter for seriousness and decide whether or not the person though not convicted can return to the project as a member of staff. It may be necessary to place the person on suspension until the matter is resolved and the police give the all clear. Should you decide to take this option you need to consult with your personnel department, which will notify the staff at the right time. Suspension is even more likely if you think the nature of the allegation affects his position in the organisation.

Staff cover

Address cover issues for the staff who may be absent for a long period. Cover may be provided temporarily by other permanent staff until a locum/bank staff is called in to fill up. Start by asking whether or not you really need a cover. Are there more cost effective ways of addressing the problem?

Consider other staff

Other members of the staff team need to know that the staff won't be available for work for some time. You can't tell them the full story but you owe them the duty of letting them know that changes are occurring within the staff team and how they can be accommodated. Discus how other staff will be affected especially in workload and execute appropriate support

Relevant support must be made available to the staff even while on suspension. If the case finished as a 'foolish' one the staff must be called back into work and full salary paid. The suspension may be necessary due to the nature of the job. For example, if providing support to vulnerable clients.

Question 46   MANAGING WORK-RELATED PROBLEMS

Scenario: You are a new team member of the Wexford project, which is one of the many owned by Equip Housing Association. The project specialises in providing support service to people living in the community. You are in your sixth month after joining and you have discovered many management errors. The situation has taken tolls on staff in several ways, which include:

- **Poor decision making and problem solving approaches**
- **Staff feeling demotivated and not supported**
- **Rent arrears problems leading to high rent arrears**
- **Low staff productivity**
- **Poor time management**

Whilst managers are complaining about work overload, their staff moan about difficult managers who have no 'heart' for motivating staff. You manage to work your way into a working party established to draw up proposals for putting things right and restoring normality.

Question   **What proposal will you make to the managers of Equip Housing Association as a way of resolving their problems?**

Your answer to this question will very much depend on how much influence you are able to make. You cannot do much if you are in a front line role. Therefore this is more likely to be a question for a management position. Nonetheless, questions based on project level problems can feature in interviews for front line staff.

I do not intend to provide answers to the issues raised in the scenario. This is because they are already covered elsewhere in *Winning Ideas* and *Evidence of Performance*. See details below.

- Poor decision making and problem solving approaches *(Winning Ideas Volume two, and Evidence of Performance)*
- Staff feeling demotivated and not supported *(Winning Ideas volume two, three and four)*
- Rent arrears problems *(Winning Ideas volume two)*
- Low staff productivity *(Winning Ideas volume two)*
- Poor time management *(Winning Ideas volume three)*

Question 47   EFFECTIVE TIME MANAGEMENT
How do you manage your time in the course of your work?

A.   Plan your work

Put your work in perspective by time, goals and objectives. Then, prioritise them according to service demands:

- Current gaols (up to 3 months)
- Short range goals (3 months – 1 year)
- Mid range goals (1-3 years)
- Long-term goals (3-5 years +)

B.   *Observe principles*

Understand your task from the beginning
This holds the key for achieving targets within the shortest possible time. Get what you need to do and how you might do them in writing so that you are clear about what is expected.

Delegate when it is possible to do so.
Some administration tasks for example, can be attended to by the admin person leaving you precious time for other things. Don't think of doing things that will consume your time unnecessarily.

Plan for breaks and take care of your health.
This calls for being aware of your own limitations and how far you can go without a rest. If you overwork yourself consistently you put your health at stake and may end up with too many days off sick or too much to do later on.

Aid & equipment
Use aids & equipment e.g. diaries or planners, so that you don't lose anything. Let them do the memory admin task so you will be free to concentrate on each days activities.

Seek help
Being aware that you cannot do everything from the start helps. Seek help from those who can help your course.

Research /clarify
This is useful where you do not have all the relevant tools for accomplishing your task. Get more information. Gather your facts and be sure you know how they fit in into your task. Establish a clear picture of all the things you need to do.

Be quality minded
This will help avoid re-working which in itself takes significant amount of time.

Work to targets
Set targets or objectives for the task, and perform regular review on them so you don't waste time on e.g. out-dated matters.

Have contingency plan in mind
Always plan for what to do if something go wrong. This way you will not loose too much time trying to locate fresh resources.

Organise your resources
Allow your strategies to reach out for your resources, taking into consideration access and speed factors.

Do a time budget for the unexpected
Leave some hours for unexpected events, and be flexible.

Regular checks
Make regular checks on your time plan as you progress. Also make the necessary adjustment to put you back on target in good time. Compensate for lost time as soon as possible instead of leaving them till the end: Transfer any uncompleted tasks into the plan for the next period so that you don't forget them.

Realistic plans
Ensure your plans are realistic and avoid setting unachievable targets. Otherwise, quality time will be wasted on getting frustrated.

Regular audit
Do a regular audit of your activities to see if you need to drop anything, or make changes to time allocated to task. This will ensure best use of time.

Short dead lines
Set short deadlines and keep to them. These may be weekly, monthly, or quarterly. It will help you to focus on one thing at a time.

Consider your team members
Always establish how your plan will affect others (team members), and co-ordinate your plan with them. The less effects, the more control you will have of time.

Prioritise your work load
This is so that you are able to achieve the most important task within quality time.

Question 48   WHAT STAFF MAY EXPECT FROM MANAGERS
What is reasonable for staff to expect from their managers?

Treat staff with respect

Respect at the work place is a mantel for every staff not just for the manager. A manager who refuses to respect his/her staff hardly gets any from them. Respect is like a mirror, what you give is what you reflect. The man who commands respect knows how to give respect himself.

Recognise staff strengths, not just criticisms

It's always a good practice to let criticism follow praises, not the other way round. Better still, good managers will place more emphasis on recognising good works than criticising bad ones. Criticisms must be constructive and delivered tactfully.

Support and motivation

It is a key duty of every manger to provide support and to motivate their staff. This is a fundamental ingredient for production. This is even more so where work is done in a stressful environment.

Managers to provide relevant information to staff

As well as having the overall duty to induct staff into their roles, managers must be custodians of those vital information necessary for achieving both corporate and team objectives.

Consult and negotiate with staff on relevant issues

Being a manager does not make one a more human being than another person. Managers have no right of domination. Managers have no right to dictate. Instead they must reason with staff within scopes allowed by corporate resources. This is not to say that managers must not issue instructions. Sometimes they need to if objectives are to be achieved within prescribed time scales.

Structured supervision that all can benefit from

Supervision must be useful and must have the development of staff at it's core. Managers must not conduct supervisions as private exercises for showing off authority or superiority. It must be structured in such a way that staff can benefit. It is a reasonable right for every staff to receive supervision. See Winning Ideas volume one for more.

Managers to ensure confidentiality about staff

Staff often provide managers with confidential information. This may be issues of personal nature forced out by, for example, an obligation to explain one's absence from work. Such information is provided in trust and confidence and should be guarded against the access of any unauthorised person. See Winning Ideas Volume two for more on *confidentiality*.

Approachable managers, and not aggressive

Unapproachable managers often have no idea about what is happening in their own teams or departments. They are also not good around people. When they are around, staff feign pretences and act up 'shows'. They feel better and more relaxed and jubilant when the manager phones in sick.

Role model

Managers must show good examples in respect of their jobs and what is expected by their organisations, e.g. good time keeping.

Consistency in management style

Stable management style is important for staff to remain focused. They must be able to fashion their work styles within a specific frame of expectations. Therefore, they must work to consistent standards and quality levels without disruptions to the service.

Be decisive and show direction in leadership

This is important especially when staff reach grey areas in their jobs where neither the policy nor the procedure documents are very clear. The manager must be able to make important decisions consistent with the objectives at hand, and without compromising his/her leadership qualities.

Managers must lead (especially in difficult time)

Managers must lead and not boss over subordinates. This test is more visible when things are tough and team members begin to feel the strain, work output begins to lose quality and pressure begins to pile from persistent under-achievements. During this time staff need to feel a sense of purpose through motivation, direction and pure leadership.

Show value for and encourage teamwork

The good manager sees his/her team as a most resourceful tool. Therefore he/she guards against damaged team interest, and places team effort high above individual whims and caprices. A good manager will always treat his team with respect and courtesy.

Show value for and encourage Equal Opportunity

A good manager always treats staff with equality. He respects and appreciates individuals with personal opinions and tastes. Favouritism has no place in his schedules. Instead, he does things in the open, consults staff on important issues and work hard to make everyone feel important in the team.

Be flexible

Change is an important subject at every business place today. Flexibility is a most important tool for change. Staff themselves go through change, face problems and difficulties (both at work and out of work). Managers must not hide behind corporate policies and procedures or indeed any text book (of some kind) and refuse to react sensibly to environmental situations. Inflexible managers find it difficult to listen, learn and to manage their staff.

Be knowledgeable

The ability to lead, direct, and stimulate others stems from a decent knowledge of the 'subject matter', lack of which there cannot be leadership whatsoever.

Be assertive

Uncertainties have no place in modern leadership, which places significant emphasis on enthusiasm and confidence. Today's employers look for motivational leadership skills.

Command respect and confidence of staff

Image of command is an important principle of management and it is an important place for the manager. Staff must be able to cherish sufficient qualities in their manager enough to feel that they can rely on him/her when it matters.

Honesty and fairness

If a manager cannot be trusted there is always lack of unity and support in the team. There is also lack of respect and confidence a situation which can be destructive to team morale.

Able to clarify the aims and objectives of team and project tasks

If any one should know what is happening, it must be the manager who has the responsibility of keeping a clear view of team and corporate objectives. With this quality the manager is able to direct affairs for the realisation of important goals.

Be professional

One of the key leadership qualities for the manger is to be professional in every respect. He/she is the symbol of what the organisation stands for. Compared to other staff a much higher standard of 'quality' will be expected of the manager in all things.

Question 49   WHAT MANAGERS CAN EXPECT FROM STAFF
What is reasonable for managers to expect from their staff?

Expectations are not the same as realities. In fact there is always a wide gap. Today's employers look for staff who understand boundaries and who can work with it. This is what this question is about.

Clarity of roles and responsibilities are key variables for building an *Effective team*. Being able to understand and appreciate issues on both sides of the equation is tremendously important. Try this during your team away-days with every member of the team on board. Discuss the points one by one and decide whether or not they are justified. Consider writing them up and hanging them in the staff room as an addition to team's beliefs and values.

- Co-operation from their staff and showing understanding especially in difficult times

- Good time keeping and attendance records

- Staff must show professionalism (a true reflection of what they were employed to do)

- Loyalty to the organisation and to manager's leadership

- Staff must show trust for their manager
- Flexibility to take on other responsibilities consistent with position
- Staff must observe confidentiality in accordance with organisation's policy
- Openness in the work place and on matters concerning the organisation and it's business
- Support for other staff
- Volunteering freely to take up tasks and to be enthusiastic about their work
- Being innovative and creative and able to reflect this in their work
- Show confidence in their work
- Able to do their job to standards expected by organisation
- Show respect to others (including manager)
- Attend supervision and appraisal meetings with line manager
- Willingness to accept instructions, directions and supervision
- Be constructive in raising issues of concern
- Willingness to share ideas and skills
- Acknowledge and respect for differences or staff diversity
- Staff must be self-motivated
- Willingness to learn from others and to teach or train others
- Seek advice where necessary
- To use supervision and appraisal structures effectively
- Use corporate resources wisely and judiciously
- To use own initiative and creativity to sole problems

Also see page 146 for more ideas on what organisations expect from their staff.

Question 50 TEAM DIFFICULTIES AND SOLUTIONS
What difficulties are encountered in a staff team? For each one say who is responsible: Managers, individual staff, or the organisation? What can be done about the problems?

Difficulties	Responsibility	What can be done (e.g.)
Lack of consultation	*Team, management, organisation*	Making views known through meetings, supervision and making suggestions, use of the Union.
Lack of flexibility	*Organisation Managers Staff*	Addressed in supervision and team meetings. Suitable organisational structure. Use of flexible methods and procedures.
Unclear aims and objectives	*Line manager, organisation, management*	Policies and procedures made simple and easy to understand, Avenues for clarifying matters e.g. meetings, information lines, forums.
Environment: physical and non physical	*Organisation, team, & management*	Acknowledging and resourcing, change, giving or accepting suggestions, good implementation of policies and procedures Creating a conducive culture, for organisation, and team's environment.
Not being able to rely on one another	*Team Management*	Team building exercises, training, good induction, Good leadership.

185

Unfair distribution of task	*Managers, teams*	Use of approved task rota, encourage staff to volunteer, consultation of staff.
Keeping things to self (being a non-team player)	*Individuals and management*	Training, team meetings, supervision, Good leadership.
Team member assuming responsibility (Self appointed leader)	*Individuals, teams management & organisation*	Induction, clarify roles and responsibilities, training and good supervision feedback.
Differences e.g. diversity (not allowing for it or working against it)	*As above*	Training, support from management, team meeting, being open, clear policies, encouraging transparency and equality.
Lack of motivation	*As above*	Team building, team meeting and constructive feedback, praise, staff supervision, New challenges and responsibility, variety, promotions.
Lack of leadership	*As above*	On-going training, Whistle blowing, (inform senior manager). Have avenues for taking staff concerns forward, project and team audits.

Breakdown in communication	*As above*	Team building, team meeting, and supervision. Effective working systems and structures, reviewing procedures, staff training, Supervision of procedures

Difficulty	Responsibility	What can be done about it
Backbiting, gossip, aggression (Fear)	*Everyone, managers, Organisation*	**Everyone/managers** Set standards at induction stage Lead by example Address in one to one's Address in Team setting (ground rule) **Organisation** Setting the culture. Keeping people informed Policy (e.g. whistle blowing) Training Resources made available **Individuals/staff** Apply learning from training. Encourage others Support others going through stress. Opt out or challenge. Raise with line manager Don't do it Don't make value judgements Familiarise with policies and procedures

Lack of support and trust	*Managers staff organisation*	**Managers** Recognise stress & put mechanisms in place to support staff. Be accessible responsible and flexible Being fair Organising team building Show respect for staff, boundaries and not moving goal posts **Staff** To say when they need support Use structures available Contributing at teambuilding Taking responsibility for roles & tasks Show respect for manager, the roles and observe boundaries **Organisation** Open communication e.g. core brief Consultation Negotiation Training on e.g. stress External specialist service for staff e.g. counselling service for staff and their families
Absenteeism and high staff turn over	*Manager, staff, organisation*	**Managers** To monitor sickness and follow procedures Ensure induction of locums. Ensure cover is arranged. To manage the environment effectively **Staff** Say if you need support or if work is causing difficulties. Plan leave Recognise everyone's right to a private life Support and trust for each other Contribute to a positive work atmosphere **Organisation** Provide a staff working environment Consistency Reviewing working conditions

Question 51   HOW CUSTOMERS BENEFIT FROM GOOD TEAMS
In what positive ways will a good team benefit the organisation's customers?

Good image

Good image comes from positive individual (clients) experience. It is essential for business. It provides the organisation the uniqueness required for effectiveness in its competitive environment.

Improved networking

This comes from an enhanced image. It refers to the point where other organisations seek to associate with your organisation for purposes that may include:

- To acknowledge and experience your organisation's success

- To improve their own profiles in the business

- To attract good or loyal clients.

Better service/ service development/ opportunities

The aggregate performance of a good team finishes in quality service. This is because efforts are concentrated on achieving fundamental objectives.

Better customer care

Clients of a good team always feel well cared for. They feel respected and valued. This is an essential business asset.

Continuity

Where everyone is out to provide support for someone and there is flexibility in the way services are provided, continuity of service can be achieved. This means it doesn't take one's keyworker to be present for a service to be delivered well.

Confidence in the service

A good team's performance commands confidence from clients. The interplay of high skills and the display of professional knowledge make clients feel they are in safe hands.

More reliable service

Reliability is a key mark of quality. It has something to do with trust and confidence of clients. A good team's activities attract credibility and trustworthiness.

Consistency

Another hallmark of a good team is consistency. Consistency in approach in information giving, support provision, and service standards. Friction is reduced when clear expectations are established around standards and services.

Safety and security

Safety and security is another hallmark of a good quality service. Every service user expects to feel safe and secured. A good team takes its legal obligations seriously and takes reasonable steps to guarantee delivery for clients.

Staff trusted and tenants becoming more co-operative

Staff of good teams feel trusted both by their clients and their manager. The feeling of oneness then reflects in the ability to work together towards a common solution. This is more obvious especially in the face of difficulties or problems.

Promotion of participation

The openness and transparency that surrounds a good team encourage client participation. Volunteers are easy to mobilise to perform tasks necessary for common benefits.

Fulfilment

The key purpose for individual clients using the service is achieved. This stems from the feeling that priority is given to this by the team. Individuals get the opportunity to discuss problems and to generate support required for meeting needs.

Value for money

Clients are able to assess their experience against their expectations as well as the opportunity costs or the alternatives foregone (as a result of using your service). When anything is unclear or complicated they have the assurance that staff will be happy to listen and to act consistently, and such a service will always reflect value for money.

Creation of valued customers

Customers who feel valued are those who believe the organisation takes them seriously, respects them, and values their custom. The reaction from them towards the organisation is often one of loyalty and making public their positive experiences. A sense of security is therefore easily born out of the feeling of belonging.

Better management of change
Every organisation must go through changes in order to compete effectively and to grow in business. Change management is more effective with a dynamic team where support, trust, and flexibility are in abundance.

Kept informed
Disseminating of information is more effective when done through many reliable avenues. This is possible with a good team where everyone is saying the same thing to the same set of client group. In most projects where 24-hour cover is operated clients can be better furnished with information on e.g. opportunities, and new services.

Tenants' interests become paramount as team priorities receive due attention

Related topics: See Winning Ideas volumes one and two for topics on how to ensure high *Quality service.*

Question 52   GENERAL BENEFITS OF A GOOD TEAM
What are the general benefits of a good teamwork?

More information on *Team work* can be found in Winning Ideas volumes one and two. The idea here is not to provide detailed information on the various factors but to give you a brief picture of what to look for. The fact that this question appears in this book is an indication that it is a common interview question. Please refer to appropriate sections of the other volumes for more details.

- Improved quality of service
- Provide a means for coping with stress
- Training and sharing knowledge
- Allows more effective supervision sessions
- Allows regular flow of information
- Allows more substantial decisions that are also easier to implement

- Helps with effective external relations

- Shared goals, aims and objectives

- It is an important demand of support practices

- It makes it possible to meet diverse clients' needs

- Allows the achievement of objectives and targets of organisation/team/project

- Crisis and emergencies can be dealt with more effectively

- It allows smoothness and continuity of service

- Leads to delivery of high quality service

- Creates motivated staff and loyal cleints

- Change management is easy

- Promotes Equal opportunities

- Leads to individuals feeling respected and trusted

- Encourages enthusiastic participation in team task

More ideas on Team *work* are also located elsewhere in this volume and in volume four.

Question 53   NEEDS OF A PRODUCTIVE EMPLOYER
What are the most pressing needs of a productive employer?

Roles and responsibilities
- Knowing what is expected of him at work. In the absence of this I am sure you will agree that you are without a job. 'What do you do in your job?' 'I am not sure'. How about that? Then the next question. 'How much do you do in your job?' 'I can't tell for sure I am afraid'. This person would hardly find anything to be motivated by.

Materials and equipment

Ability to gather relevant materials and equipment for his work (properly). The productive worker is not held back by a mere lack of equipment. He is motivated enough to locate what he needs and to reach out and grab them.

Using strengths

Opportunity to do what he does best every day. We are all likely to be motivated by the things we do best but getting the opportunity to do this is not always available. Staff must be able to be at their best using support relevant to their own strengths.

Benefiting from recognition

This is about the ability to use praise and recognition. The productive staff sees praises and recognition as a support and approval of his actions. There is a genuine drive to repeat rewarded performance.

Feels cared for by supervisor as a person

Also feels respected by supervisor and individual with individual rights. Believes that he/she is a valued member of the team.

Has someone to encourage his development

This may come from the team manager or a colleague but has a genuine touch of seeking the staff's personal development and progress. The person also feels that the team cares about his/her growth and allows time and space for this in a proactive way.

Feels that his opinion seem to count at work

Not talked down all the time. Can relate to some aspects of team achievement as his/her idea and is able to use this as a motivational sources for own satisfaction.

Knows how his work fits in with organisation's and he is motivated by it

This in itself is another source of motivation. A holistic picture around staff's work activities is gained. This yields an important sense of value and self esteem.

Surrounded by co-workers who are committed to doing quality work

From this angle the staff is challenged constantly. He raises questions about the outcome of his work as well as methods, procedures and strategies. He is provided with good reasons to review his approach to work all the time.

Has a best friend at work
Someone who provide the soft spot, understands, genuinely empathise, and willing to sacrifice for his good. Someone to share problems and difficulties with, and to draw warmth from.

Talks to someone about his progress at least every 6 months
Receives supervision in a structured way that takes his personal interest into consideration. He is listened to and genuine steps taken to ease difficulties confronted with.

Has opportunity to work to learn and to grow
Avenues for experimentation, practicing learning from training courses, for making misstates and upping one's learning curve. Eventually, growth results and a desire to seek more challenging opportunities is born.

Refer to topics on:
What you must expect from your organisation, and *What you must expect from your team* for more ideas. Also, see answer to next question.

Question 54   SUPPORTING ETHNIC MINORITY STAFF
What special support will you provide to staff of ethnic minority background in the area of personal development and motivation in their jobs? (Position: Manager)

Be sensitive to specific needs
Recognise the fact that people are individuals in their own rights in respect of taste, preferences, opinions, languages, abilities, etc. Be mindful that people of ethnic minority origin will place value on certain areas of their lives, which will make them different from other staff. This is more visible in language, social activities, family, religion, culture and festivals, customs and rituals, dressing, and food.

Be mindful of religious and cultural needs
They may occupy a very pivoting position of all priorities. Take proactive measures for ensuring that decisions affecting them do not make things difficult for them to continue practising their religion.   Rotas, shits and holiday arrangements can be used to accommodate such preferences.

Be mindful about discrimination
Show awareness of vulnerable groups that are more susceptible to discrimination. You need not wait until a request is made but rather making suggestions and offering development opportunities where you believe they are due.

Consultation
Management style must emphasise on consultation and respect. The best way to manage diversity is to talk to people. This is even more important in times of change. Whether or not the method of support is suitable or appropriate will depend on the views of the staff concerned.

Respond well to difficulties
Difficulties may be experienced e.g. because of the extended family system practiced by most ethnic minority societies, or specific illness staff is prone to because of their racial origin.

Respond to possible problem areas around the job
This may include ability and command over English language, the UK laws, knowledge of the English systems and practices, etc.

Use supervision effectively
Encourage them to take initiative around issues affecting them because of their specific identity and do your best to accommodate them. Use supervision to listen, show understanding and address staff as individuals with unique abilities and needs around their jobs.

Make effective use of internal resources
Make effort to bring to their attention resources available within your organisation and support them with accessing those resources. They may include mentoring schemes, advocacy schemes, working parties, and cultural awareness groups all of which provides avenues for making a difference in the organisation.

Build relevant resource information
Link up with external agencies e.g. Racial equality groups, following useful guidelines and bring to their attention opportunities available externally. This means being proactive and showing awareness of the staff diversity in the project's external interests.

Provisions at the work place

Ensure those facilities and other resources for development take into consideration needs of the minority groups. This may include provisions for health and safety, access to information, the availability of a quiet place (if necessary), and a space people can call their own.

Flexibility and a willingness to change

This is fundamentally essential for addressing needs of staff in general but even more important when dealing with people about whom you may have little knowledge of their needs. Readiness to learn and to change, and showing understanding and empathy freely will make you an approachable and supportive manager.

Managing conflicts

Manage conflict effectively. This may occur around organisational policy, or with other staff. When enforcing the organisation's policy aim to build a more positive attitude and promote a strong team rather than isolating individuals. This can be achieved by remaining sensitive to the diversity of staff needs. Emphasise on collectiveness and unity.

Equal opportunity

Equal opportunity practice must be vivid enough to create a healthy atmosphere where people can feel they have the ability to develop without let or hindrance. It is important your commitment to equal opportunity is seen as genuine.

Explore strengths

Use job systems like job rotation and job enrichment to explore specific abilities and to allocate tasks in ways that reflects clients' and project needs. For example if a task can be done better because of one's ethnic origin put them in charge and give them the necessary support to develop and progress.

Make full consideration

Especially when decisions are reached, which you believe will affect certain members of the team. Another area of consideration is how you interpret organisational policies for the benefit of staff development. You need to make full consideration of staff circumstances before deciding which direction to take. In doing so you will need to be sensitive to specific needs and difficulties, and where conflicts exist check with the right people or departments for further resources.

196

Other ideas

- Use team building programmes to recognise the diversity in group. Encourage activities highlighting potentials of individual staff.

- Consider staff-led activities during team functions: Going oriental can be a consideration

- Show special interest – make effort to know more, showing your interest by accepting the other person's feelings, reasoning, meanings, etc. You need not necessarily agree in order to accept them.

See other areas of this volume for more ideas on D*iversity at work*.

Question 55   CAN'T GET ON WITH YOUR MANAGER?
You do not get on with your manager no matter how hard you seem to try. You believe this is affecting your performance. What will you do?

Assess the situation for reasons.
The action to take will depend on the cause and sustaining factors. Reasons can be many and include:

- Your manager falls short in professional qualities

- Your manager does not allow you to have your own way

- You believe your manager discriminates against you

- You seem to have petty clashes over work matters

- Personality clashes or you simply do not get on

Whatever the reason is remember that you do not need to get on with someone in order to work with the person. The most important thing is your ability to put emphasis on the employers business and working hard to achieve targets. Therefore, whether or not you need to do something about the situation will depend on the effect your relationship is having on the employer's business. And before this happens the effect will first of all take tolls on you: health, concentration, comfort, and general wellbeing. The following provisions are based on the assumption that this is the case.

If you are clear that you are faulty in your relationship towards your manager, e.g. you are making his work difficult, you need to assess how this affects the quality of the service and objectively look for ways to improve. Such ways may include:

- Asking for your manager's help to set personal development targets: You may wish to work with another manager on this.

- Attending training courses

- Receiving coaching and practical help from colleagues or other staff

- Working to specifications of corporate policy and procedures

- Working with a mentor on your difficulties

If on the other hand you believe the manager picks on you unnecessarily or irrationally, bring this to his attention during supervision. You need to be:

- Specific, making reference to incidents, dates, time, etc. as much as possible

- Be constructive but objective so that you do not come across as 'an angry lion lying in wait for opportunity to strike'

- It is always best to describe how the situation affects your work rather that emphasising on your personal interest

- Be prepared to negotiate. Do not have rigid expectations given that your feelings and observations may be challenged

I will advise that you do not make a big issue out of a one off matter, which you found distasteful. It's usually important you gather significant evidence and (e.g. documented events) to substantiate your conclusions.

There may be times when you may find it necessary to talk to another person instead of your own manager. This could be a case e.g. where your manger seriously breaches an important policy of your organisation. If this is the case check for any existing procedures of your organisation and follow it. In any case, your organisation's policy is likely to advise that you report the concern directly to your manager's line manager.

Other options naturally available to you will include:

- Avoiding the situation by transferring to another project/location

- Getting on with your job and avoiding the manager as much as possible

- Mobilising other staff to share your feelings and turn against your manager's leadership, and make his/her work difficult

- Quit your job

- Do nothing about the situation and work under stress and constant conflict of job dissatisfaction

None of these is desirable to the employer whose business will suffer. Questions like these are designed to assess:

- Your awareness of the effect of weak teams on service quality

- Your ability to work well with authority

- Your devotion to the organisation and its business

- Ability to deal with conflicts in the work place

- Ability to identify source of stress and poor performance and deal with them

---

Question 56   HOW TO DEAL WITH DEMOTIVATION
What actions would you take if you feel deskilled in your job and can hardly find any motivation?

Acknowledge the situation first, and then establish what is missing. This is not always easy but at least if you can acknowledge the situation you are on your way forward.

Consider sharing your feelings with someone else (who is in a position to help). Sometimes, what you need is a set of fresh ideas or someone to extend their motivation over you.

Supervision

Discuss this at supervision and obtain help with identifying resources for addressing your problem. The fundamental question to address is whether or not you wish to remain in your job. In other words, is it a matter of boredom or disinterest in the job itself? Remember, that boredom can be addressed much more easily than disinterest, which may involve changing jobs altogether.

Set targets

Ask yourself what you really want the situation to be or look like. Then again, get help with identifying resources:

- Check in-house resources: colleagues, manager, team activities, project sessions or groups, etc.

- Check for opportunities existing through your organisation's policy and procedure. If unsure check with your human resource department.

- Check for external resources.

Self motivation: Make sure you are able to motivate your own self to progress work towards achieving targets. Sources of self motivation may include:

- Identifying your own strengths and how you can use them to achieve targets.

- Willingness and preparedness to participate actively in progress meetings, meeting deadlines, etc.

- Showing enthusiasm about the project and making effective use of opportunities, facilities, and ideas.

- Expressing confidence about your own achievements and having a strong desire to be motivated by them.

Impact on work quality: Being aware of how your demotivation can affect the quality of work you do is also very important. The indirect effect is even more elusive. It is best for you to concentrate on areas that fit in with your strengths (and which you enjoy doing), and leave others to your colleagues.

Other issues to be mindful of include:

- Not complaining openly about things and so doing trying to discourage everyone around you.

- You need to try new things, so you get the opportunity to release your creative thinking and feel challenged.

- Assess your own abilities before undertaking tasks that will most likely discourage you further.

- Take stock of your own job description, and check if there are areas, that can help your motivation and concentrate your efforts there. Sometimes the under achieved areas can be placed into the set of priority targets to give you an opportunity to learn something new.

- Consider taking part in Service Improvement Groups/Working Parties where opportunities exist for releasing your creative thinking abilities.

- Check your organisation for anything happening which you can be part of. A club may be or some educational programme. What about starting one yourself?

- Consider ways to motivate yourself. Some practical ways involve exercising, eating well, preparing well for meetings and being punctual with your appointments.

Have a mentor

This may be your own manager though I would suggest another manager in your project with whom you get on very well – informally. The person's role will be to help you get your focus and sustain your motivation by reminding you of the importance of achieving desired objectives. You may start by choosing a mentor, perhaps a motivated colleague to start with. It is best if the person is not located in the same project. But he/she must have sufficient knowledge about the competencies you require for your job.

The monitoring process and methods must be agreed as part of a plan
You need to strive towards meeting time limits and completing progress notes or assignments in order for you to benefit from the support you receive. Bring problems up for discussion so that relevant alterations can be agreed and injected into your plan.

Sources of motivation may include:

- Setting realistic, achievable and challenging targets.

- Doing different things at different times, reducing incidence of or eliminating tasks of monotonous nature.

- Taking on new (additional) tasks or roles.

- Being able to assess margin of achievements easily.

- Your colleagues and manager –recognising your work input.

- Gaining more knowledge, awareness, and skill about some important area of your work.

- Receiving a positive feed back.

See other volumes of Winning Ideas for notes on alternative ways of getting motivated using different types of job opportunities. Motivation once achieved must be sustained. One way of doing this is to constantly look for ways of improving things. This means putting into practice your acquired skills and knowledge. Such opportunities may be found by e.g. taking on a different role, something you enjoy, something new, or simply something you feel more at ease with.

PART 3
PROJECT MANAGEMENT ISSUES

Question 57   MANAGING A COMPLAINT: EQUAL OPPORTUNITY
Scenario: Whilst on duty two tenants (one black and one white) were involved in a dispute. The black man complained to you that the white man called him a 'black bastard'. How would you deal with the situation?

Investigate the matter.
First talk to the complainant noting the following

- The circumstance in which the matter occurred e.g. was the perpetrator provoked?

- Who started the problem?

- How the complainant feels

- The outcome expected by complainant

Victim-centred approach
A good corporate policy will subscribe to a victim-centred approach. In this case staff must not doubt the complaint and must receive complaints as if they are true. However the staff need to be professional enough not to draw any conclusions until after gathering a full picture of what happened.

Talk to the alleged perpetrator
Staff must also talk to the alleged perpetrator checking key issues raised by the complainant. The usual outcome can be one or a combination of the following:

1. 'Yes I said it but I was provoked'

2. 'Yes I said it. He is a black bastard'

3. 'No I never said it'

1. 'No, not quite like that'. Something else was said though with similar implications.

Follow plan/procedures

What ever the response (you receive) ensure that you:

- Follow any laid down procedure of organisation

- Any internally agreed measures by the staff team

- Any agreed service standard or plan for the client(s) involved.

The usual situation will be as follows (refer to answers above). Answer number:

1. Perpetrator will be informed that their action represents a breach of equal opportunity and therefore their licence/tenancy agreement. Warn perpetrator that such behaviours may cost him his accommodation

Depending on whether or not perpetrator has received a warning in the past, decide what is appropriate at this stage.

2. Same as above (1); follow procedure. Here the person is unrepentant and more determined to be wrong.

3. Unless witnesses report support perpetrator's claim, or there are sufficient evidence to disprove complainant's allegations, proceed as in (1) above.

4. Help the perpetrator to understand that their actions equally breach equal opportunity (if in fact it does). Follow the procedure at (1) above.

Consider mediation

If the perpetrator expresses remorse about their actions and this meets the expectations of the complainant you may want to consider mediation. In this case you want to sit them down to talk the matter through openly. A big benefit of mediation is that it facilitates mutual solution to problems using ways that help to avoid ill feelings on both sides. Mediation is not the perfect solution to all disputes. Depending on the situation it may not be necessarily.

Put in writing

Any action you take must be confirmed in writing. The reason is simple; there must be records for serious matters such as equal opportunity breaches. The people involved must also receive letters confirming the position of the organisation on the matter and also any action taken by staff on the occasion.

The matter must assure the victim of the organisation's support and encourage him to bring similar matters to the attention of staff in future.

A fabricated case
If the case was fabricated then no action needs to be taken against the said perpetrator. If this is the case it must be confirmed to both of them in writing. If complainant is thought to be in the habit of making things up and accusing others falsely he must be informed that such behaviours cannot be tolerated.

Place on file
Ensure the matter is well documented and passed on to all staff who need to know (e.g. keyworkers) and copies of report and letter placed on residents' files.

Unhappy complainant
In the event that the white man is not happy with complaint's actions (false complaint), try and explain to him how decision on the mater was reached and make him aware of any rights or options he has especially under the organisation's policy.

Acknowledgement
First of all it is important and significant that his feelings are acknowledged
- People will understandably be displeased over false accusations
- Make them aware of any relevant support that can be made available to him whilst exercising any identified rights
- Do not make any promises

Staff cannot take any action unless the person wants to make a formal complaint or exercise an optional right. However, staff need to make note of any breaches of local rules or organisational policy that may affect the way the department is run.

Question 58   PROJECT AND RESIDENT WELFARE MANAGEMENT

Scenario: You just arrived at work after a long break. The locum staff who handed over to you informed you that a tenant refused to take her medication for two weeks. When you visited the tenant, you discovered that her flat was in a mess. You also discovered that the telephone in the communal room has been vandalised. How would you address the situation?

The assumption here is that you are the keyworker for the client. If on the other hand you are playing the role of the duty staff then your duties will cover the period before the keyworker takes over.

Voluntary medication
If a tenant is taking medication voluntarily, nothing needs to be done on account of his/her failure or refusal to take medication. This is because a messy room may have nothing to do with their disengagement from medication.

Isolate the issues involved
Following on from the above: In this case you will have to address the messy room as a lapse in the person's ability to live independently, or to manage their domestic environment.

Investigate
The telephone in the communal room (smashed). This may have nothing to do with the client especially if other people can access the room. This needs to be looked at as a separate matter and investigated. Action to take will depend on findings. It will be directly relevant to the tenant in question only if she can be connected to it.

Check provisions in care plan
If client is not on medication voluntarily check if there is any provision in care plan about this and implement it. In the absence of any such plan consider the following:

- Check files for any information on effect of not taking medication

- Assess the risks involved for the purpose of what action needs taking immediately.

Check history of client

If client has a history of doing this there is likely to be some form of agreed action plan in care plan and information on professionals to contact in an emergency. Check for any information that may be useful and use it.

Check with client for reasons

Try and check with clients for reasons why she is not taking medication. It may be something that can be easily rectified and accommodated within the hostel, e.g. time of taking it may not be suitable for client. Client may also try to be difficult towards e.g. locum staff or going through some changes that may not be immediately visible.

Consider hostel/internal resources

If client is OK with an internal arrangement and there won't be immediate problem with delayed medication the matter must be accommodated within the project. In this case simply agree with client on alternatives and record the matter.

Contact a professional

However, if such agreement is not possible contact an expert.

- Follow advice of professionals, who may include CPN's (Community Psychiatric Nurses), GP's(General Practitioners), and Consultants.

Request advice in writing

It will also be useful to request for the advice in writing though you may not be able to do this in every emergency situations. If you can request for the instruction or advice in writing afterwards, you must always do so. You are not a medical professional and cannot take certain actions/decisions unless instructed or directed to do so. You need the expert's input in writing for the following reasons:

- To ensure you are following instructions correctly

- To prove that you acted professionally

- To protect yourself in case something went wrong

- To ensure you are acting within the professional health care programme already agreed with the client

- Your decision to act and your actions were out of an expert's directions, not your own

Prioritise your actions

The most urgent matter to address here is the client's medication. All other issues can wait. This is particularly so if you know the side effects can be a serious one.

Draw on previous strategies or methods

If the particular client has experienced similar problems you will probably know methods that worked with her.

Share the information with others who need to know

Make sure you produce a report and document the incident and your actions in the appropriate logs, ensuring that the staff team is aware of the situation. It is particularly important that a good handover is done to who ever takes over from you.

Accurate records

The situation could trigger off a case review for the client. Her keyworker may consider it relevant to change the care service agreement. Accurate records of the incident will therefore be vital.

Alternatives to tablet medicine

Client's refusal to take medication is very common in residential establishments. In a lot of cases the CPN can advise you on whether or not serious consequences may result. They may decide to come to the project themselves and administer the medication by injection instead. If the refusal of tablet medicines continues the care professionals may review client's medication and alter the means of administration.

Remote factors

Client's refusal to take medication is normally caused by other factors remote to the medication itself. It is therefore important to note down any unusual behaviours or actions of client.

What a messy room means

The messy room could indicate a number of things. The following are only examples:

- Disorientation or confusion

- A decline in independent living skill

- A deliberate act, with hope to achieve some objective (e.g. get other's attention)

First action determines further action

The way forward is to find out from client why. The answers you receive will in most cases tell you the mental state or mood in which she is.

Consequences of client's actions

When discussing the matter with client it is always useful to help them to explore the consequences of their actions and also other alternative actions they could have taken to meet their wants. Record client's response and expressions attracted by your input. It will help you build up a better picture of the type of support needed.

Comprehensive case or plan review

If for instance there are indications of decline in client's skills or awareness, it must be seen as a change in level of needs. This would especially be the case if the situation continues. In that case it must be met with a comprehensive review of client's support needs and the care plan changed to respond to new level of needs.

Alternative ways of channelling energy

If messy room resulted as an expression of client's anger, assist them to establish a clearer picture of the detriments and agree on positive ways of channelling that energy. It is important that staff do not jump into conclusion over client's mental state because of the mess, as there might be some justifiable reasons, e.g. room cleaning or re-arrangement.

Vandalised telephone

The issue of vandalised communal telephone must not be allowed to cloud any judgement that goes into the cases of medication and messy room. Even where it is established that the same client was involved with the telephone, it can only go to reinforce the idea of changing level of needs. Beyond this it can only be dealt with as a project management issue:

- If phone is not safe to use, remove it and store away. If this is not possible put up a notice asking others not to use it.

- Make the area safe e.g. remove any debris (the scattered remains of anything broken, destroyed, or discarded)

- Complete a report about the investigation

- Arrange for repairs (if it is within your power to do so)

- Check with any one who might have seen what happened to the phone

- If you need to challenge any client about the incident make him/her aware of:
    - What the organisation's/project's policy says about their actions

    - Any liability they might be held for

    - Any further action they must expect from staff

Question 59   THE DIFFERENCE: A HOUSE AND A HOME
What is the difference between a house and a home?

A house
A domestic structure for living in and for performing domestic activities

A home
This is about what is contained within a house. It includes the people, furniture, decorations, routines, customs, and rites. It is about the comfort that comes from living in a house.

This question may be for assessing your awareness of issues involved in working in other peoples' homes. Working with vulnerable people in their own homes calls for greater attention for creating a homely environment.

Question 60   MANAGING COMPLEX SITUATIONS: CLIENT ISSUE

Scenario: You visited a tenant who has not been seen by staff for some time. The person is now in 2 weeks rent arrears. He also has serious drinking problems and has been abusive to other tenants. How would you deal with this?

The answer to this question will depend on the type of project or scheme as well as client group. It will also depend on the position you are applying for.

The answer provided here is for a Supported Housing Officer with a prime duty to support tenants (but would also apply elsewhere). Rent control is sometimes seen as conflicting role to the core duties of support staff. On the contrary it can be argued that the support officer's support role makes him/her the ideal person to deal with client's difficulties around rent problems.

Acknowledge your position
If it is the case that the client has not been seen because staff failed to do so, this must be recognised openly. Such recognition will clear the air and pave way for effective communication. It is significant in communicating the message that you are committed to supporting the client.

Assess client upon arrival
Progress beyond this point will depend on what mood the client is in. If sober and receptive you will find it easier to talk about your concerns. If on the other hand your visit caught him when he was drunk it will be senseless to proceed with the meeting.

Complaints of abuse
I will suggest you look at complaints about abuse first. This is because he himself may have concerns about the matter. If he is going to want to pay any rent at all, it may depend on whether or not he is going to want to continue living in the property; neighbourhood problems are a cause of many abandoned properties.

Be sensitive
The response from here (above) will help you to determine the level of vulnerability and therefore how sensitive you need to be with his rent arrears. Rent arrears issues though significant must not override or endanger other concerns affecting client's ability to function rationally.

Refer to policy and follow procedures

If client admits their being abusive/disruptive to neighbours and expresses remorse make them aware of the organisation's position on their behaviour. Such behaviours will usually represent a breach of tenancy. The client needs to understand that if the situation continues he/she may lose the tenancy. It is also useful to emphasise that other tenants have equal rights to a peaceful habitation of their flats.

The matter must be documented for filing. You must confirm the conversation and your advice in writing to client especially where they think their behaviour was justifiable.

Quote licence or tenancy agreement

It is a good practice to quote the portion of the tenancy or licence agreement that is breached. This will help establish how serious the matter is and also the consequences of the breach.

Use open-ended questions

Open-ended questions are what you need for this. It allows the client opportunity to express himself freely. Therefore you are able to get deeper understanding not only of what happened but also of underlying difficulties he is confronted with. From this angle you can be in a better position to assist the client.

Consider witnesses account

Another tendency is that the client may deny being involved in the incident. If you already have sufficient evidence or witnesses account, you should proceed with the written advice/warning (depending on your organisation's policy).

A typical good procedure

A good policy will consider first of all issuing a verbal warning, then a first written warning, then a second written warning, then a final written warning before re-possession is sought. This is important to show that:

- The organisation has acted professionally

- The organisation is committed to working with client to eradicate problems

- The organisation is following its mission and objectives around providing accommodation for vulnerable clients

Warnings must be backed with positive steps to support client to address their difficulties. Therefore a support plan is in order but only if the client is prepared to work with staff on the issues.

Follow your organisation's procedures

Staff members must be sure that they are following procedures laid down by their organisations, as consistency is important here.

Separate the issues

'Rent arrears' and 'serious drinking problems' are clearly personal problems and must be addressed separately from the neighbourhood one. Each problem must be addressed separately as distinctively as possible. It is important the client is not confused over advice or warnings or any agreement reached as a result of these matters.

Drinking problems

Client drinking problems may have something to do with the neighbourhood problems. Check with clients if he is prepared to get help with this. Note that if client is an occasional drinker this may not necessarily apply. For occasional drinkers the issue may be the way they behave when they are under alcohol influence rather than the frequency of alcohol drinking. If this was the case the emphasis will be on behaviour management not necessarily 'buzz' management.

Refer client to a specialist

If client is prepared to accept help consider referring him for specialist support and get this down as part of his support or care plan. Clearly identify the roles they need to play and check if they feel comfortable with them. It is important that goals and objectives are realistic and achievable. It is also important that they take into consideration the client's own abilities and resources.

Where the client declines offer of support

If the client refuses help you must make him aware of the consequences of the decision. In this case not much can be done apart from to continue trying. This should not stop you from executing any procedure provisions of your organisation regarding rent arrears or nuisance.

Find client a more suitable accommodation

If you must eventually evict the client consider reassessing his accommodation needs and refer him on to a more suitable one. Final decision of evicting a vulnerable client must ideally be endorsed by a manager. It is a bad practice to evict a vulnerable client with no where to go to.

Check root cause of rent arrears

The rent arrears may be resulting from client's drinking habit. This spells out problems with budgeting and also prioritisation of needs. This is likely to be the case if client pays rent himself and can be covered in his support plan.

Check Housing Benefit

If on the other hand rent is paid by Housing Benefit, support client to establish the cause of non-payment and provide assistance in chasing up payment. Non-payment of Housing Benefit may result from a number of issues, for example:

- Failure to complete a fresh application form after a benefit period has ended

- Failure to supply the benefit agency with proofs or some information required

- Failure to notify the Benefit Agency about change of circumstance

- Suspicion of fraudulent claim (e.g. discovery of conflicting information)

- A claim of overpayment

See *Remnant of Accommodation* (ROA) for more information on welfare benefits. ROA covers all you need to know on Housing Benefit and Council Tax Benefit with details on how to calculate them.

The solutional approach

If in a Supported Housing scheme/project a rent arrears resulted because the vulnerable client was not provided with relevant support in order to manage their Housing Benefit claim, the staff of the scheme will have a lot to answer for. In this case the route cause of arrears problem would be staff failures and they will find it difficult to progress such a matter through the courts if it came to it. The implication here is simple: Supported Housing staff must make sure the 'supported' element of their jobs comes first, in fact well in advance of rent and rent monitoring and certainly before any arrears pop up.

First arrears problem

If this is the first arrears problem simply agree with client to pay a bit extra on top of their weekly rent. Where budgeting problem is identified with client try and reach agreement over convenient methods of payment. Your support duties extend over assisting your clients to maintain roof over their heads as well as supporting them with daily living skills. Options to look at will include:

- Direct debit

- Direct payment (deduction) from Job seekers Allowance JSA or IS (Income Support)

Once the arrears is cleared you must consider alternative methods of supporting client to budget effectively. Independent living is about making decisions and doing things out of one's own resources. You must therefore not encourage methods that deny client the opportunity of directly controlling their money. The rent payment plan must recognise this and shift the (money) control closer to client but only in doses that will not encourage them to mismanage things.

Get a written agreement on payment

If agreement is reached it should be written down and signed by client. Ensure that terms of agreement and rates of payments are clearly documented and a copy given to client. Rates of payment must be realistic or you will only be setting client up to fail.

Assure client of staff support

Continue to assure client of your support and encourage him to come to you with further difficulties. This must be done in such a way that leaves client believing that it is not a personal promise but supporting clients is a notion subscribed to by your organisation. This way, he will feel comfortable coming to the office whether or not you are available to see him.

Follow procedure

Ensure any steps taken about rents or rent arrears conform to organisation's procedures. Make rent agreement information within reach of your work colleagues so that the support will continue even in your absence.

Budget for failure

This is because it may take time for the client to get used to the new or agreed method. In the event of failures it's important that you do not come down hard on the client. Instead, show empathy and be prepared to give him another go.

Keep your eyes on payments

It is however important that when you have reached a rent agreement with a client you keep a close eye on development. If you leave arrears to mount up high before you address them you will feel compelled to be unnecessarily too strict and therefore unhelpful to your clients.

Recognise good efforts

Positive feed back is a major source of encouragement. Let the client know if he is doing well. Even if he is not let him know this in a manner that will not discourage him altogether.

Question 61 **USING YOUR SPARE TIME PRODUCTIVELY**
Once employed by us you will discover that sometimes you have plenty of spare time after completing your daily tasks. How will you occupy yourself during those times?

Spend time in communal areas.

This carries the advantage of meeting and chatting with residents and knowing them better. Establishing relationships through informal means (client's own territories) can mean a lot to most residents whose only contact with the staff is through the office.

Look at clients' files

Spend time looking through clients' files. You can acquaint yourself with their particular problems and difficulties. This brings the advantage of equipping you with relevant knowledge on their care plans, and other key provisions established for their care or support.

If residents take medication you can learn about side effects and any agreements reached with staff around their health care. You can also acquaint yourself with names and contact details of residents' care teams: Specialist workers e.g. consultants, CPN (Community Psychiatric Nurse), social workers etc. will usually be contained in residents files.

Accompany a client
You may offer to accompany clients out of the project to say the library or to cash their Income Support. Many vulnerable clients enjoy this: For many of them it is the right time to tell a member of staff all their problems, achievements or other forms of experiences. You get the chance to know them better and to learn through their comments.

Assist with admin duties
There is almost always some admin task waiting for someone to complete. Don't sit there doing nothing. Try asking a permanent staff for forms needing photocopying or notes/records waiting to be up-dated or filed away.

Acquaint yourself with office/project resources
This may include anything from first aid box to where items are stored. This will enhance your efficiency in future when you are left on your own or with a new staff.

Policies and procedures
Check through organisation's policy and procedure documents. Also look at any team or in-house procedures and agreed practices ensuring that you are aware of documents and forms to use if you need to use them.

Dairy items
Check project dairies for anything outstanding for the day and check with other staff if you can help with anything. Usually old staff do not want to come across as 'checky' and may avoid inviting new staff to join in carrying out tasks. It is important that you take the initiative.

Join in
Join in when you see people carrying out project task. Sometimes you need not ask or wait to be invited. This means being observant and showing readiness both to offer help and to accept challenges.

Routine duties
Routine duties may include patrolling the project. In some places this is done every hour. The idea is to ensure safety and security. Staff also check on 'not

seen' residents. Being out and about on residents floors sometimes means a ready assistance to draw on if a client is in trouble.

Question 62   MISSING MONEY: PROJECT MANAGEMENT
Scenario: The project has a petty cash system, which is passed on from one shift to another during staff hand-over sessions. The morning staff (who had a very busy shift) forgot to account for the petty cash when you started your Friday afternoon shift. You later on discovered that the money was £20 short. Meanwhile, there was not enough cash to keep the project running in emergency. What action would you take?

I can imagine someone whispering 'begin to pray that nothing goes wrong during your shift'. I think you would have to do better than just pray.

- Search other areas in the project where you are likely to find cash, receipt, or something to explain the missing money

- Do a thorough check of the account again. Check if some invoices/receipts are not accounted for.

- Check logbooks and other staff communication entries for messages explaining the gap in accounts.

- Get another staff to check the petty cash.

- Check for signs for forced access or the likelihood that someone entered the office without being seen.

- Agree with another person on the amount in the tin and measures taken to get things right. Ask the person to counter sign the account as 'agreed'.

- Contact the other staff (who failed to hand petty cash over) for explanation and make notes. You may have to write a report for the management in the end and any information you received at this stage may be relevant.

- If you are still out of money check and follow any organisational policy and procedure available.

- Bring this to the attention of any senior person on duty. (E.g. a manager) and give the person the opportunity to lead decisions. However, consider the steps below if no senior person is immediately available.

- You may be required to notify your project manager or on-call person of the situation. This way they are aware of things, and are better prepared to provide you with support when you need one. Follow any instructions you are given.

- Being a weekend, the chances are that someone (the manager or team leader may be) will arrange sufficient money for the project as a matter of urgency, probably by coming down to the project. Again, it will depend on the nature of the project and what may be expected in an emergency. Otherwise, look at the following ideas:

Try and be creative in emergencies
For instance, ask that you are invoiced instead of having to pay cash to service or goods providers.

Prioritise spending
Spend only on high priority need items. Also, consider items that can only be accommodated by your 'purse' and leave others till later.

Do not hesitate to explain your situation
Explain your position to residents whose needs involve petty cash expense. Also explain any temporary measures put in place as a result. You may have to conceal an activity. Change a menu or alter some routines. Make sure any one affected is informed in good time.

Do not be quick to use your own money
Though it can be an option it is not the path your interviewers expect you to take. If you decide to use your own money be sure that this won't breach any organisational policy and also that you have witnesses. You may wish to get clearance from your project manager or the on-call person before going down this routine.

Open discussion at meeting

Encourage an open discussion of the matter at team meetings for joint reviews of the system in place. The objective will be to ensure that the situation does not happen again

Ensure you have completed a report. If you need to pass on the till to the next shift you must communicate the problem. You need to be careful not to conclude that the other staff have stolen the money. What is important is how the project will continue to function well given the situation. Also, communicate any support information you received from your manager.

Question 63   TENANT PARTICIPATION
What do you understand by 'Tenant Participation' within the context of Supported Housing?

'Tenant Participation' is a two way process involving sharing of information and ideas, where tenants are able to influence decision and take part in the decision making process.

The key parts involved in Tenant Participation are:

- Information

- Consultation

- Involvement

Information

Information is critical for our service users to make informed decisions about their housing needs. It forms an important part of the enabling process of influencing outcomes of decision. It is indeed fundamental to the process upon which success can be built.

Information provided must be:

- Correct, right and relevant

- In the correct format

- In correct quantity

- Delivered in the correct dose and pace

220

- At the correct times

- Through the correct medium

Essentially, information must be useful to its audience for the purpose and purposes of using them productively.

Consultation

Tenants need to be consulted for their views and such views must be taken into consideration in both the process and outcome. This can only take place if they were previously furnished with useful information.

Consultation must be:

Democratic
Equal access, votes, voice, etc.

Transparent
Processes involved must be known to all, conducted in a non-secretive manner. Organisations must publicise when and about whom it will consult.

Fedback sensitive
People consulted must be advised of the outcome of the consultation. This also must be done in a transparent way and must come soon after the process is completed.

Flexible
Processes used must sympathise with the needs of clients. Changes must be accommodated for the purposes of achieving desired results.

Resourceful
Must be seen as being able to make a difference.

Time
Time of consultation must be relevant to time of decision and must not be chosen to disadvantage participants.

Method suitable
Method used must be suitable to ensure that consultation can be worthwhile.

Involvement

This is about sharing of power. The degree of sharing is largely dependent on the organisation's objectives and also on the tenants' ability to undertake involvement responsibilities. As expected, power sharing comes with accountability as well as responsibility.

There is a wide range of activities in which tenants can be involved. Involvement may range from direct participation in the housing management to representations in various ways within the organisation's decision making and planning organs. Involvement must be:

Resource continuous
This is about recognition and support from senior managers of the organisation. Both financial and physical resources must be made available freely.

Empowering
There must be a degree of authority to enable participants carry out their work.

Resourceful and rewarding
Individuals must feel fuelled and motivated by the outcome of their activities and the processes involved. There must be a desire of wanting to do more.

Flexible and respond to change
People change and so are their needs. The means of involving tenants must vary as and when necessary to meet changing needs and reasonable expectations.

Equally accessed
Equality of opportunity must be the theme.

Relevant to shared objectives
For the purpose of achieving the fundamental goals of tenants' participation, the involvement opportunities must be relevant, suitable, and appropriate.

Lead to change
The ultimate objective is to enable tenants to make a difference. This must be borne in mind at all times.

Acknowledged

Hard work must be acknowledged. This is important for showing support and for motivating participants. Acknowledgement is an important avenue for open reinforcements of the organisation's commitments to the idea of Tenant Participation.

Question 64   SOURCES OF TENANT PARTICIPATION

There are legal provisions and social policies backing the duties owed to tenants in the area of tenant participation and involvement. Please tell us what you know about these.

The Housing Act 1985

Section 105 of the Housing Act 1985 places a duty on housing associations to maintain such arrangement as they consider appropriate for informing tenants about any changes in matters of housing management which will affect them considerably. Such arrangement may involve areas like maintenance and improvements (e.g. decorations, refurbishment).

Information

The Housing Act 1985 instructs on the provision of information. Under the Act tenants must be given information on all aspects of their tenancy.

The Race Relations Act 1976

Section 25 of the Race Relations Act 1976 makes it unlawful for any housing provider to discriminate against a racial group in respect of either the accommodation itself or any services associated with it. Such associations may include facilities, benefits, and privileges.

The Housing Corporation Guidelines

These are specified in standard G under Residents Rights.

Information

Tenants must be furnished with information which should be easy to understand (in plain English). Information must also be available in other languages, Braille or on tape.

Carers and advocates

Housing providers must not discourage the roles of carers and advocates. Instead their roles should be made clear.

Duty towards residents

All Residential Social Landlords (RSLs) must have policies stating their objectives and methods for achieving accountability to residents. Such policies must explain how the following will be provided:

- Information

- Complaints and compensation

- Processes and methods for influencing (decisions and services)

- Confidentiality of information

- Consultation and participation

Best value

Though originally intended for local councils, the Best Value framework is now contained in the Housing Corporations guideline documents and all RSLs (Residential Social Landlords) are expected to subscribe to it.

The Framework introduced the 4Cs concept, which obliges organisations to review their services with the aim of continuous improvement in quality and value for money. In order to achieve this, tenants must be involved in the necessary processes. According to the housing corporation guideline 'RSLs should not merely consult with residents but take active steps to ensure residents' views are at the forefront when deciding and reviewing what and how services should be delivered.'

The 4Cs are:

- Challenge

- Compare

- Consult

- Compete

These are explained further in other parts of Winning Ideas.

The NHS and Community Care Act 1990

This legislation emphasises choice, empowerment and partnership.

The minimum Care Standard Act 2000
It specifies statutory standards accepted as *quality service* for care service users. In so doing, it clearly identifies areas of involvement, participation, respect and courtesy towards service users.

Question 65   IMPROVING TENANT PARTICIPATION
Though this project has several opportunities for tenants to participate in decision making and activities, many do not. In what ways do you think tenant participation can be improved within the organisation?

Active encouragement
The project management must publicly announce their commitment to involve tenants. This must reflect in management styles which must be reinforced by direct messages at e.g. tenants meetings.

Tenants groups
Tenants are likely to be more active when they meet as a group. The project must actively promote the formation of tenants' group and then support them in practical ways. Depending on the needs of the participants, staff may want to send them reminders, provide them with a meeting place and money for petty expenses.

Formal arrangements
There must be a formal arrangement about the extent to which tenants can participate in the running of the project and therefore the degree of influence their activities are likely to effect. This way tenants can be able to establish the worth of their participation efforts.

Committee or working party membership
This is a significant way of making a difference. Working parties can be formed around specific areas e.g. food and catering, and, sports and social. This allows people with specific strengths and interests to direct their resources for the benefit of achieving positive results.

Training for tenants
Those who want to participate but lack the know-how must receive relevant training and coaching. The processes used must emphasise on empowerment. This means there must be ample opportunities for people to experiment, make mistakes, and learn.

Ethnic minority groups
Appropriate action must be taken to encourage the involvement of ethnic minority groups who may be under represented in decision making.

Develop a clear policy
This must start with a clear policy statement. Policy must be reviewed regularly to sympathise with changing needs and objectives.

Clarify roles (for tenant, staff and managers)
Make people aware of the degree to which they can exercise their power of participation. This helps to avoid disappointments and conflicts.

Clarify goals and objectives around tenant participation
One cannot emphasise well enough the need to clarify goals and objectives around tenant participation. The shared vision needs to be translated into goals and short term objectives. Goals as well as objectives must be clear and simple. Above all, any changes in them must be fully communicated. This will ensure consistency in approach and help preserve the common platform upon which ideas are generated.

Ensure confidentiality and & equal opportunities
This is about respect for individual rights and security. People can only feel free to participate if they can trust officials and feel respected by them.

Acknowledge resistance
Organisations must not pretend that resistance does not exist by ignoring them. Conflicts, problems and dissatisfaction must be examined objectively and constructively. Considerable resource of efforts must be spent to listen, discuss and to find common solutions.

Allow tenants to determine pace of change
Tenants participation involve dealing with change. The change may be that arising from the need to respond to business objective, a new legislation, or

some new professional guidelines. The pace of change must recognise tenants' limitations and weaknesses. Therefore any effort leading to change must start with tenants and finish with tenants.

Ensure a clear complaints procedure
The procedure for collecting information must be clear, and also simple to use. Dissatisfied tenants who may not be regular at meetings must have alternative avenues of registering complaints.

Improved accessibility of information
Lack of information is one reason why people fail to participate. Just letting people know about things is not enough. The organisation must actively facilitate access to information which is necessary for enhancing it's influencing power.

Consider access to independent support for tenants
This may mean assisting them to access advocacy service or promoting the involvement of families and friends. It also means working in consultation with independent agencies (e.g. self help groups) which tenants are already associated with.

See Winning Ideas Volume two for more on Tenant Participation. You can also find more on this topic elsewhere in this volume.

Question 66   BENEFITS OF TENANT PARTICIPATION
Both the government and the Housing Corporation are actively encouraging housing providers across the UK to create opportunities for tenants to participate in their activities. What are the benefits of Tenant Participation?

Quality
Giving people what they ask for is about meeting needs as defined and expected by them. Quality is not down to the provider but what the consumer expects. This can only be achieved by working together and by avoiding 'assumptive' service.

Reduce incidents of friction

This comes from working with one purpose and towards one goal. Though differences of methods may exist, they will be suppressed by the common vision and the shared desire to enshrine this in the processes required for reaching the goals.

Empowering

This comes from a sense of self-esteem and fulfilment. Giving people opportunities to try, experiment, and learning paves way to motivating achievements, experience, competence and knowledge.

Quality leads to quality

The working parties, committees, task groups, etc. are all engines for realising new targets and standards. The evolving roles of these organs leap from one ground of quality to another each time with some significant degree of improvements.

Problem solving made easy

Shared power is a recipe for problem solving. The reason is obvious: Responsibility as well as accountability are shared, leaving fewer grounds for blame. As more information will be available to base decisions on, reaching agreements are more likely to be easier.

Development of a sense of belonging

Tenant participation can increase everyone's understanding of how the organisation works. The open culture, together with a transparent approach to managing tenants' interests will lead to loyalty and develop a sense of belongingness.

Promotes equal opportunity

Joint working amongst tenants where views are shared, respected and encouraged creates a platform for equality. Tenant participation is a way of reinforcing the important message of equal opportunity.

Weakens divisions

The activities weaken the division between service providers and service users. The formality surrounding the 'office people' and the approaches to making views known are distilled down to the common man's level and displayed on a common platform.

Creates an exciting environment
An opportunity to work and the feeling that you are able to make a difference helps the atmosphere: It becomes one of friendliness, equality, openness, trust and support. Incidents of suspicions, denial, and unhealthy debates are kept low. Such an environment is very important especially for tenants with other needs e.g. around health.

Source of feedback
Tenant participation provides the organisation and its staff an important source of feedback. This then becomes a trigger for change and modernisation. Adjustments and changes are necessary from both sides in order to accommodate differences, problems and pressures.

Gaining of knowledge
A 'civilised' approach to sharing and exchanging of ideas do not only lead to quality, it also equips individuals with knowledge. Knowledge is then strengthened through practice opportunities. The end result is skill and competence, both of which are no doubt very useful assets for participants.

Value for money
For many people opportunities to influence services and their delivery can lead to value for money. The obvious is that you get the chance to give yourself what you wish to buy. Because you can influence decision you can decide and demand what you believe your money is worth.

Less complaints
Frequency of complaints made about services will be comparatively low where tenant participation is freely encouraged. This is due to the clearly defined and well-recognised channels for receiving complaints in a non-confrontational manner. Complaints can be dealt with by complainants themselves before they come to the attention of staff.

Others
Other named benefits of tenant participation include:

- It helps in determining management priorities

- It leads to job satisfaction for staff

- It improves the social life of service users

- It provides avenues of personal development for service users

- The organisation is able to meet legal and professional standards expected by its stakeholders

- It leads to further involvements (internal and external)

- It enables organisations to plan well into the future

- It gives both organisations and tenants sense of security and safety

- It leads to the design and information of more acceptable service

- It improves corporate image

- It gives organisations stronger position in its market: There is security and a promised future

Question 67   BARRIERS TO TENANT PARTICIPATION
What are the barriers to tenant Participation?

Here, I will only list the key factors. This topic is already covered in Winning Ideas volume two. The fact that it has appeared here is an indication that it is a common interview question. This stresses the importance employers place on costumer satisfaction through participation. You must also read notes under *Best Value* and the *Tenants Participation Compact* covered elsewhere in this volume.

- Staff distrust for tenants and a stereotype belief that nothing good can come from their efforts.

- Unrealistic expectations from staff and the organisation.

- Inappropriate structure for informing service users on what they can participate in.

- Irrelevant involvement opportunities or opportunities are not always available or not made clear.

- Inflexible structures used e.g. policies and procedures do not always make room for tenants to participate fully.

- No resources for participation, even where tenants choose to participate.

- Extent of tenant participation not defined, so people are not aware what they can and what they cannot do.

- Bottom-down management approach where directions and instructions are issued from the top and no room exist for consultation at lower levels.

- Lack of consultation, hence staff are unable to identify suitable ways of involving tenants.

- Previous experience of inaction and failures makes tenants not want to have anything to do with staff or the management.

- Health problems in most cases forces vulnerable people out of participation opportunities.

- Ineffective communication and lack of communication skills. This makes people feel inferior and stay away for fear of embarrassment.

- Fear of losing privileges already enjoyed with staff.

- Organisation's failure to recognise important roles of carers and family members and advocates in tenant participation programmes.

- Discrimination, harassment and intimation can also isolate people from participating in social activities.

- Unequal opportunity atmosphere where little or no attention is paid to most-likely-to-be-discriminated groups e.g. women, people with ethnic minority background.

- Don't know how. Most vulnerable clients though believe there is value in making their voices heard, simply cannot bring themselves together for a lunch because of fear of not being able to do it the right way. Unless such people are supported with the 'how' and also encouraged to use the service, they can hardly break free from their chains.

- Lack of trust (for the system, procedures, or staff).

- Lack of recognition. Some do not feel recognised as people with a right to choose or voice out their concerns. Also, tenants decline in their efforts when they feel that their contributions do not make a difference or they do not receive any recognition for inputting.

See Winning Ideas Volume two for more on *Barriers to tenant participation* and *Barrier to complaints making.*

Question 68   BEST VALUE IN HOUSING MANAGEMENT
What is Best Value in Housing Management?

Best Value is a central part of the government's agenda for improving public services. With effect from 1st April 2000, it is a duty upon local authorities to abide by the Best Value practice. The purpose is to bring councils closer to their communities and promote their role in community leadership and governance.

Though Best Value is fundamentally a legal prescription for local authorities, the Housing Corporation has now introduced Best Value guidelines for all RSLs (Residential Social Landlords). Meaning, all housing associations are equally affected.

A Best Value authority must make arrangement to secure continuous improvement in the way in which its functions are exercised, having regard to a combination of economy, efficiency and effectiveness.

In carrying out the duty local authorities are made accountable to local people and have a responsibility to central government in its role as representative of the broader national interest. In simple terms Best Value can be seen as a process for achieving continuous improvement in services through a performance management framework, which consists of:

- Service reviews

- Performance indicators

- Improvement targets

- Consultation with service users and other stakeholders

- Information giving

All the above apply to housing management where tenants and residents are expected to gain significant influence in services and their delivery methods and their management.

Question 69   BEST VALUE PRINCIPLES
What are the key principles imbedded in the government's Best Value concept?

There are seven key principles in the government's Best Value concept:

1.   Local accountability

The Best Value law requires consultation with local people. Local authorities must also publicise service standards and their corporate objectives and take relevant steps to obtain feed back on progress. Using such information relevant changes can be made to ensure that services address genuine needs as defined by the people they are meant for.

2.   Joint working

The law prescribes joint working emphasising on 'joined up thinking'. This calls for activities across departments, levels and agencies. The key objective being to develop the best service for achieving the best results.

3.   Partnership approach

This is about embracing partnership actions from private and voluntary sector and other agencies in the various processes for achieving best value. Such processes include:

- Development of local plans

- Development of local targets and objectives

- Reviews of services

- Strategies for achieving local outcomes

4.   Provision of quality services

This is the sum of the Best Value idea. The concept is not about who provides services but how well they are provided. It must however, be borne in mind that whether or not a service is 'quality' depends on what the service users think. Regular consultation and involvement in the design process is therefore an important way forward.

5.   Performance measurement and management

The government has issued a set of national performance indicators for local authorities and expects them (the local authorities) to produce their own local versions (in consultation with the local people). The indicators are necessary for measuring, comparing and demonstrating performance.

The national performance indicators only provide minimum levels. Local authorities are expected to show quality management through the continuous realisation of improvement targets.

6.   **Comparability**
In order to be sure performance is of a high standard, Best Value concept demands comparability. Local authorities will need to match the best performers in private and public sectors. In some instances good private/public agencies can be used as benchmarks.

7.   **Continuous improvements**
All services should be reviewed over five-year cycle. This calls for reliable monitoring and measurement systems. Review systems must facilitate and lead to change. Therefore the process of continuous improvement calls for total involvement of all who will be affected by the change: Local people, agencies, private and voluntary organisation, etc.

Question 70   IMPLEMENTING BEST VALUE
The Best Value concept aims to involve service users as a means to the provision of quality service. What changes will you advice if our organisation was to embrace the concept?

Put a department in charge
Place the Best Value assignment in a department's care. The task of the department will be to co-ordinate all activities throughout the organisation, train, educate and coach relevant individuals (working closely with the training wing). The department will also oversee the general operations of Best Value and guard against course deviation.

Put an experienced person in charge
An experienced staff who is able to combine requirements of the concept with the organisation's own mission and values must head the department in charge. The person will hold the key responsibility for delivering the Best Value package through a systematic change management approach.

Best Value work group or steering committee

This should ideally be made up of people drawn from across different sections of the organisation. Members will collate views and concerns from other staff in their local levels and assist the committee to take relevant issues into consideration during it's deliberations. The corporate Best Value committee will have the responsibility of steering change, generating ideas, educating and training others, advising the senior management team, as well as acting to preserve a clear focus of desired targets and objectives.

Change management

It is important that Best Value implementation in an organisation is seen as a significant corporate change. This is about things like the following:

- The way people think

- The systems people work with

- Objectives, targets and goals

- Work place environment and expectations

- The job description and tasks emphasis

- Expectations from service users and staff, etc.

Therefore, the principle of change management must apply and be observed. See Winning Ideas volume one for how to manage change in an organisation.

Comprehensive Assessment

Assess the organisation's current position. This may involve the use of the minimum performance indicators. From here it must be clear what needs changing and what needs preserving. Flexibility is of an essence in that a total change process must be engaged where necessary.

Produce a service statement

The idea is to establish a clear and transparent picture for Best Value. A service statement is different from the goals in that it announces purpose and intentions where as goals defines the destination of strategies. Having a corporate service statement confirms support from senior management and gives the executive organs (largely the front line staff) a sense of purpose for achieving desired objectives. To be effective, service statements must:

- Take into consideration what service users want

- Be simple, brief, clear and available or accessible

- Respond appropriately to failures as well as success

- Take into consideration resources available to the organisation

- Be responsive to identified performance expectations

- Provide people with useful information for making comparisons

Involve service users

Service users must be involved in:

- Defining the range, type and quality of services provided and proposals for changing and improving them

- Targets-setting and the standard required for service quality as well as costs

- The monitoring and reporting on performance

- Evaluation and judging of performance

- Review process which must itself be an on-going feature of the Best Value concept

Performance plans

A clear plan for performance is required to set out targets, identify change for meeting revised objectives and new targets including a clear timetable, strategies and subsequent reviews. Targets must be set to cover year by year performance. The process involved in arriving at the plans must:

- Challenge purpose

- Compare performance

- Consult service users and other stakeholders

- Compete with others

- Ensure that all services are reviewed within five years

Performance reports

Performance reports must be easily accessible and must be easy to understand. It must set out achievements against targets (published performance indicators and local measures). Reports must be published

236

annually. This is another area for involving service users. The report must cover past and current performance.

Performance indicators

Besides the government's national performance indicators, local authorities are expected to produce their own PI's in consultation with local people. The PI provides a useful tool for setting benchmarks around quality issues.

Service reviews

Best Value commands a comprehensive service reviews. This is about an on-going review of services using the 4Cs which are explained below:

- Challenge
- Consult
- Compare
- Compete

Challenge

Examine ways of improving services. It involves questioning whether or not the service could have been delivered as a better package and/or through a better method. Some practical and challenging questions that need asking are:

- Is it necessary to provide the service in the first place?

- Should there be more or less of the service?

- Should we buy service in from another provider more cheaply than providing them ourselves?

Compare

Compare costs and performance levels to those of other organisations. Then assess whether or not there are any rooms for improvements. To do this you need to:

- Identify areas of under-performance for reviews

- Learn from other organisations and adopt more effective methods

- Show how performance compares with others in your report to stakeholders (tenants, residents, board, agencies, partners local people, etc.)

Consult

Consult service users and stakeholders on services, service reviews and performance. This is about involving people in on-going dialogues. Strategies for involving people include:

- Users' forums
- Users' representatives
- Advocates

- Surveys
- Focus groups
- Project users meetings

See Winning Ideas Volume one for more on means of involving service users. Those involved in influencing service outcome will like to know how significant their input was. A feedback is therefore important.

Compete

Best Value calls for cost savings and require local authorities to be cost effective in their operations. To this extent external organisations must be invited to provide services on their behalf where these organisations are likely to be able to deliver services to an agreed standard at a lower cost.

- Ensure services and their delivery methods are competitive
- Compare degree of meeting quality standards and corresponding costs with those of other organisations delivering similar services.

Culture

Culture is seen as the 5th in the chain process of Cs which provides the operational framework (already explained –above).

For Best Value to succeed in any organisation attention must be given to tuning the working culture in the direction of desired targets and goals. Culture is essentially *the way we do things around here*. Best Values prescribes quality, quality prescribes methods and methods prescribe attitudes, beliefs, values and these in turn prescribe customs.

Best value requires organisations to be:
- Creative and innovative
- Self-reflective
- Accommodating to ideas and methods

- Change responsive
- Quality minded
- Joint working oriented, etc.

All the above is done through a cyclical process meant to achieve higher quality performance. These processes and methods represent fundamental change in the work culture. Therefore, the dynamics of cultural change must be given deserving attention.

Question 71   BEST VALUE IMPLEMENTATION: STAFF ROLE
How do you see your role in the implementation of Best Value in this organisation? *(Front line position)*

This question is best answered with full knowledge of the benefits of the 4Cs (covered above), and how it works in practice. Most front line staff will probably concern themselves more with the *Consult*. Let us try and put the 4Cs into perspective and to the level of an individual front line staff. Look at the explanation below.

Challenge   Staff must challenge the way they deliver services on daily basis, constantly looking at ways of improving. This can be done by for example, setting new targets, and using safer delivery methods.

Compare   Staff can compare their own performance with others' within the same department or project or other departments within the organisation. There will be a case for improvement if other service users are enjoying better services from other staff. Once a gap in performance has been established, perform competence assessment. Realistically examine areas you fall short in, set gaols and objectives, and then identify strategies. Work hard to achieve them. Aim to improve all the time using corporate and external resources consistently. Involve your supervisor or another more experienced person so you can benefit from constructive feedback.

Consult   Staff must obtain feedback on the service they provide and act on it. Also, staff must make sufficient efforts to establish needs of customers and take them into account when delivering the service. Make it a point to make customers feel welcomed and comfortable. Encourage them to come back with their complaints and do your best to find answers or point them to the right direction. Complaints must also be made available to policy or decision makers.

Compete   Staff must continuously assess themselves and find justification for being in their post. Why should they be employed in preference to others? Here staff must be able to use their strengths effectively, to benefit the service, and to justify their inclusion.

Specific areas front line staff can make a difference include the following:

- Assessment of current situation using points highlighted in the Best Value concept.

- Completing survey questionnaires either by themselves or with clients.

- Using keywork sessions to encourage and educate others.

- Participate in organisation's forums, debates, social activities, etc.

- Take part in feeding back to service users and other stakeholders.

- Doing your best to resource efforts of those involved in improvement or participation programmes or activities which may include working parties, work groups, steering committees etc.

- Assist others (e.g. clients) to complete forms, provide advice and guidance on what is available and how people can participate.

- Assisting in accessing of interpretation and translation services for those with other languages.

- Taking part in self–reflective activities which may include discussions around comparing achievements with external projects or schemes.

- Be aware of professional standards and statutorily prescribed good practice and work hard to reflect this in your job.

- Contribute to change by providing accurate report on service users' complaints and concerns.

- To deliver service in a manner that is consistent with corporate promises (made to service users) via e.g. customer charter.

- Encourage tenant participation through a service that is friendly, courteous, and respectful.

- To admit mistakes and make amends without hesitation.

- Making contributions at staff team meetings in order to generate ideas towards quality services.

- Provide colleagues and service users with support especially in times of change.

- Also be flexible, willing and ready to accommodate new ideas.

- Implement and work well with any organisational guidelines available for promoting Best Value.

- See complaints from service users as an opportunity for service improvements and use the occasion to reassure them of a responsive service.

- Volunteer to serve on improvement groups and work hard to influence change in performance in a positive direction.

- Keeping accurate records on expenditure and cost to make it easier to compare cost performance with those of other organisations.

- Undertaking training to enhance ability to continuously work towards quality and setting of challenging goals.

- Take active part in forums, and sensible debates organised for the purpose of challenging quality levels or service strategies.

- Use joint-work and link-work and other opportunities like open days and seminars, to improve your knowledge on competitive service (existing elsewhere), so that you always aspire to reach higher goals

- Acquaint yourself with corporate strategies on best value so that you can make better sense of your own contributions at all times.

Question 72   DRUGS, DRUGS MISUSE AND THE LAW
What are the offences under the Misuse of drugs Act that you need to be mindful of in this job?

Tell us what you know about Drug legislation that can affect the operations of this project.

What sort of drugs can normally get misused by young people?

Given the simple nature of this question I will briefly state the category of offences. Then, I will proceed to look in more detail the Law and Drugs in the UK. The idea being to equip you with sufficient information, so you can be able to handle the topic more competently. The offences are:

- Possession

- Possession with intent to supply

- Supply or attempting to supply

- Production, cultivation or manufacture

- Import and export

- Allowing premises to be used for consumption (of some controlled drugs), supply, cultivation, manufacture, etc.

Some drugs can legally be in someone's possession if they have a prescription for them. Most class B drugs can be prescribed, e.g. methadone and morphine. See Winning Ideas volume Two for more information. Further coverage will be contained in Winning Ideas Volume five.

I will also draw your attention to section 8 of the misuse of drugs Act 1971 which tries to place obligations on occupiers and managers of premises to discourage drug related activities on premises. It states 'a person commits an offence, if … concerned in the management of premises, he knowingly permits or suffers any of the following activities:
- Producing or attempting to produce a controlled drug.
- Supply or attempting to supply a controlled drug to another; Or offering to supply a controlled drug to another

- Preparing opium for smoking

- Smoking cannabis, cannabis resin or prepared opium

THE LAW AND DRUGS

There are two main laws covering the use of drugs or their control in the UK

- Misuse of Drug Act (1971) and Registration 1985)

- Medicines Act (1968)

Misuse of Drug Act (MDA) 1971

The MDA was enacted to control the possession, supply and production of street drugs like heroin, cocaine, cannabis, amphetamine, ecstasy and LSD. It does this by classifying drugs according to their perceived potential for causing harm and the nature of penalties facing offenders.

Class A drugs: Include the following:

- Cocaine
- Crack
- Stronger opioids (opium, dextromoramide methadone, morphine etc.)
- Hallucinogens (LSD, Psilocin, etc.)
- Tetrahydrocannabinol.
- PCP (phencyclidine)
- Hash oil,
- Processed magic mushrooms
- Any class B drug which is prepared for injection

Class B drugs: Include the following:

- Barbiturates
- Stronger stimulants (like amphetamine, dexamphetamine, methylamphetamine, and methylphenidate)
- Weak opioids (like codeine, dihydrocodeine and pentazocine)
- Cannabis in herbal and resin form

Class C drugs: Include the following:

- Weaker stimulants (like diethylpropion, and phentermine)
- Distalgesic (like destroproxyphene, benzodiazepines)
- Some other mild sedatives, pain killers, and sleeping pills

The Misuse of Drug Registration (MDR) 1985

In 1985 the MDR was introduced to prescribe the way in which drugs must be:

- Stored
- Prescribed
- Documented

This law (MDR) groups drugs into 5 schedules which are explained below:

Schedule 1

These drugs have no recognised application in conventional medicine. They include;

- Opium,
- Coca leaf,
- Cannabis
- LSD.

No doctor can prescribe them under any circumstance. A special licence must be obtained from the Home Office for persons carrying out research on them.

Schedule 2

These consist of drugs that may be misused but at the same time have important medical properties. They include;

- The opioids,
- Dexamphetamine
- Cocaine
- Morphine

With the exception of Heroin, Dipipanone (Diconal) and Cocaine, any doctor can prescribe the drugs in this group. A home Office licence is required for prescribing them to drug addicts, for import, export, production, or supply.

Schedule 3

Drugs falling under this schedule include:

Barbiturate (like sedatives and sleeping pills). Tamazepam, a range of slimming tablets and milder pain killers, Buprenorphine, Diethylpropin and Mazindol.

They are those that are often subject to abuse but to a much milder degree compared to those in schedule 1 and 2.

Schedule 4

Consists of drugs which require only a modest level of control. They include the rest of the Benzodiazepines (apart from Temazepam), Pemoline and

Anabolic steroids. Authority is required for production and supply, but no authority is required for their possession, import or expert.

Schedule 5
Consists of mixtures and concoctions produced from pieces of substances from schedule 1 to 4. Some controlled drugs, included in preparations in small quantities can be bought 'over the counter' and include mild pain-relief medicines, cough medicines and diarrhoea treatments. No authority is required to possess them, but it is needed for their production and supply.

The Medicine Act (MA) 1968
This is mainly about the manufacturing and supply of medicines other than street drug. The term 'controlled drugs' therefore applies to any drug affected by both the Medicine Act and the Misuse of Drug Act and Regulation.

See Winning Volume two and five for more on drug use and in particular *Prevention of Drug Misuse in hostels/ project/ homes* with some ideas on good practice.

Question 73   COUNCILS' DUTIES UNDER HOMELESSNESS LAW
What duties do the Local authorities have under the Homelessness legislation?

The current law relating to homelessness is the one in Part VII Housing Act 1996. Before this it was the Housing Act 1985. The sections referred to in numbers 1 to 9 (below) are from the Housing Act 1985.

The duties are many. Duties towards homeless people vary depending on the findings of the authority especially on matters of 'intentionality' and 'priority need'. We will concern ourselves with the main and must-know ones. I believe you will find them self explanatory.

1. Duty to make enquiries (Section 62): Local authorities must investigate all cases of application

2. Duty to secure accommodation during enquiries if applicant may be homeless and have priority need (Section 63)

3. Duty to provide appropriate advice and assistance to those in non-priority need (Section 65 (4))

4. Duty to secure suitable accommodation for a reasonable period and give appropriate advice and assistance to the intentionally homeless (Section 65 (3) and section 69)

5. Duty to provide suitable accommodation pending local connection referral (Section 68)

6. Duty to provide suitable accommodation to those homeless, in priority need, unintentionally homeless, and with a local connection (Section 65(2))

7. Duty to take reasonable steps to prevent loss or damage to property. In this case, reasonable charges may be imposed (Section 70)

8. If the authority is satisfied that the applicant is threatened with homelessness intentionally, and eligible for assistance, and in priority need, then the advice and appropriate assistance duty arises (1996, s. 195(5)(b)), on the basis that application (once the homelessness itself occurs) should entitle the applicant to a period of temporary accommodation

9. For applicant who are found to be homeless intentionally or unintentionally, threatened with homelessness (whether intentionally or not), eligible for assistance, but not in priority needs, the authority will provide an appropriate assistance in the form of advice and support.

10. For those who are unintentionally threatened with homelessness, and eligible for assistance, and have a priority need, but did not become threatened with homelessness intentionally, the authority's duty is to take reasonable steps to ensure that accommodation does not cease to be available for their occupation (196, s. 195(1),(2)).

11. If the authority is satisfied that the applicant is homeless, eligible for assistance, in priority needs and not intentionally homeless the following must apply:

    Where other suitable accommodation is available in their district for the applicant's occupation, to provide such advice and assistance as they deem fit, reasonable, and appropriate, and which are necessary to enable the applicant to secure one (1996,s. 193(1), 197(1))

Or

If it is possible to refer the applicant to another authority, to ensure that an accommodation is available for the applicant's occupation, together with any family member who normally resides, and anyone else who might reasonably be expected to reside with the applicant (1996, s. 193(2)).

12. Duties to notify applicant of decision (Section 64):
   - If it agrees that applicant is homeless or threatened with homelessness (Section 64(1))

   - If it agrees that applicant is homeless and also that he/she is in priority need (Section 64(2))

   - If it agrees that applicant is in priority need and also whether or not he/she is intentionally homeless and whether or not it intends to make local connection referral (Section 64(3))

   - All decisions must be given in writing (Section 65(5))

   - If decision is negative or a referral is necessary it must give reasons (Section 64(4))

13. The council's duty to provide accommodation may be considered discharged by:
   - Offering own suitable accommodation

   - Securing suitable accommodation from some other person

   - Giving advice and assistance which will secure suitable accommodation from some other person or source (Section 69(1))

It is clear under section 193 of the Housing Act 1996 that a local Authority's duty to the homeless is now limited to a minimum period specified by the legislation. Where a local authority is satisfied that an applicant is homeless, eligible for assistance, has a priority need and did not make himself intentionally homeless, they will provide the applicant accommodation for a period of Two Years. This is known as the 'minimum period'. At the end of this period, the local authority will have no duty under the law to continue to provide accommodation for the applicant.

According to the law the local authority's duty may be considered discharged before the end of the two years. This provision is contained under section 193 (6) of the Act. Conditions where this is possible are as follows:

- Where applicant ceases to be eligible for assistance (as in the case of a person from abroad under Section 185 and 186)

- Where applicant becomes homeless intentionally from the accommodation made available for his occupation under Section 193.

- Where applicant voluntarily ceases to occupy (the accommodation provided to him by the council) as his only or principal home; under Section 193.

- Where applicant accepts an offer of accommodation under the housing allocation system. Such an offer may involve moving into a private landlord accommodation, shared ownership, etc.

- Where applicant refuses an offer suitable accommodation under section 193 of the homeless legislation having been informed of the possible consequences of refusal.

- Where applicant refuses an offer of accommodation unreasonably with full knowledge of the consequences of such refusal.

An applicant towards whom the duty ceases may make a fresh application (1996, s. 193(9)), provided that the applicant still qualifies for full assistance.

The local authority will still have powers to continue assistance or to accommodate after the two year period. This is however, only possible if it conducts a review 'towards the end' of the minimum period, with a view to being able to make an assessment of applicants situation. It will have to satisfy itself that:

- The applicant had a priority need ((10.21)

- There is no other suitable accommodation available in their area (10.71)

- The applicant still wants them to continue securing accommodation for him (1996, s.194 (1), (2))

Local authorities are to provide accommodation in their own area if it is at all possible (196, s.208(1)). Where this is not possible and they place an applicant in another area, they must notify the local authority with responsibility for that area and provide them with information on everyone being accommodated including anyone else who might reasonably be expected to reside with applicant. Such notice must be submitted in writing within the first two weeks from when the accommodation was made available (1996,s.208(4).

You may read more on Housing laws in Winning Ideas Volume five which will contain an extensive coverage of the 1996 Housing Act.

Question 74   MANAGING TENANT NUISANCE
Scenario: You have received reports from your client's neighbours that he has been drinking and making noise denying them peaceful sleep. They want to know what you are going to do about the matter. How will you address the matter?

Remember that whereas you are required to support your client to enable him live peacefully with his neighbours you have no direct duty to report to them on issues involving your service. This means you must not feel pressurised to respond to their demands. All the same you must respond.

You need to be cautious when you need to deal with outsiders (other people who are not party to your own contract with your organisation and your duty towards your clients). If in doubt it's better not to act at all, and seek advice from a colleague or your manager. Anyone with an interest in your work could qualify as your customer, but not all will feel obliged to act professionally towards you and your organisation or for that matter your work. You need to show understanding without feeling a deep sense of obligation to report to them.

Another important consideration is the need to separate your duty towards your client from the duty of the landlord. Neighbour problems are ideally issues for landlords, not support officers. Neighbours must feel free to report their concerns to the landlords. This will represent their right as would be enshrined within their licence or tenancy agreements.

The point I am making is that you must not rush to dive in with answers because you won't have any. Receive the complaints courteously, friendly, and respectfully, but do not make any promises.

If you feel pressurised to give answers, advise the neighbours they may direct their concerns to the landlord but remember it is not your duty to do this and in fact indulging them may conflict with your role in supporting your client.

Make sure you document what was said. Who is making the complaint? In what ways was the person affected by the claimed situation? When and how did the problems occur (as well as the frequency)? By listening carefully and attentively you may decide that three is no case in the matter, or it is too trivial to merit any serious attention. You need to concern yourself with specifics and not speculations. If you need to check the information with your client you will need facts not 'fictions'.

However, you cannot ignore the knowledge that something is wrong with the way your client is conducting himself around the block. But wait a minute! How do we know if the allegations are true? If you have received more than just a few complaints then there could be some truth in the allegation.

For the safety of your client you must bring the matter to his attention and check if any support is needed in the matter. If your client accepts faults and request for your help then this must be accommodated within the support plan, and considerations made for strategies for overcoming the problems.

It will help if you are able to explain the following to your client:
- The rights of his neighbours in respect of the problems he is causing
- How your client's behaviour affects his tenancy agreement
- The possible consequences of the behaviour if it persists

The likelihood is that the landlord will contact you about your client's behaviour. In this case you would explain that you are already aware of the problems and that you have agreed on strategies for addressing it. This must not stop the landlord from writing to your client to register concern about what is going on. Furthermore, this will help in your discussions in that it will stress the need for your client to work closely and co-operatively with you in order to eradicate the problems.

You will need to liaise with the landlord and any other authority or agency that may be involved in the matter to make sure that the relevant professionals understand and appreciate the need for more time and space to get your client to respond appropriately.

You will need to be careful of confidentiality issues. The Data Protection Act specifies that you may only give relevant and adequate (not in excess) information, and must be so than with client's consent. Remember, it is not your duty to solve the problems. You are only required to provide support for the person with the problem (if he is ready to accept it).

Question 75   DEALING WITH CONFLICTING PRIORIES
Scenario: On a very busy Monday morning you are the shift leader of the 2 staff members covering the project. The other member of staff is a locum and not very familiar with the project. You are behind schedule preparing for a meeting with a consultant psychiatrist and a CPN at 10.30 am. A resident informed you his room is flooded from a bust pipe.
Whilst talking to the resident another resident rushed in calling for help because another resident has collapsed. How will you deal with the situation?

Start by identifying the 3 main issues competing for your attention. Start by assessing the situation carefully, then prioritise. You will need to respond sensibly and sensitively, using your resources wisely. When you've finished assess effects of the incidents for lessons learnt and changes required. Also consider how your organisation and other staff, and also residents fit into the entire equation. Look at the diagram below.

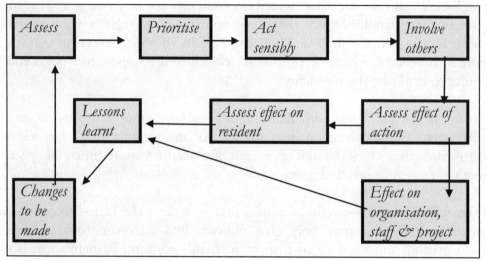

Fig.3.1   Flow diagram: question 75

Quick thinking
This is one instance you must think fast. Ability to think on your feet is very important when dealing with vulnerable people. You may not be able to provide an absolute answer or magic solutions for every situation but you must wherever possible prevent the situation from becoming worse.

Consider 360 degrees approach
Like in every scenario situation you must consider a 360 degrees solution to the problem starting by prioritising, bearing in mind what your resources are. Remember resources are always limited so good planning is important.

Prioritise
In every emergency you must occupy yourself with life-threatening matters first. This means you must give priority to the collapsed person above everything else.

Engage another staff
Explain to the resident with the pipe problem the need for you to see to the collapsed resident straight away. Check if you can use cleaners, kitchen assistance or for that matter any other member of staff to accompany this client and try, either to stop the water or remove items from where they could get damaged.

Attending to the casualty: first priority

Put the locum person into the picture and let them stand by to call the ambulance as you go straight away to verify the situation. You do not want to call the ambulance and have nothing to tell them or later discover that there was no casualty in the first place. Once you are aware of the situation and you are trained to resuscitate, go ahead and perform resuscitation. If anything would delay your having to attend to this matter immediately you must ask the resident reporting the case to go and stay with the casualty. In any case this is one instance that will by all counts demand immediate reaction. Call the ambulance in any case if you are held up or delayed in your response, just to be on the side of caution.

Once the ambulance crew has been called and any instructions given have been followed, someone must stay with the casualty until they arrive.

Second priority

Attention can now be given to the pipe problems. It must be inspected before a decision to call the fire brigade is made. Either you or the other staff can check this and call the experts, if necessary. Before engaging external help check if it is possible to cut out the water e.g. using stop valves. None of these must be done at the expense of the collapsed person – it is a matter of professional judgement over the effective use of limited resources.

Cancel meeting

The fact of your meeting with professionals would be minor compared to the situation in the project. Dealing with the emergencies may mean that you would not be able to prepare for the meeting but that is okay. They are professionals and all things being equal, they would understand. If you are able to deal with the emergencies before the time of your meeting I would still suggest you call it off unless there is something very important about it, in which case you must agree with the other parties over temporary measures instead of a formal meeting. You would hardly have any energy left in you to complete a sensible meeting after dealing with such a hectic situation unless the reports turned out to be untrue.

After incident matters

Check with the other staff how she/he is feeling and if any support is required. Agree on how you are going to proceed with after-incident matters, discuss the experience and have a clear picture how this is to be presented to staff, residents, family members (who need to know), as well as any outside agency which need to be involved. Agree on how information on casualty is to be used and who can access it. Make sure you have information about the hospital, the ward, any medical treatment given to the person before being transported to the hospital. Consider whether or not immediate further support (e.g. clothing) is required, and when contact in the hospital can be arranged.

Effect of response methods

If you had to use the stop valve to cut off water supply you will need to decide what happens next to residents without water supply on their floors. Check if you need to put up a notice or write to warn people of what is happening and if there is any temporary arrangement (those who need to know about it or have ways of finding out).

After incident actions

- Check if any maintenance works need reporting

- Check if any resident is affected by the incident and needs support

- Check that all places and areas affected by the incident is restored and made fit for normal use

- Complete your incident reports

- Complete hand-over forms

- Check organisation's policy ensuring anything that needs doing is done

- Check that the residents files (called *day files* in some projects) updated and copies of incidents filed in them, etc.

Question 76   AN EMERGENCY: PROJECT MANAGEMENT
Scenario: The staff has failed to see Mr. Jones for 2 days so a decision was made to check his room. When you arrived there you find him naked on the floor crying for help. What will you do?

The nakedness of client regardless of gender must not prevent the availability of help.

Radio for assistance
Upon hearing calls for help and discovering that client is naked, radio for another member of staff to assist you. This is even more important if you are dealing with client of the opposite sex. You do not want to be accused of 'attempted rape'. Imagine what the client's family members will think of staff if the storey is twisted against you. It is the normal approach to get the full picture of situations before deciding whether or not you need assistance yourself. But situations like this always command quick thinking, precautions, and hence the involvement of a third person.

Put life threatening situations first
Never put anything before a life-threatening situation. Your first and foremost duty must be to make the person safe. On the other hand if you are unable to tackle this because of something discomforting then get support from your team, but make sure you act appropriately to save a life even if this means taking the relevant steps whilst the person is in the nude.

Carefully assess the situation
Check if client is in obvious danger. If he had an accident assess if there are obvious signs of pain. Is anything likely to worsen client's pain if the person was to remain in the same position you found him? Any signs of drug (misuse)?

Talk to them
Talk to them. Tell them who you are and why you are there. Check if they are all right by talking to them. 'You seem to be in pain: What can I do to help?'

Keep talking the person through your actions
As you act to help or provide help keep the talking up; explain what you are about to do before you start. Explain, what you a doing, how you are doing it, why you are doing it and the way you are doing it. This is even more important if you require the person to follow your instructions.

Make them safe

Once you have established what is wrong, make them safe. Do not move them unless they are in obvious danger. This is where your first aid skills are called into action. You must not attempt to give first aid of any kind if you are not trained to do so. In that case simply call the paramedics.

Cover them up

Do this as soon as you have the opportunity, as it may be a source of distraction not only for you but also the casualty. It is important you let him know what you are doing.

Get further help.

Depending on client's answers get further assistance. Client's answers and what you see on the scene will provide vital clues as to whether or not immediate further assistance is necessary. For example, if he took an overdose and is in pain you must call the ambulance straight away. While waiting for specialist help to arrive you can fill in the time with other activities aimed at making the casualty comfortable. The appropriateness of the help you engage will reflect on the quality of your assessment of situations.

Possibilities of client situation may include:

- An accident

- Health affected due to missed medication

- Attention seeking

- Deterioration of health

Support to ambulance crew

As the first person on the scene you are in the best position to provide the ambulance crew with useful information, which may include the following:

- The position client was lying in

- Condition in which you found client

- What his answers were to your questions

- Any evidence (e.g. drug) you found around client and at what stage they were found.

- Whether or not you moved client, reasons and when

Case review

Whatever the situation staff must see it as an opportunity to review the support or care needs of the client. The care plan will therefore change to reflect the reviewed needs as soon as possible.

Case conference

A case conference will be the best of starts so that the support or care professionals can have direct input. The support needs must then be clearly identified and translated into day-to-day practical assistance (from staff as well as relevant external agencies).

Consult with other staff

If unsure of any action it's always a good practice to check with your colleagues. If you are not the only duty staff do not treat an incident of the project as a personal one. Cherish a moment of consultation with others. At the very least air your plans for endorsement or support or suggestions (which ever is appropriate).

Temporary safety measures

Always consider temporary safety measures especially if client is still in the project after the incident. You must decide (ideally with other duty staff) on measures to ease the situation. This may include the following:

- Frequent checks to see if client is okay

- Encourage client to CASS or call the office (if necessary or at time interval for you to know he is okay)

- Using pendent or intercom to say that he is okay

- Removal of drugs from client's room (especially if this was involved in the accident)

- Checking to make sure that client can use the call facility with ease

- Actually trying the call system in client's flat or other areas of the project to see if they work or batteries need charging or replacement.

Remember

Incidents like this can be a sensitive one especially if it leads to death of a client or creates troubled family members or cause concern for the external professional (care and medical) team members. Therefore, remember to:

- Follow any instructions previously issued by your senior management staff

- Follow team agreed practices and procedures

- Comply with organisational policies and procedures, and

- Any demands placed on your project and it's operations by the law

- Any advice from specialist staff

Do not get family members involved

Project incidents must be dealt with in-house. Wherever possible, liaise with medical professionals. You must not make the decision of contacting the police, family members or the public without consulting with your superiors. When it comes to this, only designated individuals with the right skills and authority must do so.

Write a report

You have a duty to write a report of the incident so that members of your team can familiarise themselves with the case. It is always useful to complete an accident form besides documenting the case in your log or day books. You must also make sure a copy of the full incident is placed on client's file.

Hand over

Ensure that staff will be able to do a good hand over using your reports. To this extent you can make notes on staff hand over sheets so that important details are not missed.

Review of client logging system

An obvious question following the incident will be whether or not the system for logging clients as 'seen' is efficient enough. Questions may include the following:

- Was there a breakdown of the system in place?

- Did any staff member fail to check on client and could the situation have been avoided?

- What must constitute a 'seen client'?

- How long must it be for a 'non-seen client' to be declared a 'cause for concern'?

- Are there effective measures for addressing *cause for concern client's* situation and how well are staff informed about this?

- How effective is the system of communicating client log information between shift workers?

- Is the system tested routinely?

- Do all clients know how to use the call system or do they need to be inducted as part of the booking in activities?

Question 77   MANAGING RESIDENTS NUISANCE
Scenario: You are the duty staff supervising dinner. Two residents get involved in a fight causing disruption to other residents. You try to intervene but they ignore you. What further action would you take?

There are two main issues here:

- The 2 residents involved in the fight

- Other residents being disturbed and possibly placed at risk because of the fight

Get help
The scenario itself suggests that situations may get out of hand so you must consider getting support from other staff. You need to be creative about this: Consider support from your kitchen staff, as they may be immediately available. In addition radio an office staff for assistance.

Invite fighting residents out
Get them away from the area if you can. Invite the fighting residents to come away from the area and talk to you about their concerns. If they both ignore you concentrate on one person at a time. You need to be careful how you do this as your action may be interpreted as siding with that person you are

concentrating on. This works best if there is another staff present doing the same with the other 'fighter'.

Consider safety of others
If the fighting residents fail to co-operate divert your resources to ensuring that other residents are safe. Ask them to leave the areas (with their food) where necessary. Close the normal canteen activities temporarily.

Do not handle physically
The fact that lives may be at risk during a fight means that you must do something about it. However, you must not handle fighting residents at anytime unless your organisation's procedures say you can. I have no doubt that you are well within your rights not to physically intervene unless you have received relevant training on how to do this. Physically separating two people engaged in a fight works well when they are being restrained at the opposite directions and at the same time.

If in the process of physically handling the fighting residents you injure yourself or some other person is injured, you may be denied your organisation's support. Though it is almost an instinctive reaction, it is best to ensure that the organisation's policies support such actions.

Show understanding
Regardless of the cause of the fight you need to understand that anger can deny people the ability to think straight and take no notice of authority (you). Therefore failure to co-operate with staff in the heights of their anger must not be held against them. This does not necessarily mean that such a response in right. However, it will help you to get your priorities right and dish out appropriate support at the right time.

Consider external help
Assess the situation for an external help. This is likely to be the case if properties are being damaged or high risks are presented to other service users, or even where the fight seems to prolong (without any luck of you separating them). Call the police.

Attend to damages etc (if necessary)
Make safe the area before allowing other residents to go back there. For example if there are any broken chairs or tables remove them and ensure the

area is cleaned up. Also arrange for any emergency repair works to be completed. This may include smashed windows, bust pipe mains, and electricals. A colleague can see to this while you speak to the 'fighters'

Give fighting residents attention
The next task after defusing the situation is to give resident fighters opportunity to air their feelings. This is the beginning of the investigation process. It is important not to be judgmental of them or have premeditations about the consequences of their actions.

Consider views of witnesses
If you did not see what led to the fight talk to named witnesses documenting comments as they are delivered, not your own interpretation of things.

Action
Action taken will depend on the following;

- Any special needs of the residents

- The extent of damage, disruption, nature of risk presented by residents actions

- Whether or not there were provocations and who started the fight

- Options available to the residents which they failed to use

- Your organisation's policy and procedures

Consider effect on other residents
It is always necessary to consider effects of major incidents on other vulnerable residents. This is an area that can be easily missed. You need to be observant about changed moods. Also consider inviting other residents to talk about any concerns arising from their experience. Perhaps a more proactive approach is more in order, so those residents live with the assurance that they can always approach staff in times like this.

Question 78   MANAGING A DISRUPTIVE BEHAVIOUR

Scenario: **Georgia suffers from mild mental health. She is also known to have a temper. She came to the office to collect her mail and discovered that one of her letters was opened. She got furious and started swearing and shouting at the admin person who gave her the letter. You were in the office at the time and witnessed what happened. How will you respond to the situation?**

Give other staff room to act

Spend a minute or two to assess the situation and to give the admin staff opportunity to respond to the situation. Being too quick to intervene may constitute a deprivation of a valuable opportunity for her to practice her professional abilities. On the other hand, do not hesitate to intervene earlier if you think she is already vulnerable.

Show interest

You can do this by drawing closer to the reception and standing next to the admin staff. Keep close eyes and good ears on development and wait for the right opportunity to cut in. An example of good opportunity will be when Georgia begins to raise her voice.

Challenge action

Using the information gathered in your presence you must challenge Georgia's actions:

- First you must ask Georgia to stop shouting and listen to you.

- You need to be assertive and perhaps you will need to repeat your request several times. Ideas on being assertive and dealing with angry customers are included elsewhere in Winning Ideas.

- Maintain a calm approach, with sturdy and firm tone.

You must challenge acts of swearing or any form of rudeness towards staff by for example;

- Telling Georgia that such behaviours cannot be tolerated.

- Informing her that she is putting her licence at risk by her behaviour.

- Advising her of alternative options: Invite her to come and talk about her concerns in a logical manner whilst assuring her that staff will listen and consider the details.

Reinforce previous comments made to Georgia by admin person (i.e. if they are relevant).

If Georgia's actions persist
You must take a decision not to deal with her at the time. Remove yourself as well as the admin person away from the reception area. Unless Georgia is in danger herself because of her action ignore her and don't allow yourself to be drawn into her anger.

Consider feelings of admin person
Check with the admin person if she is OK. She may be in shock and her ability to continue working (soon after the incident) affected. Check if she needs a break or time to recover while you cover reception duties.

Consider further action
Further action may include:

- Talking in confidence with Georgia (i.e. if she accepts your invitation).

- Considering disciplinary action against Georgia (if necessary).

- Making the reception area safe for other service users who may wish to use it.

- Considering ways of signalling clearly to service users that violence towards staff members won't be tolerated.

Report
As usual complete reports ensuring that Georgia's keyworker (especially) is aware of her behaviour. This may represent a significant twist of something else, and may be part of an entire picture providing grounds for re-examining Georgia's support or care plan.

Part 4
SCENARIO QUESTIONS

Several styles of questioning are used in Housing Support and Care interviews. Whilst the ultimate reason remains that interviewers want to be able to select the best person for the job (i.e. all things being equal), their decision is based on analysis of candidates' total response. This means your whole being is involved in the interview not just your answers. Scenario questions offer the best chance for interviewers to make tangible assessment. Recently I was an interview panel member during a management position interview. Nine questions were asked and nine of them were scenario questions. The future of interview questions lies in scenarios. They are generally accepted as the type that is able to bring the best out of candidates. It is a must for the job hunter to feel comfortable with them. Scenario questions require you to picture a scene and your position in the capacity of the same position you are applying for. You are provided with the scenario, and then given a question afterwards. Interviewers may also play a short video, DVD, or an audio tape. The answers you give are essentially restricted and defined by the nature of the scenario. Most people find it difficult answering them for several reasons which include:

- Difficulty holding information/ facts in mind
- Difficulty following some scenarios or find them confusing
- Some scenarios are either unclear or do not make sense
- They may contain trick questions or hidden agendas

Scenario questions must be seen as an opportunity than 'bad luck'. Simply follow the strategies in this book and work your way through the examples located below. You will find answers to lots of scenarios in this volume. You may find it helpful also to look at our publication *Evidence of Performance* which covers a wide range of strategies necessary for getting your next job.

Examples of scenario questions
If you are already in the industry I have no doubt of your familiarity with scenario questions. The following affords examples:

- *A client has just collapsed and another resident has approached reception with the news how would you respond to the situation?*

- *You are alone in the project when the fire alarms went off. As you were trying to organise evacuation of the premises you discovered a flood of water gushing out of the laundry. What would you do?*

- *A tenant who has suffered harassment from another tenant for a long time came to see you in the office. He is threatening to do something about the situation because of the Council's 'lack of action'. Meanwhile your manager is on annual leave. How would you address the issue?*

Scenario questions are usually based on actual incidents occurring in the project, department or organisation. If you have no previous experience in answering scenario questions your best chance is to work through chains of them. They are designed to test the following (amongst other things):

- Your ability to act on your own

- Your ability to use appropriate resources

- To be creative and resourceful

- Your ability to think well and fast on your feet

- To take appropriate action in real life situations.

Other types of questions
Other types of questions you can expect in your interviews are;

Open-ended questions	Straight Questions
Vague or trick questions	Personality (test)

These are examined in detail (including strategies for dealing with them) in our publication *Evidence of Performance*. In this section our focus is on scenarios.

What the interviewers are looking for
What exactly are interviewers looking for when they use scenario questions? 'They want your blood!' No, they really want to help you express yourself more freely. Because scenario questions bring together the essentials of the other types of questions, a lot can be expected. The following are some things they look for.

Effective communication	Ability to work alone and

- Presentational styles
- Body language
- Sense of initiatives
- Ability to think fast, on your feet
- Skills
- Knowledge
- Experience
- Commitment
- Responsibility
- Sense of purpose

independently

- Sense of directions and initiative
- Ability to be creative and innovative & resourceful

Other importance of scenario questions are:

- Used to compare notes completed on interviewees
- Provide grounds for immediate elimination
- Used to get confirmation of previous answers or suspicions

ANSWERING IMAGINATIVE/SCENARIO QUESTIONS

Scenario questions are best answered if you are able to hold the key points in your memory. You may ask the interviews permission to make notes before you answer. Here we can only provide summary of the strategies (which are featured in more detail in *Evidence of Performance*.) A very important point to bear in mind is this: Good answers for scenario questions always go beyond the lines that set the case. This will become clearer as we proceed. Meanwhile, look at the following strategies which must be considered in all answers to scenario questions.

- Always ensure you cover key areas of the question
- Identify what is expected (the quantity and type of answers required)
- Identify key issues in the scenario and concentrate on them
- Establish how the issues link to each other and use this to determine your approach
- Choose the right strategy. The approach must match the issues in the scenario
- Cover all areas using a 360 degrees approach (See below)
- Create scenarios within the scenario to make your answers more realistic and interesting.

The 360 degree approach

To be competitive your answers must follow a 360 degrees approach. This means you must provide your answers in a logical, progressive, and holistic picture finishing at the very point where you started. For example if you are answering a case involving an incident, your answers must come back to look at how similar incidents can be prevented using limits within your job description. Therefore, you must start by looking at an immediate solution (or a temporary one if the situation is a complicated one), a short term solution, and then a long term solution. You will find examples below.

STAGES IN YOUR ANSWERS	EXAMPLES OF THINGS YOU CAN DO
An immediate response/ solution	▪ Call the ambulance ▪ Seek immediate help from colleagues ▪ Remove casualty from further danger ▪ Make casualty comfortable ▪ Stop bleeding ▪ Challenge behaviour ▪ Calm other person by showing empathy
Short term response/ solution	▪ Attend to other residents who were affected directly or indirectly ▪ Make the place safe and restore normal operation or activities ▪ Liaise with professionals (short term) ▪ Complete report or relevant forms
Long term response/ solution	▪ Involve team members ▪ Complete report and follow up ▪ Liaise with professionals (long term) ▪ Use of Service Improvement Groups (SIG's) or working parties to address problems

- Use of progress meetings (with clients) and residents/tenants meetings

- Keywork sessions

- Working with altered care/support plan and strategies that takes into consideration current problems and difficulties

Things to consider

When answering any scenario question consider possible involvement of the following. The question is could any of these be required in the scenario? Do you need to mention any of these in your answers? We can only provide the main points here. See *Evidence of Performance* for more.

- Team member(s)

- Your team

- Professionals (e.g. Psychiatrist)

- Emergency services

  - The Fire brigade

  - Gas company

  - Water Company

  - Ambulance

  - The police

- First aid

- Safety of others

- Life threatening situation must always come first

- Production of incidents reports

- Hand over to other staff

- Keyworkers are informed

- A copy of incident or report on

- Think of sister projects and schemes (within your organisation)

- The law and legal requirements

- On-call arrangement or staff who can help

- Residents care plans

- Particular support needs of clients involved

- Sensitivity to confidential issues

- Exhausting in-house resources first before external ones

- Prioritising what you need to do

- Comprehensive assessment of situations

- Putting up notices (e.g. to warn people)

- Taking time to be clear of your options

- Consider arranging for staff cover

resident(s) file

- Follow organisational policies

- Consider agreed team procedures

- Consider corporate business priorities

- Consider any interim arrangement (agreed by team, with clients, etc.)

- Think of other resources e.g. residents

- Consider arranging for maintenance (subject to corporate procedure)

- Consider drawing on lessons learnt from handling similar incident(s) in the past

- Sending fax message to confirm telephone calls

- Requesting for instructions (especially from medical professionals in writing - by fax)

SCENARIOS IN BRIEF

This section contains short scenarios to help you develop your techniques even further. Using your knowledge from the previous sections, test yourself. Then compare your answers with relevant sections of Winning Ideas. You may mark out only those relevant to the position you are preparing for or your training topics, and cover them. Not all the scenarios here are treated in Winning Ideas. You are advised to discuss your answers with people who can help. Do not hesitate to contact S2S if you need further assistance. As a team you may examine the scenarios that may apply in your project.

- Assess them for good practice
- Have a team agreed procedure for dealing with the issues
- Consider using them in interviewing prospective staff
- Establish training needs that may arise from them

RESIDENT/PROJECT/STAFF

- **Refusal to take medication**

- **Causing trouble in the community e.g. to neighbours**

  - **Harassment**

  - **Noise**

- **Harassment of another resident**

- Harassment of a staff member
- Refusal to participate in social activities
- Refusal to use communal facilities with another resident
- Wakes staff at night because of panic attacks
- Wakes staff at night for no apparent reason
- Have speech and hearing problems and can't communicate effectively
- Can't read or write
- Refusal to share facilities with someone because of the other person's illness
- Have hygiene problems
- Support for a resident who feels harassed or being harassed by another resident
- A fight between 2 residents
- Resident flooded their flat or communal areas
- Resident who do not get on with other residents for reason of e.g. anger management
- Support for resident who falls out with own advocates/friends/ family members
- Malpractice of external agency staff concerning one of your residents
- Resident threatening a contractor/external agency staff
- Resident refusing to take part in reviews/case conferences
- Resident causing trouble at day centre which he/she attends (and facing sanctions)
- Suicide attempts
- Resident slipped and fell on stairs
- Resident taken unconscious because of drug overdose
- Resident refusing to bath

- Resident refusing to speak to relative: Refuse to take telephone call from relatives

- You see a resident talking to herself for the first time

- Resident accused of in appropriate advances on female resident/female neighbours

- Resident accuse staff /another resident of theft

- You discover a resident's medication has run out.

    1. Meanwhile he arrives at the office waiting for his medicine

    2. the resident's health becomes worse needing immediate administration of his medicine

- Resident not eating, losing weight and affecting his/her health

- Support for a bereaved resident

- Resident with support needs around alcohol

- You saw one of your residents on your day off. He looks disorientated, shabby in appearance and quite distressed

- Incontinent resident (hygiene issues)

- Lack of budgeting skills (affecting parts of resident's life)

- Anger management problems

- Not getting on with your client

- Client avoiding you: Not wanting to meet with you though you are concerned about his welfare

- Resident with problems getting on with people

- Resident with difficulties coping with changes e.g. in staff team

- Drug abuse problems

- You witnessed a resident's inappropriate action in communal room

- Resident tells you about a secret which concerns another member of staff

- Resident complains he/she does not like the colour of his room

- You witnessed a resident having a go at a member of staff

- Resident complains that someone has opened his letters

- Resident complains of severe stomach pains

- Resident refuses to eat his food when prepared by a particular member of staff

- A resident not eating for religious reasons. You become concerned because of the effect on her health which begin to show in paleness, and weight loss

- Supporting a distressed resident following a bad day at the day centre

- Resident threatens you (e.g. to beat you up)

- You feel uncomfortable working with a resident

- Resident lacking basic living skills now affecting his self esteem

- Supporting a resident without much relevant background information

- Resident persistently breaking the hostels policy/rules

- You discover a resident vandalising property of the organisation (in his room). What act will you take?

- You are informed that a notorious resident is responsible for vandalising a communal facility

- You witnessed a fight between a resident and a member of staff

- Resident lost his money or belongings

- Resident reported loosing his giro/income support book

- Resident always complaining of financial difficulties

- Resident with health problems affecting eating, mobility, or sight

- Resident looking for job but lack relevant skills

- Resident phoned you out of hours to report that he lost key to flat

- Resident having difficulties with changes being introduced by your organisation

- Resident persistently failing to comply with agreed care/support plans

- Resident refusing medical appointment because of a nasty experience with medical staff

- Resident persistently tampering with Health and Safety provisions in the hostel/unit

- Resident having problems with class/academic work (outside the unit)

- Resident requesting for your support to sue his landlord/ social worker/ GP

- Resident's neighbours complain of nuisance and wants you to do something about it

- Resident being pursued by debtors and fails to use his flat as a result

- Resident using his flat as an extension of 'rough sleeping' habit – always full of friends drinking and drugging

- You receive a formal complaint about one of your residents from an external staff who is also a member of that resident's care team.

STAFF/STAFF/ORGANISATION

- You do not agree with a policy of your organisation

- Implementing an aspect of your organisation's policy is difficult for you

- You do not get on with one member of the staff team

- You disprove of your manager's action over a matter

- You are aware that your manager is breaching the organisation's policy

- You are a member of a dysfunctional team. You decide to make a difference using your strengths

- Your work is affected by demotivated staff around you

- You witnessed a colleague in an action that is against the organisation's policy

- Your job content makes it difficult for you to achieve targets/objectives

- Working with a difficult team

273

- Working with a non supportive team

- A member of staff confides in you that a colleague is a gay/lesbian or suffers from Aids

- You become aware that a colleague is stressed out in his work

- You become aware that a colleague is struggling with certain aspects of his/her work

- How you cope with change

- Dealing with another staff with deferent approaches (e.g. disruptive) to work

- You become aware of discriminative practice by one staff towards another.

- You witnessed a colleague being abused by a resident.

- You believe that your manager treats you less favourably than other staff.

- You disapprove of methods used in sharing task.

- You become stressed out in your job which affects quality of service delivered to client/staff.

- Dealing with a non-team player (staff).

- You are often picked upon by one particular member of staff, and the situation is stressing you out.

- Dealing with and working with new policies and procedures.

- How to progress your task despite other staff failure to do the same because of their disagreement with the method prescribed by the organisation/manager.

- You caught a member of staff stealing from the organisation.

- Petty cash tin money is missing whilst you are on duty with a colleague.

- A Colleague with whom you are on duty dealt with an incident in a manner you disapprove of.

- You and your colleague were unable to agree on how to deal with an incident which occurred on your shift.

- You witnessed a colleague looking through your manager's confidential documents.

- Another member of staff makes a complaint about you to the manager and you know the matter is untrue.

- You are denied the opportunity to use your strengths in your job.

- You become aware that two of your colleagues are gossiping about you. Your relationship with them is deteriorating.

- A colleague touches you inappropriately. You are not happy about this.

- Whilst you were out with a colleague and accompanying a client, he engages in a dishonourable/disgraceful behaviour. How will you deal with it?

- You receive a telephone call from a relative about an emergency at home requiring that you leave the project immediately.

- The other person with whom you are on duty was taken ill and transported away by ambulance crew.

- You have a serious incident while on shift. You try to contact the on-call person (following approved procedure) but there was no answer.

- You are confronted with a situation whilst at work and you are unsure of what action to take.

- The police arrive in your project to search a client's room and request access.

- Lights/power in hostel goes off and you are getting several queries from clients.

- You received a complaint from the manager of an external agency about conduct of your colleague.

- You disagree with procedures used by your team in solving problems.

- You begin to feel that your job does not motivate you anymore.

- Problem erupts due to differences in style of working between yourself and an external staff.

- On your day off you receive a telephone call from a work colleague querying you about an omission.

- Other staff you work with do not adhere to agreed procedures. This is affecting your work.

- You do not get on with your manager

- You feel disliked in your job and can hardly find any motivation

- You discover a serious health and safety problem in the project

MANAGER/STAFF/ORGANISATION/RESIDENTS

- You are concerned about contractors working in your unit because their methods present serious health and safety issues.

- You are on your way to attend an urgent meeting when you received the news that one of your residents is taken into hospital following a motor accident.

- You have a difficult staff who seem to oppose whatever you do or say.

- You received a complaint from a relative of a resident to the effect that he must not share a communal facility with gays / lesbians.

- Following a major incident involving one of your residents you receive a call from a media representative asking for a brief.

- You become aware that a staff member has stolen from the organisation.

- You are running thin on budget and confronted with unavoidable expenditure which will take you beyond your limits.

- You become aware that you are approaching your budget limits and you must make adjustments in your expense and at the same time maintain a high level of quality in services.

- You lack a key managerial skill. This is showing in your work output.

- A staff is under-performing persistently and not responding much to coaching and support.

- You become aware that a staff has breached an important organisational policy.

- You received a complaint from a manager of an external organisation about conduct of one of your staff.

- You are confronted with a number of tasks all of which seem to be urgent.

- You are required to implement a new organisational policy which you yourself do not believe in.

- You have a difficult staff team and making changes is a nightmare though this is inevitable.

- A member of staff has asked you to reassign one of his residents because they do not get on.

- You are on-call and received a telephone call requesting for permission to evict a client following a violent incident.

- A resident is dissatisfied with the organisation's service. He is now very angry at all staff and this seem to be affecting his health

- Your organisation is changing its client group and you need to prepare yourself for the new service and clients in order to ensure that service quality is not affected

- You are a member of a dysfunctional staff team and you need to make a difference through your own contributions

- A client is racist towards you and it is obvious that this is due to the person's mental health

- You discover that you have made a very dreadful mistake because of a decision you made about a client

- Your manager is very disruptive in his working style and demands that you do things his way, causing inconvenience to the rest of the team

- You strongly disagree with your colleagues on a decision made (without you) during a previous meeting

Part 5
PRACTICE QUESTIONS

The questions here are for your own practice and development. You may work as a team or as an individual with an action plan to self develop. Some of the questions are already covered in Winning Ideas. Those not yet covered will be featured in future editions of Winning Ideas. We encourage all users of winning Ideas to contact us with specific interview/development questions they want help with, and we will do our best to help. See page 2 for contact details.

For those of you in management position you may find this section useful during staff interviews (promotional, development, or recruitment), quiz programmes, and team building programmes. Also located behind this section is a profile of all the questions covered in this volume to help revision and self examination.

1. What qualities would you look for when recruiting a Tenancy Support Worker?

2. How do you show commitment to Equal Opportunities?

3. How do you see your responsibility under the Community Care Legislation?

4. How can the service benefit from other services provided by external agencies?

5. What is your understanding of the housing, care and support needs of people with mental health and learning difficulties

1. What welfare benefits are the clients likely to be assessed for and how will you ensure that the staff provide them with full support in making the claim? (This question is already covered in our publication *Remnants of Accommodation*)

2. What legislations are relevant and can be used whilst providing services within the project to meet the needs of service users?

3. How would you ensure that the project's management meets a high level of health and Safety standards?

4. In what ways has your previous experience prepared you for the post of a manager?

5. What are some of the problems around communication in a project of this type and how would you ensure that communication is maintained to a high standard?

6. How would you ensure that budgets are monitored and accounted for effectively?

7. How would you ensure that your staff is provided with good leadership, motivation, and feel supported?

8. What sort of challenging situations do you expect in your job and how would you cope with stress?

9. What are your leadership qualities?

10. If appointed as the manager how will you develop close and effective working relationship with residents outside agencies?

11. How would you go about in developing policies and procedures and also implementing ones already existing in the organisation?

12. How would you use supervision, support and motivation to develop and train your staff?

13. As part of your duties you will be required to assess the care and support needs of the project's service users and to co-ordinate planned programmes to meet these needs. How would ou go about this?

14. What makes a good complaints system?

15. How would you encourage service user's involvement (including clients' relatives and carers) in the service provided in the project?

16. What steps will you take to establish and maintain a healthy maintenance system?

17. How would you ensure that service users receive a quality service through keyworking?

18. You duties will include co-ordinating assessment of needs and individual care plans for service users. How would you do this?

19. What services (statutory and non-statutory) are available for meeting the needs of the service users?

20. What good practices are there for ensuring that prescribed medication and their administration are managed professionally?

21. The project runs on a limited budget. How would you ensure effective use of the funds available? Hint: Look at both sides: good expenses, and control of expenses

22. Rent arrears (amongst tenants) are the most-known cause of eviction. What measures would you take to tackle this problem?

23. How do you prepare budgets?

24. What do you consider to be included in a good maintenance procedure /policy document?

25. What local community organisations would you liaise with in the course of your work?

26. If you were to draw up a list of good practice on networking, what will be on it?

27. How would you improve and develop yourself?

28. What issues may arise from working with a wide range of referral agencies, and how would you deal with them?

29. What issues may arise from managing a large number of specialist staff (from partnership organisations)?

30. What liaison strategy would you put in place for working effectively with our partnership organisations?

31. If successful you will be one of two deputies/manager managing a staff of 15. How would you ensure consistency in the way they are managed?

32. If successful you will share an office space with other managers of other departments:
    - What issues may arise?

    - How would you benefit from their presence?

    - How would you support them in meeting their objectives

    - What contribution will you make to help create a healthy, motivating, and supportive atmosphere for every one?

33. What is your experience in relations to this job?

34. How can this organisation benefit from your skills gained in previous experience?

35. Tell us a moment you failed and what you did to put things right.

36. Give an account of a moment in your previous job when you used your own initiative in dealing with a problem.

37. Give account of a moment you represented your organisation/team/project.

38. How do you approach/problems you encounter in the course of your duties?

39. Give an account of staff problems you successfully dealt with in the your previous jobs.

40. How do you use your strengths to overcome your weaknesses?

41. Tell us about a moment in your previous work experience when you encountered problems with an external agency and how you dealt with it.

42. Give us an account of a change you managed successfully in your previous experience.

43. What part of the job description would you find difficult and what would you do about it?

44. How would you use the multi-disciplinary nature of the team to help achieve project objectives?

45. What changes will you make when appointed into this position, and why?

46. Which areas of team operations will you prioritise when you start working with us, and why?

47. Scenario: You have received a complaint of harassment from a tenant. The tone of the letter sound very urgent and it contains sensitive information. You would normally discuss the letter with your line manager but he is on annual leave due to return in two weeks time. How will you address the issue?

48. Scenario: You have a client with needs around basic living skills. He finds it difficult to budget and prioritise what he must spend his

money on. As a result he is in rent and service charge arrears. What measures would you take to support the client whilst ensuring that the arrears do not become worse?

49. What skill do you need for counselling a tenant who is in debt?

50. What will you take into consideration when counselling your tenants on debts?

51. What makes good presentation skills?

52. What Tenants participation /involvement opportunities are there?

53. Two members of your staff are on bad terms and seem to have problem working together on the same shift. The situation is affecting team performance. How would you deal with it as a manager?

54. What would you do if a colleague of yours is making your work difficult and as a result you are unable to achieve your work targets?

55. What would you do if you walk into a group of residents dealing in or doing drugs in the hostel/project?

56. If your manager take an action that is not consistent with the organisation's policy what would you do?

57. How would you support a resident who suffer from sudden changes in mood and becomes aggressive or agitated?

58. One of your clients is having rent arrears problems. She informs you that she has completed all the relevant benefit forms and sent them off to the benefit office, and yet it appears she is not getting any payment. How would you support her?

59. What sort of benefits can be claimed by a resident who suffers from severe mental health problems and needs help with managing his own domestic tasks?

60. A resident of the opposite sex approached you with health problems which he/she finds difficult talking about. How would you manage the situation and ensure that the person can get appropriate help?

61. How would you communicate with those residents with speech problems?

62. Most of our clients suffer serious health problems which affect their ability to live independently. What measures would you take to help them develop independent living?

63. What will you do if a resident you are supporting is not cooperating despite all your good efforts?

64. Whilst on duty you receive a telephone call from a resident's advocate/ family member who is querying an alleged (staff) malpractice against the resident. How would you manage it?

65. The police telephone the project to inform you (at midnight) that one of your clients has been arrested for stealing. What would you do?

66. How will service users be affected by the quality of service they receive from staff?

67. What would you consider *good practice* when dealing with family members of our service users or their advocates? What issues must you bear in mind or show awareness of?

68. This organisation is changing it's client group. How would you prepare yourself for the new service/clients in order to ensure that service quality is not affected?

69. What management principles do you consider important and useful for managing a project?

70. As a manager how would you use your interpersonal skills to help front line staff in dealing with clients?

71. A client who suffers from incontinence is having problems dealing with it because he finds it discomforting talking about it. How would you support the client?

72. A tenant whom you provide support to have received a massage that the bailiffs will execute an eviction order tomorrow. How would you support the client?

73. Your client has been informed by his landlord about a court action against him for a breach/offence which he says he did not commit. How would you support him?

74. How would you provide support for a client who is being unlawfully evicted by his landlord?

75. You are required to inspect a room of a client who is suspected to be a heavy drug user, and who may also be injecting and supplying. What precautions would you take?

76. How will you go about improving customer participation in the project?

77. How would you use your interpersonal skills to help create a homely environment for all service users and staff?

78. What will you do if you discover that you are having difficulties in some aspects of your job?

79. In what ways can this organisation benefit from your previous experience?

80. In what ways can we benefit from your computer skills?

81. In what other ways can you tell if a resident may be in discomfort apart from the person telling you?

82. In what creative ways can you involve clients in the project's activities?

83. Diana suffers from severe depression. How would you support her with her problems?

84. Sheila suffers from severe diabetic condition. How would you support her with her problems?

85. Mary suffers from epilepsy? How would you support her with her problems?

86. During your patrol you discovered traces of blood (or what you suspected to be blood) in the residents' communal sink. What steps will you take?

87. How would you support a colleague who is new in the job and seems to be having problems getting used to the job?

88. How do you deal with emergencies?

89. According to the Health and Safety Act 1974 what provisions do you expect in your work place?

90. How would you support your client to maximise their income from welfare benefits?

91. This organisation is changing the way it provides service to it's clients. How would you accommodate the change so that you are able to help your clients adjust to the new system?

92. You discovered that a resident is vandalising a fire extinguisher (a health and safety equipment) what action would you take?

93. A resident who finds your work admirable writes a cheque for £500.00 for your personal use. What will you do?

94. What makes a good staff recruitment? What issues would you consider when recruiting staff (to join your team)?

95. In what way do you see the Minimum Care Standard Act 2002 improving service and service delivery?

WINNING IDEAS VOLUME THREE
(Questions in profile)

Part 1
TENANT AND RESIDENTS WELFARE ISSUES

Question 1

Scenario: Whilst on duty in the project a tenant comes to you and complains of hearing voices. What action will you take to address the situation?

Question 2
How can you tell if a resident/tenant is attempting to commit suicide?

Question 3
Which groups of vulnerable people would usually be considered as being at more risk of suicide?

Question 4
One of our clients has attempted suicide several times. If you are appointed to the post and you become the person's keyworker what practical ways will you consider for supporting the client?

Question 5
What do you consider a good practice when working with the benefit system or when supporting client with their benefit claim?

Question 6
Scenario: Florence has a chiropody appointment. She approached you for £10.00 for cab fares, which she said, was promised to her by another member of staff. Meanwhile there is not enough money in the petty cash tin. Her appointment is clearly confirmed in the staff diary and by her appointment letter. What support will you provide to Florence?

Question 7
Scenario: Whilst on duty you received a telephone call from a resident's brother (NOK) informing you that the resident who left the project to visit

his brother three days ago has not arrived. Meanwhile the project staffs are completely under the impression that the resident is with his brother. What action will you take?

Question 8
Scenario: David is in serious rent arrears and his landlord has started court action to repossess his flat. You are David's support worker with a duty to help prevent David's return into the streets. You have already written to him several times with appointments but he is never around when you call. Meanwhile his neighbours tell you that he still lives in his flat. What further action will you take?

Question 9
Scenario: You are charged with the responsibility of supporting a fresh tenant to complete a Community Care Grant application. What argument will you support the client to put forward as justification for the grant?

Question 10
You have been invited to give a talk on the effect of alcohol misuse. The objective is to discourage individual service users from senseless drinking. What key information will your script contain?

Question 11
What are the give-away signs of alcohol misuse?

Question 12
How can you tell if one of your clients with a history of alcohol problems and who is engaged in a rehabilitation programme is drifting back into serious alcohol misuse?

Question 13
Scenario: Colin is a heavy drug addict and a tenant of our supported housing scheme. He has been allocated to you as a key client. What practical support will you consider in order to enable him live life as full as possible?

Question 14

Working with drug users takes understanding, patience, and tolerance. This means staff needs a firm understanding of circumstances that drives people into 'doing' drugs. Why do people 'do' drugs?

Questions 15

What warning signs in a client's behaviour or attitude can indicate signs of drug/alcohol misuse?

Question 16

The staff team has received several reports that one of your key clients does drugs. Meanwhile he has denied any drug use and therefore does not give you the opportunity to visit the resident's room, and you decide to check out the truth by looking for clues. What are some physical signs that may confirm your suspicions?

Question 17

Some of our residents have serious drug addiction problems. What steps will you take in providing support for them?

Question 18

A significant part of this position is about accompanying (prospective) clients on viewing after successful interviews. What sort of things will you support the client to check during the viewing?

Question 19

It is a well-documented fact that most tenancies of ex-rough sleepers collapse within the first six months. What initial support will you provide to client to enable him/her take up tenancy successfully?

Question 20

The person appointed to this position will have the responsibility of providing on-going support to the client with a view to sustaining the client's interest in the community. What considerations will you make **in** order to ensure client's interest?

Question 21
If you are successful you will be providing support for clients with long history of rough sleeping, some of whom also have mental health and living skill problems. If you are to draw a checklist for ensuring that they will be safe and reasonably independent in their new flat, what will it look like?

Question 22
What problems do people with long history of rough sleeping face?

Question 23
In what ways can you tell if the tenancy of a person with long history of rough sleeping is at risk of breaking down?

Question 24
What general support can you provide to vulnerable people to enable them maintain their tenancy for as long as possible and to prevent a return into the street/becoming homeless?

Question 25
What practical support will you consider in your working relationship with your clients in order to help them maintain successful tenancies?

Question 26
A client has approached you asking that you support his application for a transfer because he is no longer interested in their present accommodation. As a Tenancy Support Worker/Officer what do you consider to be justifiable grounds for supporting such an application?

Question 27
Scenario: George is a heavy drinker. He also smokes heavily and doesn't care for food. The staffs are now concerned that his situation is not helping his incontinence problems especially as his hygiene has reached very low ebb. George has now been assigned to you as your latest key client. How will you go about addressing this case?

Question 28
What skills do residents need for looking for and remaining in employment?

Question 29
A resident is refusing to participate in social activities. He is one of your key residents. What action will you take?

Question 30
How would you work with a resident who do not get on with other residents because of anger management problem?

Part 2
TEAM MANAGEMENT & STAFF MANAGEMENT ISSUES

Question 31
What problems have you experienced in your previous employment and how did you solve them?

Question 32
What area did you have problems in your work and how did you overcome this?

Question 33
You will be working as part of a staff team if appointed. How will you deal with your colleagues who have a different approach to dealing with tenants?

Question 34
If successful your job will include visiting clients (tenants) in their homes on your own. What precautionary measures will you take to ensure your own safety?

Question 35
What do you expect from your team?

Question 36
What managerial skills do you expect from your line manager?

Question 37
What can we expect from you?

Question 38

This organisation seeks to maintain a professional image amongst it's competitors. In many ways we rely on our managers for effectiveness in service. It is therefore important that our managers are of good qualities. What qualities would you bring into your work?

Question 39

What qualities in a leader/manager motivate you?

Question 40

As a manager you will need to delegate some of your duties in order to meet deadlines. In what ways will delegation benefit your staff and the organisation at large?

Question 41

In what ways can the organisation benefit from training its staff?
What are the benefits of staff training?

Question 42

How will you identify the training needs of your staff?

Question 43

What types of training programmes or activities can you make available to your staff as part of the staff development function?

Question 44

This organisation is committed to training and development of its staff. As a manager you will have a key role to play in this. What suggestions do you have for making this (training and development) effective?

Question 45

Scenario: You are a manager of one of our housing schemes. You receive a call from the police informing you that one of your staff has been arrested for shop lifting. What measures will you take?

Question 46

Scenario: You are a new team member of the Wexford project, which is one of the many owned by Equip Housing Association. The project specialises in providing support service to people living in the community.

You are in your sixth month after joining and you have discovered many management errors. The situation has taken tolls on staff in several ways, which include:

- Poor decision making and problem solving approaches
- Staff feeling demotivated and not supported
- Use of effective accounting principles
- Low staff productivity
- Poor time management

Whilst managers are complaining about work overload, their staff moan about difficult managers who have no 'heart' for motivating staff. You manage to work your way into a working party established to draw up proposals for putting things right and restoring normality especially in respect of staff care.

Question

What proposal will you make to the managers of Equip Housing Association as a way of resolving their problems?

Question 47

How do you manage your time in the course of your work?

Question 48

What is reasonable for staff to expect from their managers?

Question 49

What is reasonable for managers to expect from their staff?

Question 50

What difficulties are encountered in a staff team? For each one say who is responsible? Managers, individual staff, or the organisation? What can be done about the problems?

Question 51
In what positive ways will a good team benefit the organisation's customers?

Question 52
What are the general benefits of a good teamwork?

Question 53
What are the most pressing needs of a productive employer?

Question 54
What special support will you provide to those staff of ethnic minorities in respect of their personal development and motivation in their jobs? (Position: Manager)

Question 55
You do not get on with your manager no matter how hard you seem to try. You believe this is affecting your performance. What will you do?

Question 56
What actions would you take if you feel deskilled in your job and can hardly find any motivation?

Part 3
PROJECT MANAGEMENT ISSUES

Question 57
Scenario: Whilst you were on duty two tenants (one black and one white) were involved in a dispute. The black man complained to you that the white man called him a 'black bastard'. How would you deal with the situation?

Question 58
Scenario: You just arrived at work after a long break. The locum staff who handed over to you informed you that a tenant refused to take her medication for two weeks. When you visited the tenant, you discovered that her flat was in a mess. You also discovered that the telephone in the communal room has been vandalised. How will you address the situation?

Question 59
What is the difference between a house and a home?

Question 60
Scenario: You visited a tenant who has not been seen by staff for some time. The person is now in 2 weeks rent arrears. He also has serious drinking problems and has been abusive to other tenants. How would you deal with this?

Question 61
The nature of the job is such that you will have times when there is hardly anything to do. How will you occupy yourself during those times?

Question 62
Scenario: The project has a petty cash system, which is passed on from one shift to another during staff hand-over sessions. The morning staff (who had a very busy shift) forgot to account for the petty cash when you started your Friday afternoon shift. You later on discovered that the money was £20 short. Meanwhile there was not enough cash to keep the project running in emergency. What action will you take?

Question 63
What do you understand by 'Tenant Participation' within the context of Supported Housing?

Question 64
What legal provisions and social policies are there to back the duties owed to tenants in the area of tenant participation and involvement?

Question 65
Though this project has several opportunities for tenants to participate in decision making and activities, many do not. In what ways do you think tenant participation can be improved within the organisation?

Question 66
Both the government and the Housing Corporation are actively encouraging housing providers across the UK to create opportunities for tenants to participate in their activities. What are the benefits of Tenant Participation?

Question 67
What are the barriers to tenants Participation?

Question 68
What is Best Value in Housing Management?

Question 69
What are the key principles imbedded in the government's Best Value concept?

Question 70
The Best Value concept aims to involve service users as a means to the provision of quality service. What changes will you advice if our organisation was to embrace the concept?

Question 71
How do you see your role in the implementation of Best Value in this organisation? (Front line position)

Question 72
What are the offences under the Misuse of drugs Act that you need to be mindful of in this job?

Tell us what you know about Drug legislation that can affect the operations of this project.

What sort of drugs can normally get misused by young people?

Question 73
What duties do the councils have under the homelessness legislation?

Question 74
Scenario: You have received reports from your client's neighbours that he has been drinking and making noise denying them peaceful sleep. They want to know what you are going to do about the matter. How will you address the matter?

Question 75
Scenario: On a very busy Monday morning you are the shift leader of the 2 staff members covering the project. The other member of staff is a locum

and not very familiar with the project. You are behind schedule preparing for a meeting with a consultant psychiatrist and a CPN at 10.30 am. A resident informed you his room is flooded from a bust pipe.

Whilst talking to the resident another resident rushed in calling for help because another resident has collapsed. How will you deal with the situation?

Question 76
Scenario: The staff has failed to see Mr. Jones for 2 days so a decision was made to check his room. When you arrived there you find him naked on the floor crying for help. What will you do?

Question 77
Scenario: You are the duty staff supervising dinner. 2 residents get involved in a fight causing disruption to other residents. You try to intervene but they ignore you. What action will you take?

Question 78
Scenario: Georgia suffers from mild mental health. She is also known to have a temper. She came to the office to collect her mail and discovered that one of her letters was opened. She got furious and started swearing and shouting at the admin person who gave her the letter. You were in the office at the time and witnessed what happened. How will you respond to the situation?

REFERENCES
A wide range of references resourced this publication
References used in this volume is contained in *Winning Ideas volume one and five*

CONTACTING US
If you have benefited from Winning Ideas we will like to hear from you.
Please write to us at S2S 4 Suffolk Road. London E13 0HE or call us on
0207 474 5411. Other volumes of this publication are available.

QUESTIONS IN THIS VOLUME
Most of the questions in the PRACTICE QUESTION section of this volume
are already covered in Winning Ideas (volumes 1 – 4). If you would like
further help you may attend out workshop where one-to-one attention is
available to all participants. The workshops are:

Application and Interview Strategies (AIS)
You learn how to produce winning application forms and how to win the job
at interviews

Answered Interview Questions (AIQ)
You learn all the various types of interview questions and strategies for
answering them as well as answers to a wide range of questions (with
emphasis on scenarios). You also learn how to generate your own interview
questions before our interview

More information is available on
0207 474 5411

Wishing you the very best in your career
**To inquire about any of our publications please call as on 0207 474 5411
or write to us at 4 Suffolk Road. London E13 0HE**

You may also provide the ISBN numbers (located at the back and second
page) of the books to your local book shops and they can arrange your copies
for you.

HEARTS

375 High Street Stratford. E15 4QZ tel. 0208 519 0089
WWW.hearts.eu.com

Example of Courses available

Intensive Housing Management
Foundation Certificate in Housing
NVQ levels 2 & 2 Housing
Housing Training for New Deal Candidates
Information and Communication Technology
Workshop and Seminars
Institute of Public Sector Management courses
(available on demand)

One day workshops on Applications and Interview
Strategies
One day workshop on Answered Interview Questions

Training for corporate bodies available
Wish to change your career? Wish to start a new job?
Speak to us 1st.
Free advice and information available
We specialise in getting you back into work